HANGAR FLYING

Hangar Flying

GENERAL MERRILL A. McPEAK
Former Chief of Staff, US Air Force

*For Cody, Natalie,
and Logan,
With best wishes.*

[signature]

Lost Wingman Press
Lake Oswego, Oregon

LOST WINGMAN PRESS

123 Furnace Street, Lake Oswego, OR 97034

www.LostWingmanPress.com

Editor: Holly Franko

Airplane illustrations and map: Keith Buckley

Cover and book design: Jennifer Omner

Set in Myriad Pro and Century Schoolbook

PUBLISHER'S CATALOGING-IN-PUBLICATION DATA

McPeak, Merrill A., 1936–
    Hangar flying / General Merrill A. McPeak, former chief of
staff, US Air Force.
        p. cm.
    ISBN: 978-0-9833160-1-5 (pbk.)
    ISBN: 978-0-9833160-0-8 (hardcover)
    ISBN: 978-0-9833160-3-9 (leather bound)
    ISBN: 978-0-9833160-2-2 (eBook: ePub)
    1. McPeak, Merrill A., 1936– 2. United States. Air Force—
Generals—Biography. 3. Fighter pilots—United States—
Biography. 4. Vietnam War, 1961–1975—Aerial operations,
American.   I. Title.
UG626 .M435 A3 2012
358.4`0092—dc22

                                                    2011910441

For Ellie

Contents

Prologue

It's 14 August 1961, on the coast of North Africa. Here, near the city of Tripoli, the Air Force owned and operated Wheelus Air Base. Its principal attraction: a 23,000-acre gunnery range etched into the Libyan desert at a place called El Uotia, 50 miles west of the base, up against the Tunisian border. Pilots stationed at NATO airfields had access to smaller, specialized ranges near their continental bases, but bad weather and crowded European airspace made it a good idea to come down to Wheelus periodically to sharpen the full assortment of gunnery skills.

I'd recently reported for duty with the 79th Fighter Squadron at RAF Station Woodbridge in the United Kingdom. The squadron was equipped with F-100s, an aircraft I'd not flown for a while. That Monday morning, I was flying the number four aircraft in a sortie to the El Uotia range, getting "recurrent" in the jet, as well as renewing bombing and gunnery qualifications. It was a great time of day for flying—early, the sun not yet pounding thermals off the desert floor. Our four-ship worked its way methodically through the air-to-ground events: skip bomb, dive bomb, rockets, panel strafe. I could see Arab boys darting through the strafing lanes, scavenging the expended shell casings that would turn into brass coffee tables on offer in Tripoli's souk. No doubt they kept the range clean, cut down on ricochets. They seemed sure of their footing. Still, I caught myself wishing they'd wait until we stopped shooting.

Suddenly, the control tower back at Wheelus began broadcasting the recall word on the guard channel. At Wheelus, pilots carried a pair of recall code words, changed each day: a practice word and one reserved for the real thing. The practice word got occasional use, as when we were tested to see how quickly aircraft aloft could be brought down and reconfigured for combat. No one remembered the real word being broadcast, ever, but now the control tower was surely using it.

Our flight leader, Capt. Cecil LeFevers, came up on the radio: "OK, guys, let's hold high and dry and I'll go over and straighten out tower." We orbited at low altitude in a box pattern while Cece switched to guard and clarified the procedure in plain language: if they wanted to do a recall exercise, they should use the practice code word. Ignoring the advice, the control tower repeated the real word, a little urgency in their transmission this time. Uneasy now, we safed up our weapon systems and headed back to base.

I was the last pilot in the last flight to recover at Wheelus that morning. Decelerating down the runway, drag chute stretching out behind, I glanced across to the parking apron. It was a color-ful sight, heavy with aircraft, upwards of 100 fighters of all the current types, decorated in the livery of every Air Force squadron assigned to the alliance.

Our ground crews quickly downloaded training ordnance and hung the external fuel tanks needed to give us range to home sta-tion. In less than three hours, I was on the runway again, acceler-ating this time, afterburner cooking, and now the parking ramp was a concrete moonscape—aircraft and everything moveable flushed out, gone.

The flight to Woodbridge was unremarkable. After landing, we learned that Khrushchev had finally decided to stop the bleeding through Berlin, the only real gap in the Iron Curtain. The East Germans were busy knocking over buildings, clearing a no-man's-land on which they and the Russians would erect the Berlin Wall.

Beyond bringing our aircraft back, we did nothing about it, at least nothing I could see firsthand. Over the next couple of months, a few fighter units flew in from the States to reinforce bases in France and Germany, but on the ground at Woodbridge, we didn't load live ammunition or go to any advanced state of alert. I mean no criticism; considering the then-existing nuclear stalemate, it would not have been easy to choose an appropriate yet prudent response. I suppose the Russians watched us scramble out of Wheelus and were perhaps impressed by how quickly we regathered NATO's air order of battle. Nevertheless, they went on to build a wall that stood for nearly three decades as a symbol of the Cold War. Our acquiescence meant the West would accept a divided Europe, at least for the time being.

Among the pilots in my four-ship flight to El Uotia range that day in 1961 was Lt. Mike Dugan, a razor-sharp West Pointer, one of the most creative officers I ever knew. Our families were neighbors in base housing, had babies about the same time, became friends. I liked him and learned a lot from him. As much as anything, Mike's example led me to stay in the Air Force.

It turned out both Mike and I ended up wearing four stars. Only a handful of officers attain this rank, so the odds are against two lieutenants from the same squadron doing so. Nevertheless, by the autumn of 1989, when the Berlin Wall finally cracked and fell over, Dugan and I were in charge of the overseas operations of the Air Force—him in Europe and me in the Pacific. Each of us had begun our service a little before the wall went up and each stayed on a while after it came down, but the rise and fall of the Berlin Wall is a sort of metaphor, bookends for two careers that spanned much of the Cold War.

I know of no public monument to the Cold War, no campaign to decorate Washington's Mall with such an object. But make no mistake, it was a real war, with everything at stake: real battles won and lost, real killed and wounded and missing in action, much treasure spent, many mistakes made. Maybe calling it "World War III," or "The Forty Years War" would give a clearer idea of its importance. Against a background of domestic opposition, there were many opportunities to quit. Too often, it was a close thing. But somehow we found the determination to hang in there, to hold a dreadful system at bay until its own people could bring it down, a seismic event that ushered in the possibility, if only just that, of a safer, more prosperous, more democratic world.

———◆———

Shortly after the collapse of the Berlin Wall, the Air Force turned its attention to selecting a new chief of staff. Mike Dugan and I were finalists for the job. Naturally, I was disappointed when he was chosen to become the Air Force's 13th chief. As it happened, I would replace Mike after he'd served only a few months, but when his selection was announced in the spring of 1990, it sure looked as if I'd run out of options. I began to contemplate retirement from active service, to consider what I wanted to do when I grew up. It was anything but an easy question because, from the beginning, all I had in mind was to be a fighter pilot.

. . . the pilot in training must consider the nature and sources of information. "Hangar flying," while an impressive and pleasant pastime from which some information may be gained, is a poor means of resolving problems and gaining knowledge. All too often, exaggerated tales of wild experiences or "war stories" are related merely to impress the less experienced pilot.

—Federal Aviation Administration,
Flight Training Handbook

Chapter 1

Hondo

We turned north, in search again of our landscapes of solitude.

　　　　　　　—William Langewiesche, *Inside the Sky*

Flying is best done alone.

I began learning this in Hondo, Texas, in 1958. A village 40 miles west of San Antonio, Hondo was home to one of the contractor-operated primary flying schools then used by the Air Force.

The principal business of the Air Force is to fly airplanes, and in those days there was no mistaking this. Barely a decade old, the organization's first concern had been to create a new, separate service while concurrently repairing the damage done in a rapid postwar demobilization, work only just begun when the Korean War came along. Thus, by the late 1950s, we were still getting organized, hadn't quite figured out *what else* besides flying we should be doing. Half our officers and nearly all our commanders were pilots, as were 200 of our 207 generals. Whatever an airman's later assignment, pilot training was likely his introduction to the Air Force and his single most important, formative career experience.

By agreement, the Air Force took some of the yield each year from the two existing service academies. In the decade after 1947, about 30 percent of West Point and nearly 10 percent of Annapolis graduates volunteered for Air Force commissions. The other services were unhappy about this, and, in fact, the new Air Force Academy was up and running, on track to produce its first graduates in 1959. Meanwhile, the Aviation Cadet Program, which combined officer candidate school and flight training, was our largest source of officers. Aviation cadets typically had some college credit, but most lacked a degree, making Air Force officers on average the least educated of any service, a serious concern for an organization seeking leadership in the age of technology. We had resolved to get rid of the Aviation Cadet Program as soon as other officer sources—mainly college ROTC—could be expanded to provide enough pilot candidates. However, in 1958 the Aviation Cadet Program was still going strong. My class, designated 59E, divided about evenly between cadets and commissioned officers who, like me, were ROTC guys.

I was born in Santa Rosa, northern California, in the middle of the Depression. A sister, Norma Grace, came 18 months after me. We didn't get to know our father, who managed a quick getaway and is lost to memory. He left behind the reputation of a dreamer who couldn't keep a job. As "Scotty Merrill," he composed sentimental lyrics that eluded publication ("It's Been Fun to Play the Field," "My Honey with Honey-Colored Hair," "When It's Payday It's Lei Day in Oahu"). His teaching invention, the Merrill Melody Method for Stringed Instruments, didn't catch on. He was more successful chording a country-and-western guitar, which is how he met my mother, an occasional bass fiddle player. I do remember my grandparents on both sides, though I didn't see much of the elder McPeaks, who lived in Santa Rosa. On my mother's side, grandfather Stewart gave sound advice: "Never get a tattoo. The police use them for positive identification."

After our father left, Mother raised my sister and me on her own, which is to say in combination with a succession of stepfathers, some worse than others. We moved a lot, mostly around California, but there were episodes in Washington, Oregon, Idaho, Nevada. I have almost no recollection of the series of lodgings we occupied, except that a few were still off the electric grid, and two or three did not yet incorporate indoor toilet facilities. We were transient not so much out of restlessness as owing to matrimonial dynamics and the need to get fed and housed. I went to school all over the place, always the new kid. A slow developer, I wasn't much good at sports, the deficiency making playground life even more unforgiving for a boy. I failed third grade in Kellogg, Idaho, but we moved and the record was lost. I never had a paper route or joined the Boy Scouts. Early, I discovered the pleasures of withdrawal into the world of books. Only a sporadic Sunday school attendee and never baptized, I leaned on Zane Grey rather than scripture for help in building a value system. Later, I dived into science fiction, Ray Bradbury a special favorite.

At age 12, I got my first job for wages, hoeing weeds at a commercial nursery, tough going and 35 cents an hour. My sister and I had always done chores at home, but with this first outside employment I got a painful lesson: you owed the house one day of every week's pay for rent, plus you bought your own school clothes. Ignoring the disincentive, I've either had steady work or been looking hard for it ever since. I scrubbed pots and pans at a chicken pie shop in east San Diego—hellish, Orwellian labor. In summer, I picked berries, peaches and apples in Washington, harvested hops in Oregon, cleared brush at the Josephine County Fairgrounds. I developed an appetite for savings, a deep distrust of debt.

My academic record was up and down, but in high school I began to achieve some success at public speaking. I was good in the individual events, writing and delivering orations, and maybe better at debate—a combative, two-man team sport. By my junior year, spent mostly at Hoover High School in San Diego, I was getting some recognition in interscholastic contests. At one tournament, I managed a win over Dennis Hopper in an event called dramatic declamation. Hopper's stage skills had made him already something of a local legend and, of course, he went from strength to strength as an actor and director in Hollywood. I don't remember the piece he performed. I'd done an adaptation of Bradbury's short story "There Will Come Soft Rains," about an automated house that continues to function for a while in the time after a massive nuclear exchange. My pretending to be a house was what beat Dennis Hopper, much better than me at playing people.

And it was at Hoover High that I met Elynor Moskowitz, a leggy, brainy star of the girls' debate team.

Mother gave my sister and me fresh last names for the usually abbreviated duration of each remarriage, so I accumulated multiple identities. In 1952, the delegates to California Boys State elected me governor under the name Tony Fuller. Because of this unexpected feat and my public speaking exploits, I got quite stuck-up. I squirm to think of it now, but in those adolescent years I worried my celebrity would dissolve in a confusion of names. Midway through my senior year, at Grants Pass High School in southern Oregon, my sister and I took on the social pain of reverting to our natural father's proper name.

The early years of confrontation with the Soviet Union gave rise to many topics chosen for high school debate. The issues were important, worthy of the analysis we did, but there was little to inspire in this "cold" war, no "greatest generation" storming the beaches, no John Wayne in *Flying Tigers* showing us how fighter pilots do it. Romance was replaced by grim realism: an Iron Curtin falling across Central Europe, civil war in Greece, the Berlin blockade, a containment policy erected against Communist spread, the misery in Korea grinding to an inconclusive stop. Stalin's death in 1953 loosed the attempted jailbreak in East Germany, precursor of other uprisings, notably the fateful Hungarian Revolution of 1956.

At least at the start of the Cold War, our international actions seemed reasoned and proportionate, the domestic reaction unbalanced and in many ways foolish. The House Un-American Activities

Committee conducted venomous hearings that led to blacklisting Hollywood writers and artists whose unorthodoxy posed a threat to the republic. A young Navy veteran named Richard Nixon was on the committee and parleyed red-baiting into promotion from House to Senate, then on to the vice presidency. The loathsome Joseph McCarthy was abroad in the land. My friends and I cheered when the junior senator from Wisconsin was at last brought low by the Army-McCarthy hearings and Edward R. Murrow's telecast attacks, but we wondered why a warrior like Eisenhower hadn't the courage to stand against him. In what would become a recurring theme in the years ahead, the judicial branch seemed the only reliable source of progress: in *Brown v. Board of Education*, the Supreme Court ruled that segregation in the public schools violated the Constitution, that separate was inherently unequal.

In the late summer of 1953, I hitchhiked from Grants Pass down the length of California, headed for San Diego State College, the first of my family to begin a higher education. Andy Brown, a friend already a student there, had seen to it that the college offered me an academic scholarship covering tuition and books. In those years, San Diego State was a feared competitor in intercollegiate debate, and Andy was recruiting top draft choices. He also convinced the Sigma Chi house to hire me as a hasher, meaning I could offset the cost of room and board by washing dishes and waiting tables. These blessings were much appreciated but put no cash in the pocket, so I looked for supplemental employment. I did minor auto repairs and pumped gas at a service station, updated plat drawings in the county tax assessor's office, worked the night shift at one of the new hotels being built in Mission Valley.

Following my freshman year, I returned to southern Oregon one last time. That beautiful summer of 1954, I worked as a lifeguard on the Rogue River and taught swimming at a newly opened municipal pool. Altogether, I lived in Grants Pass perhaps a year and a half but always after claimed the town as my home of record.

By my junior year, I (gratefully) put dishwashing aside, instead earning my keep by managing the fraternity house—hiring and supervising the cook and housemother, ordering goods and services, paying bills, keeping the books.

One problem with boarding at the fraternity house: Saturday breakfast was the last meal until Monday morning. Weekends were spent foraging, a sort of recurring survival school. Often, though, Ellie Moskowitz, who also had decided to attend San Diego State, made life easier by getting me invited to Sunday dinner. I came to know the family pretty well, maybe better than my own. Asher Moskowitz, Ellie's father, had roots running back to Romania. He'd established a successful fruit and vegetable business in Salt Lake City, there wooing and winning Fern Clawson. The Clawsons made up a large Utah clan, Swedish Mormons, and if the family was not famous for its handsome women, it should have been.

I recall taking Ellie to the movies often, once to watch Kim Novak slow-dance William Holden in *Picnic*. There is an ancient stratagem for success with girls: tell the pretty ones they're smart and the smart ones they're pretty. In Kim Novak's case, you might have to stick with plan A. With Ellie Moskowitz, you had a choice.

Those days, the Military Academy at West Point sponsored an annual tournament that was a sort of national championship, the pinnacle of college debate. Schools from all over the country came there after surviving regional eliminations. I went three times, never winning or coming close. Still, being invited to West Point three times running would be a hard record to beat. As a sophomore, I teamed with Andy Brown, and as a junior with Ada Picaisen, an attractive and persuasive advocate.[1] I was always second speaker for my team, closing in for the kill. My strengths were preparation, pushiness, and the ability to think on my feet. A blunt instrument, I relied on my partner for any charm needed to win

---

1 As this is written, Andreas Brown is an expert on rare books and first editions. For many years, he owned and operated New York City's Gotham Book Mart. Ada Sands is a successful attorney in Los Angeles.

over the judges. My third shot at West Point was with the former Ellie Moskowitz, now a partner in life as well as debate, after I talked her into crossing the state line to Yuma, Arizona, where, in 1956, we married in a civil ceremony.

San Diego State had an Air Force ROTC unit, which ordinarily would not have interested me. As I entered college, active combat operations in Korea had long since stopped, and there was little chance of being drafted. On the other hand, ROTC academics were dead easy, a criterion I always applied when selecting course work, and the government paid upper-class cadets a dollar a day, clinching the deal. I certainly did not intend a military career. I disliked the parade ground and avoided it whenever possible, earning an appearance before the Cadet Honor Council to explain my numerous absences and coming quite close to being tossed out of the program. Even so, I managed somehow to be named a distinguished graduate of ROTC and, like everyone in this category, was offered a regular commission, the same kind then given to service academy graduates. I turned it down, thinking this enhanced status should go to someone interested in long service, and opted instead for the standard Reserve commission, obligating me to only four years of active duty—or five, if I went to flying school.

My academic standing put me at the head of the line to enter the Air Force following graduation, but I saw no reason for haste. In Moscow, Khrushchev had become first secretary of the Communist Party. A brief struggle for power ensued, but by 1956 he felt secure enough to denounce Stalin in a famous "secret" speech to the party faithful. What could be better? Khrushchev was distancing himself from the Stalinist past. We needed to be watchful, of course, but just maybe he was onto something with this idea of peaceful coexistence. Anyway, the Communist bloc seemed increasingly less monolithic—unsettled, headed toward schism. Stalin's death had Mao Zedong thinking he deserved to be recognized as the movement's senior leader, and that wasn't happening. In fact, Khrushchev attacked many hard-line policies that Mao had supported with gusto. The developing Sino-Soviet split gave us strategic maneuver room.

There was a small dark cloud, an insurgency brewing in Vietnam. When, in 1954, the French were defeated at Dien Bien Phu, President Eisenhower cited a "domino theory" to warn of consequences. At Geneva, a conference of interested parties split the country temporarily into a Communist North and anti-Communist South and promised unifying elections in two years. Ho Chi Minh, a major political figure with nationalist legitimacy and widespread popular appeal, led the North. In the South, former emperor Bao Dai, who had carried water first for the French, then for the Japanese, then for the French again, fronted the government, with Ngo Dinh Diem, a Roman Catholic in an overwhelmingly Buddhist country, as prime minister. We had begun sending aid to the Saigon government directly—not, as previously, laundering money through the French—and our Military Assistance Advisory Group switched its 700 advisers from helping the French to training and equipping the South's army. Diem soon rigged a referendum, ousted Bao Dai, and declared South Vietnam a republic, with himself as president and family members and friends occupying many key posts. Armed insurgent activity, supplied and supported by the North, began almost immediately. Diem held the opposition up to scorn, calling them Viet Cong, meaning Vietnamese Communists. When Diem made a state visit to Washington, Eisenhower praised him as the "miracle man" of Asia.

In the summer of 1957, the situation seemed messy, but recoverable. The deadline for countrywide elections promised by the Geneva Accords had passed, with Diem refusing to cooperate, but Moscow had gone so far as to propose making the partition permanent, with North and South admitted separately to the United Nations. We rejected the idea, overestimating our ability to control events. We'd already "lost" China, and our experience in Korea had not been positive. We weren't about to recognize a Communist North Vietnam.

As if to show that Vietnam was a minor disturbance far away from Cold War center stage, the Russians orbited Sputnik 1, opening the space age and casting a long shadow over American scientific and technical achievement.

For Ellie and me, the important things were the birth of a first son, Mark, within a few days of college graduation, and a balance of $700 I owed on a loan from the Daughters of the American Revolution. We resolved to retire this obligation before going into the Air Force. I got a job at Ryan Aeronautical Corporation in San Diego and spent several months there, learning something of the game played by defense contractors. Then, debt free, we came into the Air Force at the end of 1957.

In due course, an officer's seniority is established by his active duty date of entry, so I had spotted my year group a six-month head start up the promotion ladder. But this was of little consequence as I planned only a brief stay in the Air Force.

—✈—

A new flying training class stood up every six weeks, the students shared out to five civilian primary schools operating in the South. Primary lasted six months, after which graduates reported to regular Air Force bases for an additional six months of basic flying training. Primary, the introduction to flying fundamentals, was the same for everybody, but students streamed into two basic tracks: about half went to B-25s (the equipment used in Doolittle's Tokyo Raid), where they prepared to crew multiengine, prop-driven aircraft, mostly transports. Prospective jet pilots went instead to T-33 training. Those who made it through both the primary and basic phases were awarded wings—and aviation cadets, their commissions as second lieutenants—in just over a year.

—✈—

The Army Air Corps graduated 301 pilots in 1938, all the training done by military instructors at military bases. The next year, Hitler invaded Poland, and the Air Corps couldn't keep up with the workload. By May 1943, 56 civilian contract flying schools were in operation, enjoying an effective monopoly of primary flight training.

Civilian instruction was of good quality and somewhat cheaper than the military variety. Typically, instructor pilots (IPs) were middle-aged men with impressive credentials—ex-airline guys, crop dusters, barnstormers, a few with military experience. They could be exceptional teachers, having seen most of the mischief nature and man can cook up in an airplane.

But the Air Corps, and later the Air Force, was never happy to outsource pilot training. The institution's principal asset was its airmanship. We therefore prized flying experience and didn't want to give it away to civilian instructors, even if it meant we had to ride around in some student's backseat. Moreover, officer instructors were thought to be more professional; civilian schooling, adopted reluctantly, was always seen as a short-term expedient. As a consequence, contract flying schools began phasing out in 1943— the last one folded in 1945—then had to be reopened to meet the surge demands of the Korean War.

Now, in early 1958, the Air Force was once again pulling the plug on civilian schools with a view to consolidating flying training in-house. Class 59E would be the last through Hondo. The base was closing, and as classes ahead of us graduated and moved on to the basic phase at six-week intervals, they were not replaced. The drawdown thinned out the civilian instructor force, a development highlighted every 45 days as IPs with greater seniority exercised bumping rights. My instructor, Bill Robinson, was an old hand who provided stability, but some of my classmates struggled through a succession of IPs, many of them preoccupied with concerns about their own future.

———————◆———————

Three kinds of instruction comprised our training day: academics, military, and flying. In the classroom, platform instructors covered the core disciplines—aerodynamics, engineering, radio communications, navigation, weather, aviation physiology—in considerable detail. We listened to enough Morse to pass the test: decode five three-letter groups a minute. In addition, for each new aircraft type, an equipment course was devoted to its various systems: engine, fuel, electrics, hydraulics. Theory was held to a minimum, the emphasis on a practical understanding of normal and emergency procedures.

Military instruction consisted of lectures on ethics and behavior, a little professional reading, and lots of marching and in-ranks inspections. Air Force regulations granted the chaplain a minimum of five minutes to plead with each of us. We received a healthy dose of physical training and sports. If we didn't know how, we were taught to swim. Seven of us from 59E put together an officers' basketball team and won the base tournament against depleted competition.

For officers, the students themselves ran military training, with leadership positions going to a sprinkling of youngish captains who'd served time in other career specialties before recycling through pilot training. A small cadre of regulars made military training for aviation cadets a lot harder. Cadets were separated from officers and lived in barracks, subject to 24-hour supervision. Worse, if a student officer washed out, he was still an officer and could go on to other professional schooling. (Often, this was the route to becoming a navigator.) For aviation cadets, washing out meant finishing an enlistment in ranks. Not surprisingly, a little friction showed in the relations between student officers and cadets.

But even for cadets, the strictly military training, the development of "officership," was subordinated to the task of learning to fly. Thus, of the three types of instruction, flying training was by far the most important. Half the duty day was spent on the flight line or in the air. When not flying or briefing about flying, students hung around, studied, or performed flight line chores of varying importance. We carried the IP's parachute to the airplane, stood fireguard during engine start, pulled and replaced wheel chocks, refueled the planes. I liked every part of it. Even at this modest level, flight line operations were exotic, fascinating.

We sat for hours in the aircraft, practicing the steps of each normal and emergency procedure and memorizing the location of gauges and switches, preparation for the blindfold cockpit check administered before first solo. Here on the ground we established habit patterns that would keep us alive in the air: tighten the lap belt and shoulder harness until there was no more give; lower the seat to the exact same position every time; adjust the rudder pedals to a comfortable distance, making sure you can get full rudder throw and still compress the brakes completely; check every switch, knob, gauge, handle, and circuit breaker from back-left around to back-right. At first, this was done methodically, using a bulky checklist, but gradually the lodgings became familiar and the checklist was relegated to standby use, there only in case something went wrong.

We came to appreciate the importance of human factors in cockpit layout and design. By the mid-50s, we had finally figured out that the airplane is not a machine but an extension of the pilot. The most important gauges—attitude indicator, altimeter, airspeed indicator—were grouped at the top center of the instrument panel. Control knobs were of different sizes and shapes so they could be identified by touch. As obvious as these design basics may seem, they'd all been learned the hard way.

We got our first actual flying hours in the T-34, a small, tandem two-seater developed from the Beech Bonanza. Delivered starting in 1954, the planes were still pretty new. Weighing just over 2,000 pounds empty, a 225-horsepower Continental O-470 gave the T-34 a cruising speed of about 170 mph. All metal and fully aerobatic, it was safe and easy to fly.

T-34 training was followed by checkout in the T-28, built by North American. Three times as heavy as the T-34, it looked serious, and big as a house at first. Powered by a Wright R-1300 radial engine reminiscent of many World War II fighters, it cruised at more than 200 mph and had a max speed of nearly 300, performance impressive enough that an up-engined version was used by the French in Algeria and by the air forces of South Vietnam and Thailand as a light attack aircraft.

Both the T-34 and T-28 featured tricycle landing gear, a major improvement over the T-6, the Air Force's primary trainer until the mid-1950s. The T-6 Texan was a tail-dragger, a configuration making it a handful when taxiing and during takeoff or landing. But as the Air Force moved to jet-powered aircraft that couldn't drag tailpipes along the ground, the T-6 was phased out in favor of trainers with tricycle gear.

For flight training, the class operated out of a building next to the parking ramp. Activity was organized around tables, arranged for an instructor and three students. The IP led briefings before and debriefings after each flight. All the students at a table listened in on these and could follow one another's progress toward the first important milestone: initial solo in the T-34. It soon became clear that one of my tablemates, an aviation cadet, was already a pilot. He had a private license and claimed hundreds of hours of flying time. Aviation cadets in general showed little deference to student officers, and when our IP, Mr. Robinson, was absent, this cadet was especially generous with suggestions. Judging by debriefings, he was progressing smoothly through the initial stages of instruction. I concluded he was our table's best bet to solo first.

But it has never been easy to predict who will do well in flight training. In the early days, a celebrated nostrum held that men who could ride well, sail fast boats or handle a motorcycle were good prospects. Promising candidates were likely to be athletic but not necessarily smarter than average. Hap Arnold, father of the independent Air Force, was the prototype. Graduated from West Point in 1907, he wanted cavalry but, owing to class standing, ended up in the infantry. It was largely to escape this fate that he volunteered for the aviation branch of the Signal Corps, attending the Wright brothers' school in 1911 to become one of the first military pilots.

Over the years, preflight screening became somewhat less haphazard. During World War I, applicants were blindfolded and twirled in a spinning chair to test equilibrium. Just before World War II, the Army developed a written test, called the standard nine or "stanine," supposed to assess a range of aptitudes in nine bands centered about the mean of normally distributed scores. As a practical matter, the emphasis remained on hand-eye coordination, good eyesight, and motor skills. Most people believed that academic achievement, especially in the humanities or social sciences, did not markedly improve chances of success.

My stanine scores had been quite high, and I was enthralled, entirely captivated by my initial experience with flight. Nonetheless, I was anything but a natural pilot. In the air, the format never varied: Mr. Robinson explained each new maneuver, then demonstrated it. I tried to imitate; he corrected mistakes; I tried again. Deliberate, mechanical, I did things by the book. Never far off the mark, I got it exactly right only rarely.

In later years, I would learn that few really good pilots trust their lives to natural ability. They may seem awfully casual about it, but the ones who survive do little that isn't meticulously prepared. ("Lucky Lindy" never came close to describing Charles Lindbergh.) But at this point in my own flying career, I worried about not being able to make flying seem effortless, as it wants to be. So it was a mystery why Mr. Robinson decided I would solo first, not just for our table, but for the whole class.

That initial solo flight didn't amount to much—a few circuits of the traffic pattern, a couple of touch-and-goes followed by a full-stop landing, all under the watchful eye of Mr. Robinson, standing at the edge of the tarmac. Still, nothing I'd done before evoked simultaneous emotional opposites: exhilaration layered over an inner calm. Alone, I relaxed, experimented, allowed mistakes. Still an awkward apprentice, I somehow came under the spell that's cast when a craftsman loses himself among his tools.

I decided what I wanted most was to be alone in the airplane, to be a fighter pilot.

———✦———

The days galloped by at Hondo as Class 59E moved through the primary curriculum. Before soloing, we'd become familiar with the general operation of the airplane, starting with straight-and-level flight and progressing to the turns, climbs, and dives that make flying interesting and useful. We came to recognize the numberless ways of getting in trouble. We forced the airplane into its various stall modes—power on, power off, accelerated stall, cross-control stall, elevator trim stall, secondary stall—and got proficient at recovery from each of these, as well as from the spins that develop when one wing is more fully stalled than the other. Reacting to power loss became second nature. Mr. Robinson yanked the throttle to idle and yelled, "Forced landing!" so often I flew in my mind's eye from one cow pasture to the next, always ready to set it down.

In the next phase, we worked on precision control, flying standard courses and patterns, elementary 8's, lazy 8's, pylon 8's, chandelles. We developed proficiency in the various kinds of approaches and landings, learned how to handle crosswinds, organized a spot-landing contest. We got a fair ration of aerobatics, doing loops, cloverleafs, Immelmanns, split-S's, the menu of rolls.

Flying is never mastered, but we either got better at it or washed out. One way or another, we lost 40 percent of my classmates, all of whom had tested well for aptitude, and almost all because of flying deficiency. (It was understood that anyone who failed the relatively simple academics did so on purpose.) At first, much of the attrition was due to airsickness, rooted in physical causes but usually amplified by anxiety. Our instructors, convinced every pilot's life must include some memorable moments, probed to see how we would handle stress. Hazing technique varied with instructor style. Some IPs yelled over the intercom during the entire lesson. It was pure luck if you did anything right for these guys. But even the most benign IPs cranked up the tension as needed, and more than a few students folded under pressure.

Once past being airsick or terrorized, many who had hoped to become pilots failed because they lacked one or both of the twin skills essential to safe flying. The first is division of attention, the ability to collect and evaluate a lot of information from a variety of sources and thereby develop a heightened awareness of the situation.

At one end of the scale, some students seemed incapable of recognizing even ominous changes in their circumstances. Their eyes glazed into a hundred-yard stare. We said of them that they had their "head up and locked," a play on what happens when the wheels are raised after takeoff. It was the IP's job to identify and eliminate such people quickly.

But even for those with good ability to observe, the act of flying reshapes everything all the time, inside and outside the cockpit. Most of the changes are of little consequence. Nonetheless, safe flying requires that the variables be noted, analyzed, a decision be made to act or wait. With time and experience, much of the workload will be taken over by the subconscious. But it's far from automatic in the beginning, and I pushed myself: check altitude, airspeed, and the rates at which these are changing; look around for traffic; make a quick scan of the engine instruments. What's the weather doing? Check fuel quantity and flow. Am I feeding from the proper tank? Now where am I? Look at the map. Like quantum events, the act of inspection itself produces a result, triggering another cycle of observation, evaluation, action.

The best pilots—there will be two or three in any fighter squadron—seem to have the human version of a fly's compound eye. They pay attention to everything at once, all the time. Parallel observation of the many variables is important because no one acts effectively on the unnoticed. An aircraft accident is the climax of a sequence, beginning from an infinite number of initial conditions and moving through a succession of events, each event reducing safety margins by some amount. Finally, there comes an additional, culminating event, you run out of options, and an accident occurs. This sequence is true of every accident and can be interrupted at any point if someone notices and acts on available information. By seeing everything all the time, the pilot builds up situation awareness in layers, like a composite material. The glue's secret ingredient is this knack for dividing attention.

The second essential quality is the ability to prioritize. Several important things may be happening at once. For instance, unintended altitude loss is likely to be accompanied by undesired airspeed increase. Which should be fixed first? If at medium altitude, airspeed buildup may be more threatening; close to the ground, better take care of altitude. The ability to recognize and work on the most important of competing priorities is also at the heart of safe flying.

These two indispensable skills seem in tension with one another. At the least, they have a sort of duality about them. Dividing attention illuminates, prioritizing spotlights. When to do which?

There are no easy answers in flying, even at the beginning, even if it will never be more than a hobby. But we were becoming professionals, so one further skill had to be added to the mix. When we can see our surroundings and orient on them, nearly all of us can visualize space and time relationships well enough to roller-skate or climb a stepladder. But aviators must learn how to make a mental picture of time and space when there is no visual reference to the real world. We started on this problem in the famous Link Trainer.

———♦———

In the early 1930s, Ed Link put together the first true flight simulator in the basement of his father's piano factory. Mounted on a fulcrum and painted blue, it had a stubby wooden fuselage with an organ bellows attached to provide air pressure that banked, pitched and yawed the whole assembly. When Link tried to sell what he called the Blue Box, amusement parks rather than flying schools bought most of them. He nevertheless went into the flight training business when the Depression closed down his piano operation. A few years later, the federal government contracted with the Army to fly domestic airmail. The adventure cost the Air Corps 11 pilots the first week, all lost in bad weather, and the Army ordered six Link Trainers at $3,500 apiece. It purchased 10,000 more in World War II.

Some of these Blue Boxes were still in use at Hondo. We spent 25 hours in them, instructors monitoring our progress at an outside console. We climbed in, closed the lid, and entered a world in which you could not see what the airplane was doing but had to measure it, like a sort of laboratory experiment.

Soon, we graduated to the rear cockpit of the T-28. The backseat featured a cloth hood, a bag pulled down over the pilot's head to hide the outside. Flying under the hood was at least as tough as flying in cloud, plus an element of claustrophobia made it seem even worse. We polished the basic maneuvers learned in the Link, including hooded takeoffs, and soon progressed to the added complication of navigation instruments. We learned how to intercept a course and track to and from ground-based radio aids, how to hold at fixes, how to penetrate safely to lower altitude. We didn't do hooded landings, but we did fly hooded approaches to published minimums. It was a nice feeling when the IP told you to come out from under the hood and your first sight was the runway, just below, on centerline, in great shape to land.

Here in the South, a nascent civil rights movement was underway. Emmett Till had been murdered only a couple of years before, in Money, Mississippi. An all-white jury acquitted his killers, the case causing nationwide consternation. Recently, Rosa Parks had refused to give up her seat to a white man, sparking the bus boycott in Montgomery, Alabama, that gave Martin Luther King Jr. a major role to play. Still more recently, President Eisenhower had sent troops to Little Rock to enforce school integration, pushing Gov. Orval Faubus aside.

On this Texas air base, progress was not yet visible. There were no black faces among my classmates, officer or cadet.

No women either.

———✦———

In important ways, flying school was as much an initiation as a place to learn a craft. If the trainee survived the winnowing process, he entered the fraternity. Pilot skills and *attitude*—a controlled response to pressure, a veneer of false modesty—defined one's status inside the brotherhood. Ancestry, education, even rank, were secondary considerations. There was the undeniable, ever-present fact of accident and death. The base salary of a second lieutenant was $222.30 a month, but flight pay added a fat $100-a-month premium for hazardous duty. (Officers in ground jobs said we didn't make more money, we just made it faster.) Inside the club, the shared experience of flight, including its acknowledged risks, produced less rigid, more informal officers and a loose, casual association that appealed to me.

But it was flying, the thing itself rather than its sociology, that became a dominant force in my life. For me, flying was a replacement childhood. My own had been virtual. I'd gotten through by being watchful, risk averse, a fake adult. Now I was given a second chance at the unmixed pleasure only children experience. Flying was simply great fun, replete with small but consequential tasks that could in theory be done perfectly every time, leading to instant gratification every time, over and over again.

———✦———

We lived on base in what passed for family housing—modular clapboard, set on cinder blocks. A tiny oil stove positioned at the exact geographic center of the structure took the edge off a raw Texas winter. The small clothes closet had no doors; Ellie juryrigged bedsheets to shield its contents. With a baby on hand, she was not happy about the occasional cruiserweight scorpion that put in an appearance.

Its renowned city-limits sign—"This is God's country, please don't drive through it like hell"—earned Hondo a *National Geographic* cover. The town was otherwise unremarkable. (It played no part in the early 1950s filming of *Hondo,* based on Louis L'Amour's breakout Western novel.) Even grocery shopping was limited. When Ellie cooked up a Middle Eastern casserole calling for cashews, none could be found in Hondo. She improvised to produce "peanuts Turkistan," the dish becoming part of family folklore. At the end of the pay period, if we had any cash left, we drove to a local ranch and ordered two or three chickens killed and cleaned, putting them away as a buffer against future consumption. A small cafe in town served family style. At night, the cockroach army mobilized in the light rings of half a dozen street lamps, exoskeletons crunching as we motored through the beams, headed back to the base.

But, imagine! They were paying me $300 a month and providing free, heated housing, all for doing something I loved, that I'd pay *them* to do. We budgeted and were able to save on the salary. I financed a slightly used 1957 Chevy and began putting aside $50 a month for the next automobile, resolving never again to make car payments (which I did not).

—✦—

As flying operations at Hondo continued to fade out I got my first exposure to the remarkable process of base closure. Hard as it was for someone with the habit of frugality to believe, I saw it with my own eyes. Workmen swarmed over sleepy little Hondo Air Base. Every building got a fresh coat of paint. Trees said to be worth $50,000 were planted. Base closure came with a budget that had to be spent.

—✦—

As graduation from primary approached, we were scheduled for a final check ride in the T-28. This was a biggie. Student preference for jet training far exceeded availability. Half of us had to go to B-25s; only those with high class standing could count on getting the T-33.

The check-ride format was an out-and-back cross-country, with a stop at another of the civilian primary flying schools, the one at Mission, Texas, in the Rio Grande Valley. We'd fly out in daylight, back at night; one leg solo, the other dual, an IP accomplishing the flight check on the dual leg. It was not an instructional flight. The idea was to see how we would plan and fly a cross-country, the IP a silent observer. I drew the check on the outbound, daylight leg.

My check-flight instructor was new to the class, having recently bumped his way onto our staff. Thus, he was an unknown quantity, but it didn't much matter, as my approach would in any case be by-the-book conservative. Mission briefing, start-up, taxi, takeoff, and initial climb were uneventful. I took pains to do everything just right, making continuous small adjustments to engine controls, airspeed, climb rate. Everything seemed to be going well until I leveled at 10,000 feet and pulled the throttle, rpm, and mixture knobs back to cruise settings. Correct engine management requires these controls to be set precisely, but no sooner had I established the proper values than the IP pushed his backseat levers forward, adding power, making clear his desire that we cruise well above textbook airspeed. This troubled me a bit, as the check ride was supposed to showcase what I would do by myself. Also, the higher cruising speed would throw off the flight planning I'd done; my leg times and fuel figures would be all wrong. So much for preparation, but . . . OK.

En route, we began to encounter the puffy cumulus cloud typical of a summertime Texas afternoon. I'd filed with Air Traffic Control for flight in accordance with visual flight rules (VFR), meaning I should keep clear of cloud. At first I was able to weave between the buildups, staying semi-legal, but sky conditions gradually worsened, and I decided to descend below the cloud deck. By now, I was cruising at rather high speed and needed to reduce power for descent. As I pulled back the throttle and started down, the IP once again shoved the lever forward, telling me to climb instead. Apparently, he did not want to lose speed, as we would by letting down into the thicker air at lower altitude.

A couple of things were wrong with climbing. First, the cloud cover was now so solid I'd have to punch through to get VFR on top. So far, I'd been fudging, but it was flat, undeniably illegal (and unsafe) to enter cloud on a VFR clearance. Second, it looked like I'd need to climb well above 14,000 feet to get into the clear. Air Force regulations prohibited flight at such an altitude without oxygen, which we did not have. (The T-28 was unpressurized, so the air outside was what got delivered to us, inside.) Thus, I was about to break the law on at least two counts. Anyway, I climbed and was able to level at 17,000, dodging cloud tops while continuing at high speed toward the base at Mission.

As we neared destination, I again pulled back power for an en route descent and watched as the knobs moved forward. I had no alternative except to descend to traffic pattern altitude, and now airspeed really began building up. The gauge had a red index mark at the maximum allowable indicated airspeed. I quickly got to this redline, and beyond, which made me uncomfortable. In ground school, platform instructors had talked us through the phenomena associated with flight above the limit, unpleasant things like wing flutter and other forms of aeroelasticity, aileron reversal, critical gust, and the stability and buffet problems associated with compressibility effects. To provide some margin for safety, aircraft are usually flight tested to 1.2 times the redline speed. Going faster than this would likely cause aircraft structural damage or even failure.

It was impossible to hide my surreptitious efforts to cheat the power back, but I kept trying, and the IP, even-tempered until now, got upset.

"Where do you want to go for basic?" he asked—loud, agitated.

"T-33s, sir."

"You better forget it," the sarcasm clear in his tone. "You just don't have what it takes. If I were you, I'd go multiengine, where there's less challenge and you have a crew to look after you."

Right. This would be a self-fulfilling prophecy if he graded me down so that I fell behind my classmates.

I managed to get the aircraft lined up on initial approach for landing but was way too fast in the traffic pattern, had to delay putting the gear and flaps down because of their extension speed limits, flew a wider base leg than I liked and, following standard Air Force procedure, executed a go-around, rather than try to salvage a bad approach. It was too late for the IP to do anything about it when I advanced power for the missed approach, and he was furious. I heard fingers drumming on the instrument panel cover in back, as he described my shortcomings in detail.

"You're going to kill yourself! You're never going to make it! I'll be reading about you in the obituary column of the *Air Force Times!*"

Eventually, I would acquire the confidence and skill to venture outside the sheltering heart of the envelope, but at this early, pupal stage, I saw myself as guilty only of trying to fly by the rules. Nonetheless, the chance of going to fighters, the only thing I really wanted from the Air Force, seemed to be fading fast. With nothing to lose, I decided to punch this guy in the nose as soon as I could get the airplane parked—which would have ended my Air Force career. However, taxiing in, we passed a low structure, "Civilian Personnel Office" lettered on its side. The IP ordered me to pull over and stop. He unstrapped, climbed out, and jumped off the wing, the engine still running. As I resumed taxiing to a parking spot, it hit me: The contract flying school at Mission Air Base would continue to operate for a while after Hondo closed. For him, the check ride had been a race with the other IPs to be first in line with an employment application.

———✦———

Returning to Hondo, the night sky staged an extravaganza—farfetched, somehow make-believe. The magic that earlier conjured afternoon clouds had in turn obliged them to vanish, leaving the Milky Way to spin out a chorus line behind bankable, Van Gogh stars that carried the production. The Summer Triangle—Vega, Deneb, Altair—beamed overhead, the points not winking much at my altitude, solid and fastened to the canopy like a paint job. Scorpius crawled across the southern horizon, at its heart a flame-red Antares, of a bulk to fill our solar system out to the orbit of Mars. Arcturus, another red giant, extended the graceful arc of the Dipper's handle. My engine murmured a raspy baritone, its best Bing Crosby imitation. Instruments glowed in dim red light.

I was at peace in this separate, cockpit world, alone with the sight and sound of flight.

Logbook: Hondo

1957–58	Dual	Solo	Night Dual	Night Solo	Hooded	Total	Landings
T-34	18:10	7:20				25:30	83
T-28	24:05	40:35	3:30	6:20	25:00	99:30	196

Chapter 2

Silver Wings

"In a way," Cleve answered. *"I can't explain it. At first
it's dangerous. Then it changes. It's a sport. You belong
to it. More than that. Finally, it becomes, I don't know,
a refuge. The sky is a godlike place. If you fly it alone, it
can be everything."*

—James Salter, *The Hunters*

I reported to Vance Air Force Base in Enid, Oklahoma, in the
summer of 1958 for six months of basic flying training in the jet-
powered T-33.

In retrospect, we count generations of jet fighter aircraft. Beginning in the mid- to late 1940s, we produced general-purpose fighters, including the F-80, F-84, and F-86, and interceptors such as
the F-89 and F-94. These first-generation jets resembled the World
War II fighters they replaced, relying, like their prop-driven prede-
cessors, on machine guns, unguided rockets, iron bombs, and optical sights. The T-33 was a two-place version of the F-80 and thus a
first-generation jet trainer. Decades of US and foreign pilots earned
their wings in the more than 5,000 T-33s Lockheed produced. It
had the same official nickname as the F-80—Shooting Star—but
everyone ignored this label. It was simply the T-bird.

At an empty weight of about 8,000 pounds, the T-bird was only a little heavier than the T-28, but its slick shape and an Allison engine producing 5,200 pounds of thrust took the airplane to nearly 600 mph. At that speed, it needed an ejection seat—young technology, the first US testing done as recently as 1946. No more baseball caps or earmuff headsets; instead, we wore crash helmets and oxygen masks. This gear, together with a bubble canopy that clanked shut over a skintight cockpit, confined and isolated in a way I found not unattractive, but some of my fellow students didn't like it much, and in the first days of basic we lost a few more candidates on account of this.

The mission for basic schools was to make military pilots out of ordinary pilots. Hence, these schools were not on civilian airfields, like Hondo, but at real Air Force bases, completely controlled and operated by the military. In most other ways, basic training repeated the primary format: on the ground, lots of academics and simulator. The flying syllabus was nearly identical: aircraft handling, traffic-pattern work, aerobatics, and instruments, the difference being all of it was done at jet speeds and altitudes.

But, formation flying! Now, here was something new and different, something we hadn't done at Hondo.

———◆———

Near the midpoint of World War I, the great German ace Oswald Boelcke made a pioneering discovery: two airplanes could be maneuvered to fight as a team. Ever since, combat aircraft have traveled together for mutual support—and not just fighters. The film *Twelve O'Clock High* reminds us that, during World War II, bombers formed up in large cells to concentrate defensive firepower and hold fighter-interceptors at bay. The Luftwaffe got though anyway, and the big, cumbersome formations meant bomber crews were committed to holding course and position for long stretches, solving the tracking problem for flak. Consequently, the Air Corps lost aircrews faster than the ground Army lost infantry, not the result expected by early aviation enthusiasts. For bombers, the large, boxy formations disappeared with the evolution to jet aircraft and nuclear munitions. However, the intercontinental reach of the modern bomber and transport fleets imposed a requirement for aerial refueling. Joining up with a tanker and holding the receiver position within close tolerances meant that both bomber and transport pilots needed good formation flying skills.

In basic, we learned several types of formation, starting with one called "close." (A four-ship version, "fingertip," takes its name from a resemblance to the look of outstretched fingers.) Close formation has no useful combat function because wingmen are so tight they can't look around, or in fact do much else except stare at the leader. It's a show formation, used when returning to base, entering the traffic pattern, doing flyovers—anywhere there might be spectators—and a building block for more advanced, combat-oriented formation flying.

We began by taking up and trying to hold a position next to the leader—not just any position, but one described by the alignment of reference points on the lead aircraft. All aircraft have prominent parts, panels, paint, decals, or other features that can be used as reference points for formation alignment. For many aircraft, the T-bird included, the classic advice is, "put the light on the star." The light is the wingtip navigation light and the star is painted on the fuselage, at the center of the roundel that brands US military aircraft. For the T-bird, wingmen should be able to look up a line running from lead's wingtip light to the star on his fuselage. (Later, we would joke, "*What part* of the light on *what part* of the star?") This line established a front-back reference. In level flight, the wingman should also be a little below lead, about level with the belly of his aircraft, this being a second, up-down reference point. For a final reference—in-out—we used a gap of three feet between wingtips. In close formation, the wingman's eyes should be at the point where these three references triangulated.

Although it doesn't look like it when seen from a distance, formation flight involves a lot of relative movement. Even when straight and level, the highly dynamic character of flight makes for constant change. Wingmen are almost never in precisely the right position, instead making continuous small adjustments to *return* to position. As we notice unwanted movement out of position, we (1) stop the movement, (2) initiate movement back to position, and (3) stop the remedial movement. Rudder keeps the fuselages aligned, elevator holds the up-down reference, ailerons maintain wingtip clearance, and the throttle takes care of positioning fore and aft. Thus, every aircraft control moves at least three times when we adjust any one of them, a complicated waltz in four dimensions.

A good lead makes the job easier, which is why, even in the training setting, a bond develops between leader and wingman. A "contract" between the two is the beginning of the air warrior culture, based on trust. Leaders *trust* wingmen either to be in position or trying to get there. Wingmen *trust* leaders to maneuver in a way that makes this possible. Since wingmen anticipate what lead will likely do and cheat a little, it's essential that lead actually does what makes sense, what was planned for and briefed on the ground—no surprises. If lead is erratic, a wingman can be forgiven for hedging his bets. It's not necessary to follow the leader into the ground, though many have.

Staying in position would seem a straightforward proposition but can be a test in bad weather or at night. Large formations pose special difficulty. Any change in pitch, bank, or power by lead is amplified as each of the wingmen tries in sequence to make adjustments. Moreover, close formation is, in fact, quite close, the other aircraft looming large in the windscreen, midair collision always a live possibility. For this reason, a modified version of close, called "route" formation, allows for roughly two wingspans lateral clearance from lead, along the same fore-and-aft and up-and-down reference lines. Holding this position requires alertness too, but it's possible to do housekeeping chores—radio frequency changes, map folding, fuel checks, and so forth—without fear of impact during very short excursions inside the cockpit.

I delighted in flying formation, a feeling not easy to explain. It's an unnatural act, highly stylized, entirely lacking in the spontaneity that makes single-ship so much fun. At its best, flying opens up a kind of sanctuary, a release not only from the constraints of terrain, but also from the afflictions of social life. This feeling of being alone, potent, and therefore superior to everyone else is especially prized as our individuality comes under comprehensive assault by modern forces of standardization. Undoing all this, the covenants of formation flying impose regimentation, fence off the open range. It's also hard work, physically demanding, and in many ways more a test of character than skill. If, in the end, you don't *want* to be in position, no amount of effort will put you there. Even so, somehow, formation flying was pure pleasure, a fresh entry in the slapstick struggle between humans and logic.

In fact, all the flying at basic was wonderful, though maybe just short of the unadulterated joy of primary. The instruction was indeed more military, more professional, though in my view too many IPs were themselves recent flying school graduates, one lesson ahead of the student. Once again, I was lucky. My IP, Ken Thomas, was a great pilot who had come back to the training business from service in a fighter squadron, with an attitude and operational experience that added much value.

———◆———

A smallish, midwestern town, Enid was the economic and political center of a dry county. (The local newspaper did print front-page notices about where to party on New Year's Eve.) We rented half of a nice duplex, a big step up from our Hondo digs, though the railroad ran by, just east and pretty close. For balance, the Chisholm Trail was on the other side of the house. Over the years its ruts had filled, the rumble and lowing of longhorns no longer a bother, unlike the trains.

In Tornado Alley people took their weather seriously. By now, I knew enough about meteorology to be impressed by the expertise of local TV weathermen, so unlike San Diego's version. Our duplex featured a shelter, dug beside the back door. A couple of times the sky did churn up some excitement, but the one funnel cloud we saw came no closer than a few miles.

———◆———

As graduation approached, we were briefed on assignments. Many of us would end up in bombers, some in the incipient B-52 fleet. The Air Force was taking delivery of a jet tanker, the KC-135, and quite a few would be posted to the right seat of that aircraft. Only a dozen or so of the top graduates (out of 40 in my class at Vance) would get a shot at fighters, and half of these would be interceptor assignments.

By the end of the Vietnam era, the distinction between fighters and interceptors had disappeared. Instead, we would speak of air-to-air, air-to-ground, and dual-role fighters. But in the 1950s, President Eisenhower wanted a reduced defense budget and "more bang for the buck," so we turned to the supposedly less expensive doctrine of massive retaliation. The shift meant most Air Force money went to buy the bombers, tankers, and missiles of Strategic Air Command (SAC) and to make these systems ready for long-range use against the Soviet Union. Second priority went to funding the defense against a similar attack on us by the Soviets. At its peak, Air Defense Command (ADC) operated nearly 1,500 interceptors, providing point defense of American cities and other high-value targets. Many pilots ended up in ADC, then flying F-89s, F-94s, and starting to get F-101s, F-102s, and F-104s. Not much money was left for general-purpose forces, though the Korea experience had shown we could still get involved in conventional wars. Tactical Air Command (TAC) and its overseas counterparts in Europe and the Pacific operated shrinking fleets of fighter-bombers or tactical fighter aircraft, designed to provide air support for conventional conflict in a theater of operations. At the time, the workhorse of the tactical fighter fleet was the F-100 Super Sabre.

A divide existed between two fighter communities. In Air Defense Command, it was all about speed. Interceptors scrambled off an alert pad, accelerated, climbed rapidly and made a single, fast pass on a large, non-maneuvering target. (In the old days, the guys doing this sort of job flew "pursuit" aircraft—hence the "P" in airplanes such as the P-38 and P-51.) There was a premium on head-down, instrument-flying skills, since the country needed defending at night and in any sort of weather. Interceptor pilots wore highly visible, bright orange flying suits. If they bailed out, it would be over friendly territory; they wanted to be found. The mission would be gangbusters if it ever turned real but, day to day, it was mostly sitting alert waiting for an attack that never came.

On the other hand, the tactical fighter pilot was a jack-of-all-trades. Fighters did both air-to-air (air superiority, or fighter-versus-fighter combat) and air-to-ground (bombing and strafing, or close air support and interdiction) missions. These tasks required a combination of speed and maneuverability. It always helped to be good at instrument flying, but most fighter action would happen in daylight and good weather. Not glued to static defense, fighter pilots went to where the action was. Much of the tactical fighter force was stationed abroad, and even stateside-based units rotated overseas often. No orange flight suits for these guys; any combat bailout would likely be behind enemy lines.

All things considered, in January 1959, Air Defense Command was large and vigorous, with what seemed an important role, whereas Tactical Air Command, the parent organization of fighter pilots, was going nowhere as it hustled to find a role in the nuclear age. ADC might be the more attractive option if your primary concern was an Air Force career—which, of course, cut no ice with me.

This assessment of prospects also turned out to be wrong. In the years immediately ahead, Air Defense Command would wither and die as we moved from the doctrine of massive retaliation to that of mutual assured destruction (MAD), the organizing principle being that each side must stand utterly exposed to destruction by the other. The logic of MAD (a truly appropriate acronym) never connected, but, given a decision on this approach, we gradually abandoned the air defense mission in favor of other claims on Air Force resources. By contrast, the Vietnam War produced a renaissance in fighter aviation.

———⊥———

I finished high enough in the class to be named a distinguished graduate, an honor having the practical consequence that I got an early choice of assignments. The training squadron commander tried halfheartedly to recruit me for continued service in Air Training Command, but riding around in somebody else's backseat was, for me, the aerial equivalent of empty calories. I was single-minded about becoming a fighter jock. I hesitated briefly between interceptors and fighters but decided to head for Luke Air Force Base, near Phoenix, Arizona, and combat-crew training in a tactical fighter, the F-100.

———⊥———

The last months of 1958 were unremarkable, except at age 23, Van Cliburn won the first International Tchaikovsky Piano Competition in Moscow, easing Cold War tensions momentarily. In Cuba, Batista fled Havana on New Year's Day. Almost immediately, Che Guevara's column entered the city; by 8 January, Fidel Castro had arrived. In France, Charles de Gaulle was inaugurated as the first president of the Fifth Republic.

And in Enid, Oklahoma, my classmates and I pinned on silver wings. An aeronautical order was published, declaring that, effective 28 January 1959, we held the rating of pilot and were therefore "required to participate frequently and regularly in aerial flight."

I liked that "required" part.

Logbook: Vance

1958–59	Dual	Solo	Night Dual	Night Solo	Hooded	Total	Landings
T-33	61:55	10:20	4:10	1:50	36:15	114:30	100

Rating:

    Pilot

Qualifications:

    Single Engine Jet

    Instruments (White Card)

Chapter 3

Fighter Pilot

Here comes the trout that must be caught with tickling.
—Shakespeare, *Twelfth Night*

Setup time, the gestation period from concept to realization, lengthens as we come to grips with ever-more complex systems, the social echo of biological fact. The stages of pilot training, primary and basic, end with a pinning-on parade, the wings worn with pride, to be sure. But we could be put to no practical use at this point, the graduation ceremony signaling little more than the beginning of another round of revision. We moved on to yet another base and took on yet more instruction, starting with a period of "transition," the term for learning how to operate any unfamiliar airplane. Already, we'd transitioned from the T-34 to the T-28, and from the latter to the T-33. The transition now to a combat aircraft was a larger undertaking, involving not only a complicated, high-performance jet, but also a new set of flying techniques.

In the air, the Korean War had been a clash of first-generation jets, notably on our side the F-86 Sabre and on the other the MiG-15. Both aircraft benefited from Germany's wartime swept-wing research and were therefore transonic—that is, could operate at or near the speed of sound. The F-86 was easy to fly, quite stable, and had the edge in agility, being able to roll faster so as to reposition itself either to fend off gun attack or realign its own guns. However, the MiG was lighter, had a more powerful engine, and could turn tighter, climb quicker, cruise higher and go faster at altitude. We regarded the outcome in Korea as a success mostly because our pilots had a training edge on the Koreans and Chinese (and Russians). We needed better equipment and got it in the Century Series, a set of second-generation jet fighters characterized by supersonic speed, avionics—the new buzzword for aviation electronics—and reliance on air-to-air guided missiles instead of guns.

The first of the Century Series, a prototype of North American's F-100 Super Sabre, flew in mid-1953. The A version—a single-seat, day dogfighter—had an afterburner that increased thrust by dumping additional fuel into the engine exhaust. Using afterburner, the F-100 was supersonic at sea level, a first for any combat aircraft.[2] (The Hun's landing speed was nearly as impressive, so

---

2 It went supersonic on its initial test flight, winning a bet for North American's test pilot, George S. "Wheaties" Welch. "You owe me two beers," he radioed Col. "Speedy" Pete Everest, chasing him in an F-86.

Lt. Welch was one of the few pilots to get off the ground during the 7 December 1941 attack on Pearl Harbor. Having partied all night, he hadn't yet gone to bed when the Japanese struck. He managed to shoot down four enemy aircraft that day, one of them probably our first aerial victory in World War II. Allowing for cinematic license, the story is told in two films, *Tora, Tora, Tora* (1970) and *Pearl Harbor* (2001). With Hap Arnold's blessing, Welch was submitted for the Medal of Honor, but intervening authority downgraded the decoration on the grounds that his take-off that morning had not been authorized. He ended the war with 12 kills.

Heir to a grape juice fortune, Welch had no need to work. Nevertheless, after the war he signed on with North American, becoming that company's chief test pilot. He may have broken the sound barrier in an F-86 a week or so before Chuck Yeager did it officially in the Bell X-1. In October 1954 he was killed testing the F-100.

Welch might have been a little relaxed in his approach to engineering test work. (See Bob Hoover, *Forever Flying*.) Sometimes people don't respect what they are by nature good at. In flying, this would be a mistake.

fast it was our first fighter to require a drag chute.) The F-100A was optimized for air-to-air combat and hurriedly flight-tested in an attempt to get it to Korea, but the airplane had to be grounded after several crashes caused by inertial coupling between the roll and yaw axes that made it nearly uncontrollable in some flight regimes. Lengthening both the wings and the vertical fin rectified this problem in the F-100C, a fighter-bomber with reinforced wing stations where munitions or fuel tanks could attach to pylons. But no version of the jet was rock solid, and stretching the fuselage to accommodate new weaponry (F-100D), and again to provide for a two-seat trainer (F-100F), further degraded stability. The pilot had to hand-fly the airplane continuously, couldn't let go of the control stick for more than a second or two or the aircraft would go stupid, quickly working itself into an unusual attitude. Even so, the Hun was without doubt a great airplane. In all, we built nearly 2,300 of them, the last rolling off the line in 1959, the year I checked out in the bird. It would see much service in Vietnam, logging more combat missions than 15,000 P-51 Mustangs had in World War II.

—◆—

From altitude, it was still possible in Arizona to see a hundred miles, though the coming of air conditioning had inspired Del Webb to build Sun City, "a master-planned community for active adults," just north of the base, and soon we would enter the age of smog and noise complaints. Ellie and I settled in the little town of Goodyear, renting one of the cinder block, "temporary" houses built to hold the World War II workforce of a nearby aircraft plant. No air conditioning for us, though a noisy evaporative cooler squatted on the roof. We had a parade ground for a front yard, the workers' cottages bordering a large, grassy rectangle partitioned for gravity-fed flood irrigation. Friends from college, John and Paula DeBlanc, lived in the same bungalows, and the four of us spread blankets on shaded Bermuda grass for picnics or games of bridge. Approaching his second birthday, Mark ran wild and barefoot with the other kids, roasting under azure skies. One day, when I was left to look after him while Ellie did the shopping, my attention wandered and he fell into irrigation water, scaring me. I pulled him out unhurt but muddy and rinsed him off with a garden hose. His mother was not amused.

———◆———

Luke Field was a combat-crew training base, belonging not to Air Training Command but to a fighting organization, Tactical Air Command. Sure, we were still in training, but we'd left behind flying airplanes with a "T" in the name. And something mysterious had happened. Because we wore wings, the IPs treated us like pilots, not students. It was assumed we knew how to fly. We'd now be taught to fight.

On 26 March 1959, after classroom academics, simulator training and just over six hours of dual instruction in the F-100F, I got my first ride in an airplane with only one seat, the F-100C. A cause for celebration: not only was nobody back there, there was no furniture back there either.

We now began the real training, learning the basics of air-to-air and air-to-ground combat.

———◆———

At its origins in World War I, dogfighting was single combat at its best. Success depended on getting to a position behind the other aircraft and within the effective range of guns. Closer was better. In fact, you wanted to pour in a lethal burst quickly, which meant waiting until you were as close as you could get without running into the pieces when he blew up.

Getting close is easy enough when the other guy doesn't know you're there, which is why over 90 percent of all the aerial kills in history have been the result of unobserved six o'clock shots, proof of the dominating importance of surprise in combat.[3] On the other hand, if the opponent does know you're there, attack choreography

---

3 Modern aircraft and missiles capable of killing from any angle, including head-on, are changing the picture. Even so, today's fighter pilot continues to build strong neck muscles, swiveling to "check six."

can be quite complex, the outcome now much less certain and depending more on skill than cunning.

To provide early warning needed to eliminate surprise six o'clock attack, pilots abandoned single combat. The German ace Manfred von Richthofen devised a V-shaped, or Wild Goose, formation, with wingmen charged to clear the space behind one another. Raoul Lufbery, an American serving in the French Air Service, invented (or maybe only popularized) a defensive maneuver that later bore his name.[4] When attacked by German fighters using Richthofen's Wild Goose formation, Lufbery's Lafayette Escadrille formed a circle, something like the pioneers may have done with covered wagons. Each plane protected the one in front, and the circle gradually withdrew toward friendly territory.

The war ended before such primitive tactics could be refined, but the advantages of teamwork and mutual support were so obvious that fighter aircraft have ever since flown in pairs or larger formations. The Germans solved many of the tactical problems in the Spanish Civil War, deploying ME-109s in loose, line abreast *Rotten,* or pairs. Two of these *Rotten* formed a four-ship *Schwarm.* All major air forces subsequently adopted this formation, known in the West as Finger Four.

By the late 1950s, Air Force tactics had given up some of the *Rotten's* flexibility. The basic fighter formation, an "element," consisted of two aircraft: a leader and wingman. Element wingmen

---

4 After America entered the war, Lufbery integrated into the US Army Air Service. He may have been the most brilliant of the glittering cast of America's early combat aviators. He scored 17 official kills with the Lafayette Escadrille, all shot down over front lines and therefore witnessed from the ground, but claimed 23 more far enough behind German lines that they could not be counted under the scoring rules. Had he gotten credit, he would have been far and away our leading ace, displacing Eddie Rickenbacker.

Lufberry said, "There won't be any 'after the war' for a fighter pilot," and, for him, there wasn't.

pulled well back from line abreast—perhaps 45 to 60 degrees—
into a position called Fighting Wing. (Our nickname: Welded
Wing.) For routine operations, two elements employed together as
a four-ship flight, with one of the element leaders designated the
overall flight lead. Flight and element leads, the more experienced
pilots, had an offensive orientation: find the competition and do
some damage. Wingmen gave first priority to defense, keeping the
lethal cone behind their leader under observation. When a maneuvering fight developed, wingmen cut to the inside of every turn,
weaving back and forth across lead's six o'clock and keeping it
clear. If a wingman did his job well and survived long enough,
he graduated to lead, got his own wingman and could reorient to
offense.

This separation of responsibility for offense and defense was not
absolute. Element and flight leads were expected to divide their
attention, to include clearing their wingmen's six o'clock, visually.
And a few famously aggressive wingmen blackened their reputa-
tions by repeatedly abandoning lead to chase after glory.[5] This sort
of behavior was frowned on, justified only if lead avoided a fight
for no good reason, with the burden of proof on the wingman. The
Welded Wingman took vows: get in position, hang on for dear life
and, whatever else happened, keep lead's six o'clock clear.

In the typical mid-20th century turning engagement, two core
tactics were used. The first was an "angles" fight. When you could
out-turn your opponent (when, for any reason—slower speed,
lighter wing loading, better controllability—you could get inside
and stay inside his tightest turning radius) the angular advantage

---

5 Most notably Jim Low, who recorded nine kills in Korea. Some see
Low as the model for Ed Pell in James Salter's *The Hunters*. (Those
checking the records for Salter's own MiG kill will find it credited to
James Horowitz.)

could be used to reduce distance, closing you gradually to firing range. This tactic was easy to visualize and execute. We did it all the time when joining up with another aircraft to fly formation. Simply point your nose ahead of his and along his projected flight path, making a lead turn. The disadvantage in a fight was you used more energy than the other guy, pulling the *g*'s needed for a relatively tighter turn.

The complementary tactic was the "energy" fight. In any air engagement, one of the fighters is likely to have or be able to generate an energy advantage over the other—in airspeed, altitude, power loading, or some combination of these. The idea was to exploit this advantage against the angles fighter, who dissipates energy getting nose position. Adept use of the vertical dimension was important in the energy fight. Climb and dive, instead of making flat turns. Lag, rather than lead turn (aim your nose behind the other guy's tailpipe). Keep your lift vector (the top of your wings) pointed directly at him. Eventually he would run out of airspeed and ideas. That's when you converted excess energy into a killing pounce. Patience was the key.

What we learned at Luke were the rudiments of the angles fight, a worthwhile foundation on which we could build later.[6] We began with 1 v. 1 mock combat against an instructor. We learned quickly that hard turning produced high angles of attack (AOA) as the wing plowed into the air to generate turn rate. In the F-100, high AOA gave rise to adverse yaw and compressor stall—either development an attention getter.

---

6 Moreover, given the opportunity for a quick kill, the angles fight might be a risk worth taking, though my advice is to stay away from it. If you are badly mounted, you may have no alternative. Luftwaffe Stukas flying against Spitfires and Hurricanes in the opening days of the Battle of Britain had no choice but to hope for an angles fight. Easy pickings—the engagements were known in the RAF as "Stuka parties"—they had to be withdrawn from battle after a few weeks.

Turning is done by banking the wings, which tilts the lifting force and pulls the aircraft around to a new heading. Thus, "turning" and "banking" are practical synonyms.[7]

But how to get the wings banked? Ailerons are a good way. A streamlined section of metal on the wing's trailing edge is made to turn up on one side and down on the other, producing a lift imbalance that banks the airplane around its roll axis. But in aerodynamics, nothing good is ever free. The downward-deflected aileron generates drag at the same time it is producing more lift. Adverse yaw is the tendency to turn opposite the desired direction caused by this increased aileron drag. It affects all aircraft to some degree, and the pilot's correction is the same: add coordinating rudder into the turn. Early aircraft produced large amounts of adverse yaw and were known as rudder airplanes, but most modern aircraft incorporate aileron design features that practically eliminate adverse yaw under normal flight conditions.

This was true also of the F-100: normal maneuvering didn't require much in the way of rudder use. However, during the tight turning, high-g flight characteristic of close-quarters air combat, the F-100's large, paddle-style ailerons, when lowered to create more lift, stuck far down into the airflow under the wing and produced an abundance of drag—more than enough to offset the increased lift. So, just as the engagement was getting interesting, the pilot jammed in an armful of aileron and—surprise!—it snap rolled in the opposite direction. Not good.

Compressor stall was easier to understand. The compressor blades of a turbine engine are little airfoils, miniature wings. They stall just like any other wing if airflow across them is too disorderly, and the flow down the F-100 air intake could get pretty bumpy at high angles of attack. The onset of compressor stall could

---

7 It wasn't always so. Many early aviators, the Wright brothers included, thought an aircraft should be turned by skidding it around with the rudders, using any roll control available to keep the wings level.

be insidious, sounding like a rumble, or sudden, sounding more like an explosion. When the aircraft was loaded up with *g*'s during heavy maneuvering, an engine stall coughed rejected air back up the intake, belching flame out the nose, the shock wave kicking your feet off the rudder petals. If not corrected, the stall would deepen, accompanied by rising engine temperature and rpm decay, eventually leading to engine failure.

When you got snap rolled and compressor stalled at the same time, you knew you were in a good fight.

Before really understanding much about basic maneuvering, we pushed on to 2 v. 2 mock combat. We set up so that one two-ship element had a positional or altitude advantage, then rolled in, or "bounced" the other. As soon as he saw it coming, the wingman called the attack: "Bobcat Lead, two bandits, eight o'clock, slightly high, closing."[8]

The defending element leader's reaction required nice judgment. If when first seen the bandits were far enough away, he might neutralize the attack with a low-*g*, energy-preserving turn into the attack, leading to a head-on pass. At the merge, both sides would have plenty of speed, and each had the option to engage or separate. On the other hand, if the bandits were already closing on a firing position, the defending element leader might have to execute a "scissors"—a high-*g* break turn followed by a turn reversal that dissipated energy and forced the attackers, with their greater airspeed, to overshoot, sliding them out in front. The intended victim now occupied an offensive position. However, when the attacking element leader saw a scissors developing, he knew he had lost the

---

8 Fighter pilots use "brevity code," much reducing radio chatter but making proper nomenclature important. A BANDIT is a confirmed hostile. When another aircraft's status is unknown or uncertain, use BOGIE or STRANGER instead. A multiaircraft turning fight in which BANDITS and FRIENDLIES are mixed is a FURBALL. A call of BINGO means someone is low on fuel, WINCHESTER, out of ammunition, and so forth, through an entire specialized vocabulary.

element of surprise. He could "unload" his aircraft in a sort of zero
g floating maneuver that allowed for a marked increase in acceleration, separate from the engagement and go home to fight another
day. Or he could try to retain positional advantage by pulling up
into the vertical, a "yo-yo" maneuver intended to trade the kinet-
ics of airspeed for the potential of altitude. This presented another
opportunity to exercise judgment. Against good opposition, yo-
yoing too early or too late could be a fatal misstep.

No two scissors or yo-yo maneuvers were exactly alike. Moreover, these two tactics were themselves only building blocks to
other, more elaborate moves and countermoves. And the fight could
get considerably bigger than 2 v. 2. Toward the end of the air-to-air
syllabus, we had a go at 4 v. 4. Exponentially more difficult, the
4 v. 4 scenario usually degenerated into a swirling, eight-aircraft
"furball," terminating only when the ground got close.

What's described here is the barest outline of the most basic,
opening moments of an early 1960s-style dogfight. In the decades
ahead, following the lead of the Navy, the RAF, and the Israeli
Air Force, we would return to the much better, more flexible tactics used by the Germans in Spain. Called "double attack" or
"loose deuce"—a four-ship version was known as "fluid four"—we
moved the wingman up to a position line abreast with lead. Now,
either pilot could assume the role of attacker—could, as we say, be
"engaged"—while the other became the wingman. Still, many of
the basics would not change, including the initial, major-league
judgment call: either turn hard into the attack to generate a large
crossing angle at the merge (the angles fight) or do an airspeed-
conserving lag turn (the energy fight). This decision is not unlike
the choice gunfighters must have made: either draw fast for a quick
first shot or be a little more deliberate and send that first bullet
home. I'd guess the success of Wild Bill Hickok or Wyatt Earp had
something to do with keeping the pulse rate in check while making this decision. It's much the same with dogfighting, the ultimate
test of controlled aggression.

———◆———

Air-to-air combat requires native talent, which all of us had in some measure; confidence, which most of us had in excess; and training, which none of us got enough of at Luke. About the best we could expect from this introduction to air fighting basics was to get on lead's wing and try hard to stay there.

Our training in conventional air-to-ground gunnery was much the same, little more than an orientation. To deliver with accuracy any of the conventional ordnance then in use—free-fall bombs, 2.75-inch folding-fin rockets, 20 mm bullets—we had to get the dive angle, speed, and range to the target exactly right. Or, we could try to make offsetting errors: if a little shallow in dive, which will cause a bomb to fall short of the target, compensate by being a little fast, which will make it go long, and so forth. Even if delivery parameters were perfect in all respects, we had to correct for wind, so each drop or firing became an improvisation, with success requiring adjustment of many independent variables. At Luke, we didn't have time to get good at it, though that didn't stop us from betting on scores.

By contrast, we gave lots of attention to nuclear weapons.

———◆———

During this period, it was not clear that conventional, non-nuclear warfare had much of a future. Defense thinking embraced the idea of deterrence, that our nuclear muscle would inhibit potential opponents from testing us at any significant conflict level. Should deterrence fail, we'd resort to massive retaliation. Conventional, general-purpose forces seemed not to play a large role in this scheme. Following normal survival instincts, conventional forces reinvented themselves. The fighter community reconfigured with nuclear explosives to become a sort of minor league Strategic Air Command.[9]

---

9 The Pentomic Army idea came along at about the same time and for much the same reason: stay in business during the lean years.

In theory, the concept of a nuclear fighter force aligned with the orthodox view of the military situation in Europe, which was that our ground forces would be rolled up rapidly in any conventional fight with the Soviets. The Warsaw Pact array of forces certainly looked intimidating. Based on numbers alone, especially of armored units, they seemed sure to overwhelm NATO in any test. (For the Soviets, the tank was as much a culture statement as a piece of military equipment.) When we played European force ratios in computer simulations, lead-echelon Pact formations typically reached the Channel ports in something under a week.

This bleak assessment proceeded from intelligence estimates I'd later come to regard as a social construction, the faithful servant of friendly force structure. Nevertheless, the idea that we'd be forced to use nuclear weapons quickly was accepted, and a role for the fighter force was carved out in a theater-nuclear phase, hypothetically wedged between pure conventional war and an all-out nuclear exchange.

Our classroom instruction on nuclear weapons effects made me doubt there could be a contained nuclear phase of this kind. Especially in Europe, were either side to employ atomic weapons, distinguishing between tactical and strategic use would be next to impossible. If there was a reliable firebreak, it seemed to me it had to be between straight conventional and unconstrained nuclear warfare.

On the other hand, the evaporation of many Eastern European targets—airfields, ground installations, port facilities, weapon-storage sites, and so forth—that were not quite important enough to make SAC's hit list, would no doubt seriously disrupt a Warsaw Pact attack. Moreover, if the Soviets responded in kind, we had the option of turning SAC loose into the Russian homeland. In fact, our principal allies welcomed the linkage between theater and strategic forces, which they regarded as the most sincere evidence that our fates were intertwined.

So, at Luke, we spent most of our time learning how to use

the F-100 to deliver nuclear weapons. Success would require us to get over a series of high hurdles, the first being the matter of navigation.

⎯⎯⎯✦⎯⎯⎯

The basis of all navigation is dead reckoning. Make a prediction about where you should be, based on your direction, speed, and the elapsed time since you knew for sure where you were. Then update the prediction by checking what you see out the window against what the map shows—a process called pilotage—or by reference to cockpit avionics that provide position information relative to radios of various kinds. The radio navaids would certainly be shut down in the opening stages of a major conflict, and as for cultural features, every European city seems to have a river, a railroad, and a big church. Anyway, odds were we'd launch on actual combat missions in darkness or bad weather, making visual pilotage nearly impossible. In brief, the navigation part of theater nuclear war looked semi-difficult.

For long-range strike, the F-100 carried external fuel tanks and a roughly 2,000-pound nuclear bomb tucked under one of the wings (later, centerline, under the fuselage). If intercepted en route to the target, we could drop the fuel tanks but would be understandably reluctant to jettison the nuke, except as a last resort. On the other hand, in a turning fight, the weapon's extra weight and drag would be a sizable handicap, particularly when carried under a wing, an asymmetrical configuration producing all sorts of complications for hard maneuvering. Therefore, if we could get around the navigation problem, the second challenge would be to avoid intercept en route to the target. We planned to do this by flying very low, under radar coverage. In training, we started at 1,000, then stepped down to 500, and finally to 200 feet above ground. (We told ourselves, in the actual event we'd go even lower, at "clothesline" height.) We also planned to go fast, around 400 knots, increasing to 500 or more as we approached the target. Even if detected by radar, we'd be hard to catch. Using these tactics meant we'd have to give a lot of attention to avoiding ground impact, leaving few spare brain cells to deal with the navigation problem.

Since our defense against interceptors was to go low and fast, we wouldn't need the mutual support provided by a wingman. The nuclear attack mission would be flown single-ship.[10]

Leaving aside the question of night or bad weather, flying low and fast solved one set of problems. But best use of nuclear weaponry often requires an airburst, meaning the bomb detonates high enough so the fireball does not quite touch the ground. This type of explosion produces maximum heat and blast, as well as a relatively small dose of radioactive fallout. Airbursts pose no problem for ICBMs, because they approach the target from space, or for bombers that penetrate the ring of perimeter defenses at low altitude, then climb to attack interior targets from high altitude. By contrast, our Warsaw Pact targets were essentially in the perimeter defenses, and survival against surface-to-air missiles and interceptors would depend on staying low. Approaching the target from low altitude, we'd need to loft the bomb, to toss it high enough into the air that there would be time for the internal arming mechanisms to activate and a radar altimeter to trigger the weapon as it fell back through desired burst height.

Nuclear low angle, a sort of bomb tossing that's practical if the munition has a retarding parachute, was one way to do this. Approaching the target, we selected afterburner and started an aggressive pull-up. Around 40 degrees of pitch, the bomb released automatically, deployed a parachute and detonated as it fell back through the triggering altitude. The maneuver was easy to perform, but the escape route was straight ahead, which for most targets meant deeper into enemy territory.

---

10 For routine training at Luke and later in operational squadrons, another pilot chased us, flying loose enough so he could function as a safety observer and still pay attention to the ground, an unforgiving adversary.

The delivery technique invented to solve this problem, the one we practiced most, was known as nuclear high angle. In concept, the pilot performed an aerobatic maneuver, a partial loop.[11] A complete loop is entered and exited on the same heading, whereas what we needed in an escape maneuver was to head back toward the friendlies. Our nuclear delivery maneuver would therefore be a loop segment, something like an Immelmann or the first half of a Cuban Eight. The Immelmann starts out as a loop, but, inverted at the top of the maneuver, the pilot rolls upright, making this a half-loop and half-roll.[12] The Half Cuban is pretty much the same, except the roll to upright is done after 5/8's of a loop, the aircraft well past inverted, nose down in a 45-degree dive.[13] We wanted something roughly in-between the Immelmann and Half Cuban and ended up calling it Over the Shoulder.

---

11 The loop is a 360-degree turn in the vertical. The term's origin is American, borrowed from the loop-the-loop ride at county fairs.

12 We have to be skeptical, but if anybody could perform this maneuver in the fragile Fokker monoplane he flew—top speed, maybe 80 mph—it would be Max Immelmann. After his eighth kill in January 1916, he and Oswald Boelcke were the first pilots awarded the Blue Max. Kaiser Wilhelm, at work writing congratulations following Immelmann's 12th victory, learned he had just scored a 13th. "Immelmann shoots faster than one can write," he said.

Immelmann abstained from tobacco, red meat, strong drink, and loose women—a great, but perhaps not typical, fighter pilot.

13 Len Povey was the first to perform the maneuver in public. In the 1920s, Povey was a mechanic in the Army Air Service. He learned to fly and managed, by special permission of Billy Mitchell, to get transferred to a flying job as an enlisted man. After leaving military service he became a barnstormer and in the mid-1930s helped establish the Cuban Air Force. Flying in one of its aircraft at the 1936 Miami Air Races, he intended to do snap rolls on top of a loop but was going too fast, so he rode it over the top, then on a whim decided to do a half roll and pull up into a symmetrical figure in the other direction. Afterward, asked what it was, he said, "just a Cuban Eight."

At Luke, we repeated this maneuver many scores of times: at the designated ground zero, offset for forecast winds, select afterburner and start a 4 *g* pull-up, as though entering a loop. The Hun had a gyro system that released the bomb automatically as the aircraft passed through vertical, tossing it up and "over the shoulder." Continuing through the loop until nose down in a moderate dive, we rolled upright and accelerated away in afterburner. It was hoped this escape technique would increase the odds of surviving flash and blast effects, though many were skeptical concerning this latter point.

Considering the handling qualities of the F-100, the extended ranges involved, the difficulty of low-level, high-speed navigation, and the prospect of tough terminal defenses guarding targets that might be pretty hard to locate and identify, the whole idea of a weapon delivery maneuver that culminated in the pilot's having to fly himself into a position *upside down* in space so as to peel a ton of mass off the underside of one of the wings was nutty on the face of it.

But the fighter force needed work. And the other guy couldn't count on us not being able to do it.

—⚓—

The days at Luke went by quickly as we settled into a routine: academics, simulator, physical training, flying, Friday beer call. Our class consisted of 20 top graduates from the Air Force's five basic flying schools. By contrast with primary and basic, where I soon lost contact with classmates as they went on to transports or bombers, here at Luke I made friendships that would last.

One of my buddies was John Harlin. A muscular, blond Stanford graduate, a world-class rock climber, and semi-crazy, John was one of the strongest flyers I ever knew. I'd call him a genius pilot, but that doesn't get it exactly right. A genius—a Beethoven or a Picasso—never returns to a problem once solved but immediately sets to work on variations. By contrast, pilots repeat again and again exactly the same simple, finite tasks, all easy to do poorly but for some reason deeply satisfying when done right—like golf or carpentry. Thus, flying is craft rather than art, and already, at this early stage, Harlin was a craftsman. Following a sortie in which we flew together as wingmen in a four-ship to the gunnery range, Harlin told me his formation work had been so precise he needed to make only tiny adjustments, "an eighth of an inch." He was good enough that I believed him and acted as if the same thing happened to me, too, but some time would pass before I fully understood what he'd meant.

Harlin was not cocky but was quite positive, a man completely sure of his bearings. Even more than the rest of us, he made no attempt to hide his disdain for supervision and was not always careful to show dogged adherence to prescribed procedures. Although this did him no harm with the younger instructors, themselves still a little unruly, it never sat well with the squadron's senior leadership. Like the establishment everywhere, they regarded independence and creativity as threats to order.

One evening while nearly everyone in the class was aloft, a single F-100 buzzed downtown Phoenix, flying at traffic-signal height up one of the main streets. Harlin's name, and mine, surfaced in initial speculation, but we were among the few not flying that evening. The whole class was grounded, John and me included, while authorities sought the wrongdoer. (My flight records show no activity for 10 days, a long gap during a formal training course.) Agents from the Office of Special Investigations, the Air Force's counterintelligence arm, appeared, took sworn statements, administered lie detector tests. We all sat around the squadron playing hearts or chess. They never identified the guilty party, though many thought the F-100 might have come from Nellis, soon to be our last training stop before joining operational squadrons. Nellis, near Las Vegas, was within fighter range of Phoenix, so we figured someone from the class ahead had come back to leave a calling card.

———◆———

As we approached graduation from Luke, we were once again lined up by class standing and given a choice of operational bases to which we would report after the brief top-off training at Nellis. Unhappily, only four assignments to much-sought-after overseas bases were available, two each in Europe and the Pacific. Harlin wanted to go to Europe so he could indulge his passion for Alpine mountaineering. Based strictly on performance, he was number one in the class, but the squadron commander arbitrarily lowered his standing because of a "bad attitude." Still, Harlin chose second, selecting Hahn Air Base in Germany.

In making my choice, I noted that our current relationship with the Soviets, though uneasy, was far from its worst. On the other hand, China had recently put us through a second major flare-up over the islands of Quemoy and Matsu in the Taiwan Strait. Beijing ended up calling off the confrontation, perhaps in part because the Chinese judged Moscow's support lukewarm by contrast with our more ardent backing of Taipei. Moreover, we were hearing (again) some loose talk of "unleashing" Chiang Kai-shek to retake the mainland. Mao went on record saying that even if a nuclear war killed half of mankind, the other half—he meant the Chinese— would survive to build a socialist world. One way or another, Asia seemed a more likely scene of action than Europe.

So I also chose an overseas assignment, to the fighter wing in Okinawa, Japan.

———◆———

In March 1959, Ho Chi Minh declared a "people's war" to reunite Vietnam under his leadership, a Second Indochina War to go with the first, his defeat of the French. Construction of the Ho Chi Minh Trail began. In July, in a hut at Bien Hoa, north of Saigon, eight US military advisers were watching a movie, *The Tattered Dress*, starring Jeanne Crain. The Viet Cong attacked during an intermission, wounding six and killing two, our first combat losses in this new theater.

———◆———

Between Luke and Nellis, my class attended survival school, located at Stead AFB, near Reno, Nevada. This three-week course featured academic and practical training to prepare downed aircrews for survival, evasion, capture, and prison-camp life. The Air Force had not been happy about the performance of captured airmen during the Korean War. Too many had yielded to brainwashing, signed germ-warfare confessions or cooperated in other embarrassing ways. Maybe worse, 38 percent of our Korea POWs died in captivity. Survival school was meant to convince us we should avoid capture entirely or—second best by a wide margin—meet high standards, to include taking care of one another, if we fell into enemy hands.

About midway through survival school, we were given a night escape-and-evasion problem, requiring us to penetrate various border-crossing obstacles—concertina wire, simulated minefields, tripwire flares, that sort of thing. It was hard going. We covered perhaps a mile and a half of desert, much of it on our bellies, with obstacles coming one after another and instructors assigned to "capture" us when we made a mistake. I managed to get through without being tagged, but it made no difference: everyone was interned at the end so we could get a little practice POW time.

Instructors dressed in Russian and Chinese uniforms ran the prison camp. They interrogated us forcefully enough that some people broke and cooperated. A favorite punishment was to fold us into boxes stacked so they looked like the luggage lockers in bus stations. Once inside, there was no way to stand up, lie down, or otherwise get comfortable. Because I was not being helpful, my turn in the box came early. Still dog-tired from the border-crossing exercise, I managed to doze off, doing nothing for my popularity with the guards. They finally gave up and returned me to the bunker that served as a barracks. There, I fell asleep again, notwithstanding weird, Oriental music played at high volume all night.

The entire prison-camp ordeal lasted only 24 hours but seemed to some a lot longer. Not John Harlin. From the guards' point of view, he was the prisoner from hell. He organized an escape committee, started digging a tunnel. He was caught, of course, and condemned to carry buckets of water back and forth across the yard. This Sisyphean task was intended to affect his morale, but John turned it to advantage, spilling water on guards and repeatedly leaving the faucet running, always provoking a sharp reaction. It was a pleasure to watch someone with a bad attitude at work.

Survival school's graduation exercise took us into the High Sierra west of Reno, where we embarked on an eight-day trek of about 50 miles. Of course, in a bailout scenario, fighter pilots hit the ground alone, but for administrative purposes, we were organized in six-man teams and paired with an NCO instructor, a real outdoorsman who taught us much woodcraft over those several days. We were given a few items of the sort we might expect to have after bailout: some parachute harness and shroud line we could rig as a backpack, canopy sections that would do service as a small shelter, a hunting knife, some water-purification tablets, matches, a compass, a police whistle—not much, really, and almost nothing to eat. We were expected to forage. Each of us got two bars of pemmican, a lard-based food concentrate with the consistency of candle wax, though not as tasty. We could mix the pemmican with wild onions and other forest delicacies to make a barely edible stew. Each six-man team got a live cottontail. We took turns carrying the rabbit, an enforced fellowship making for a certain poignancy the nearer we got to eating it.

Our NCO advised us to eat nothing the first day in order to shrink our stomachs. This was supposed to make the oncoming hunger less intense, but the concept ran counter to my view that food always travels easier inside. The question was academic, as we had nothing to eat anyway. For comic relief, each of us was given a roll of toilet paper.

We hiked eight hours a day through rugged terrain, walking 50 minutes and resting 10, standard practice except for forced marches (which are overrated). We rotated the lead at each stop. Though everyone covered the same distance, walking seemed easier at the front of the column. On the move, you mustn't let a large gap develop or you'll lose mutual support—that is, support for you, since the bad guys will pick off stragglers. So, at the back, the station-keeping requirement uses energy as you accelerate and decelerate to maintain spacing. En route, hungry and daydreaming, I thought of Stonewall Jackson's "foot cavalry" creating havoc in the Valley. I could see Jackson astride Little Sorrel, watchful, his men hurrying by in the gloom: "Close it up, boys, close it up."

The hiking part of the day usually ended early, in time for a little practical instruction at the campsite. It was soon obvious that long-term survival on your own in the wild is not very likely. But you could get through today, and the rules for doing so are few and pretty simple, like "keep your feet dry." Our guide drummed in such basics as the universal plant edibility test. Nature spreads a salad bar, but contrary to the popular view, you can't just wolf down any flower, fern, or weed. Mushroom "experts" bite the dust every year, so if you going to die in combat, don't do it from eating mushrooms. We spent a lot of time building and setting traps and snares for small animals and even more on fishing, learning how to weave gill nets and construct fish traps. We got the theory on fish tickling, said to be an ancient technique. If you stand very still in the water with your hands cupped below the surface, a fat trout will swim over and let you tickle his belly, the fish supposed to enjoy this right up to being tossed on the bank for barbecue. Some of the guys tried it, without result and feeling dumb, knee deep in snowmelt. Still, if you got hungry enough . . . maybe.

At dawn one day, I saw John Harlin hiking through the area where my crew had camped for the night. He'd gotten wind of a distant ranger station and trekked there to beg or steal food. He was feeling good, the trip a success. The rest of us were content to crawl into improvised sleeping bags. Harlin went hunting.

———————

This summertime stroll in the Sierras turned out to be excellent training, leading to unavoidable conclusions on the subject of escape and evasion. If you live through the high-speed ejection and get to the ground without being shot up, the first few decisions will settle your fate. The enemy has likely seen you in the parachute and therefore knows your location with fair accuracy. You're probably hurt, or at the very least in a state of mild shock, so at this point self-control is the most important factor in the survival equation. You must have the presence of mind to do several things simultaneously and very quickly: prepare to defend yourself (meaning die, but make it expensive), do expedient physical repairs (stop the bleeding), and move away from the landing site, taking such equipment as you can and hiding the rest.

Though it's not the school solution, I'd immediately drink deeply from the water supply in the survival kit because water helps with shock and also weighs a lot. As a priority, I'd take any remaining water with me. Weapons and ammo are next on the list, though I'd have seen to these straightaway as a function of preparing a defense. I'd want my handheld survival radio and any other signaling devices, such as whistles or mirrors. Deciding what else to take and what to leave behind would be double tough, with not a lot of time for deliberation. If you could fend off initial capture, exposure posed the next immediate threat, and most of the stuff that's useful for making clothing or shelter—the life raft, the parachute canopy—is pretty heavy. Pick and choose quickly, then move as far and fast as you can without making noise. The bad guys will establish a search radius and widen it every day, but they won't sustain the effort for very long. If you can get to the edge of the circle, the search will be much less concentrated and you can go to ground, hopefully someplace with good natural shelter and running water.

If you're lucky or good enough to do all this and avoid accidental discovery by some civilian, then you're probably going to die anyway because it's so hard to survive in a state of nature. Maybe Robinson Crusoe did it, but you're not going to land on a nice, warm island with a cargo ship to ransack. Plus, rescue is a long shot no one should ever put any stock in. (If you are a fighter pilot because you think you'll be rescued when you're shot down, you're in the wrong line of work.) But a pilot who knows what he's doing may be able to stay alive a day or two longer than he'd last otherwise, maybe long enough to work his way back to friendly territory.

———◆———

I lost a pound or two, not much considering the menu. I did develop an appetite, a mental rather than physical reaction, thinking about food all day and dreaming of it at night. Returning to austere barracks at Stead, I headed across the yard to gang showers that served several buildings, in flip-flops, a towel around my middle. I came across a dead sparrow, the carcass not fresh, ants already at work. Before I could stop myself, I imagined carving it six ways, so each of the crew could have a bit.

Harrah's casino in downtown Reno bought returning heroes of the forest a steak dinner. Dessert was a mix of fresh peaches and strawberries. I cannot remember a sweeter taste. Unhappily, my stomach was not prepared for real food, and it wouldn't stay down.

The other entertainment was furnished by Louis Jordan and the Tympany Five, at work on the bridge from swing to rock 'n' roll.

———◆———

Because a few flying-training events were taught only at Nellis, my class reported there for top-off. We checked out in the D model, fired our first guided missile, the AIM-9B Sidewinder, and did our first aerial refueling, qualifying both day and night. At Luke, we'd shot at a banner target to begin learning aerial-gunnery skills. The banner didn't maneuver; a T-bird simply towed it in a box pattern. Here at Nellis, we got more realistic training, firing at a new style of maneuvering target called a dart, towed behind another F-100. We also further refined nuclear-delivery skills, flying more elaborate and difficult mission profiles, many of them single-ship, without a safety observer, just as we would do in combat.

———◆———

The class went to Nellis TDY, that is, on temporary duty, not as part of a PCS, or permanent change of station. Our furniture was crated and put in storage as we left Luke. Along with many

married classmates, Ellie and I rented a furnished place in North
Las Vegas, at the Van Der Meer Apartments. There, Ellie fought
a holding action against cockroaches, arguably first-round draft
choices. They usually won by early evening and she and the other
wives evacuated to lawn furniture, waiting for us to come home
from flying. Like us, our friends were recent college graduates,
newly wed, making a first sortie into the larger world. Some were
excited to be in Las Vegas, still a small town but with the Strip
building momentum. Casinos offered cheap dinners and entertainment as loss leaders for gambling. Ellie and I sometimes took the
dinner and let the gambling go, neither of us much interested in
losing money.

———————

Nikita Khrushchev made an official visit to the United States in
September 1959, welcomed by Eisenhower "in the spirit of Camp
David." Owing to a State Department foul-up, Khrushchev couldn't
get cleared for what he wanted to do most, visit Disneyland. Miffed,
he flew on to Beijing, received an icy reception, and never visited
China again.

———————

John Harlin got into trouble again at Nellis. Alone and at low altitude in southern Utah, some phone lines jumped up at him. Parts
of the town of Kanab lost voice service for a while, and his airplane
took a beating, but John got it home, enduring only minor discipstrongin-
ary action. He went on to the NATO base at Hahn, Germany, there
going through the new-guy treatment all operational squadrons
have. Finally declared combat ready and eligible to begin pulling
alert, John confessed to reservations about using nuclear weapons.
He was removed immediately from the squadron and spent the rest
of his hitch coaching Hahn's football team.

As soon as he could, Harlin left the Air Force for a full-time
climbing career. In 1962 he and a German comrade scaled the
north face of the Eiger. Writing in the 11 April 1966 edition of

Sports Illustrated, John described the time spent on the mountain in prose as compact and sinewy as the man himself:

> It was now certain that darkness would catch us for still another night, our third . . . In addition, we had begun to have that old feeling of doubt. You know, that slow realization that maybe the road you are on is a one-way street in the wrong direction. No panic, not even fear, just the strong impression of high odds against one—an unfair twist of luck after winning so much . . .
>
> I renewed my efforts to place a piton somewhere, anywhere, but could not. With our ax we excavated a ledge on which it was possible to sit if our heels were dug into the snow lower down. Even though we had down socks and pied d'elephant sacks they were useless because in our position we could not risk trying to put them on. The only thing we dared to do was loosen the straps of our crampons. Avalanches would hit the bivouac sack, with most of the snow sliding off the front. Underneath the sack, our principal problem was staying awake. Since there was nothing to which we could tie ourselves, to go to sleep meant a fall of 5,000 feet. We solved this by having one of us hold a candle with his fingertips placed up near the wick and the reservoir of hot wax. This way, if he nodded the candle would tip and the hot wax would hit his fingers and immediately wake him. In addition, we exercised our toes to a count rhythm throughout the night. As the hours passed our hopes of surviving the night increased.
>
> Toward morning the temperature fell sharply, and the sky showed a break in the bad weather. At daylight we began climbing the chimney above. It was difficult . . . but we were gaining altitude. The summit, although still out of sight, now seemed attainable . . .

This 1962 climb was by an "easy," zigzag route. In 1966, Harlin put together a five-man Anglo-American team to attempt the more difficult, perpendicular assault. As his group prepared to start, a rival West German team showed up and the race was on. After

18 days that included appalling weather and many avalanches, the teams joined forces. On 22 March, falling rock cut a fixed rope John was ascending, and he fell 4,000 feet to his death.

Some members of the combined team continued and managed, in the end, the first-ever conquest by a direct route of the Eiger's north face.

Logbook: Luke and Nellis

1959	Day	Day Weather	Night	Night Weather	Hooded	Total
F-100C	94:40		6:00			100:40
F-100D	6:35	1:30	3:00	1:00		12:05
F-100F	32:15	1:30	4:05	1:00	11:15	50:05

Qualifications:

Combat Ready, F-100C/D/F

Aerial Refueling, Day/Night

Gunnery Qualifications:

Conventional Events:

Air to Ground

Level (Skip) Bomb

Low-Angle Dive Bomb

High-Angle Dive Bomb

Rockets, 2.75 Folding Fin

Low-Angle Strafe

Air to Air

Banner

Dart

Aim-9B Sidewinder

Nuclear Events:

Low Angle (Loft)

High Angle (OTS)

High-Altitude Dive

Chapter 4

Starfighter

I was always struck by the insignificance of the world we had left behind. Nothing looked real. Once I had climbed into the airplane, all of life seemed concentrated inside the loud space of it, shaking but steady, with my father's hand at the controls. We were completely self sufficient, completely safe, rock-solid in the center of the sky.

I found it a little monotonous, frankly. My father did the same things, and said the same things, loudly, over and over.

—Reeve Lindbergh, *Under a Wing: A Memoir*

Six of my classmates were headed for George AFB near Victorville, California, the home base of two fighter wings, one flying F-100s, the other, F-104s. Orders didn't specify which wing they would join, and it soon became clear that some of them would have a shot at flying the Starfighter. I could trade away my coveted overseas assignment, if willing to gamble that doing so would get me into F-104s, a jet so hot the press was calling it "the missile with a man in it."

I swapped assignments and left Nellis immediately following the graduation ceremony, making the short drive to Victorville. Somebody at George would determine which wing I ended up in, and I wanted to get there quickly and help with the decision. Arriving on base, I looked up the F-104 wing commander. Though I didn't know it at the time, Col. George I. Ruddell was a double ace, with eight kills in Korea and two and a half in World War II. After bluffing my way into his office, it was easy to convince him I should be in his wing. After all, there I was, pleading the case in person. He picked up the phone and arranged it with the personnel shop. Great! I was to be a Starfighter pilot.[14]

The jet era began in August 1939 with the first flight of a German experimental aircraft, the He-178, but the first practical jet-engined aircraft, the Me-262, did not see service until late 1944. Astonishingly, F-104 development started only eight years later. Under Kelly Johnson's leadership, Lockheed's Skunk Works began designing a solution to the speed, altitude, and acceleration problems the Air Force was having in Korea. The result was Model 83, a lightweight air-superiority fighter tendered to the Air Force as an unsolicited proposal. General Electric's afterburning J-79 engine was the key to the aircraft's performance. Johnson had a weight budget of only 10,000 pounds for the empty airplane, so the J-79's 10,000 pounds of dry thrust would give the airplane a world-beating one-to-one thrust-to-weight ratio. At usable weights—which include fuel, ammunition, and pilot—the aircraft would be heavier, but afterburnering added another 50 percent to dry-engine thrust, enough to make the F-104 the first operational aircraft capable of sustained flight exceeding twice the speed of sound.

After testing, Johnson's prototype gained weight, as seems always the case. Still, we fielded an interceptor version (F-104A) of high quality, nicknamed the Starfighter. It had a radical appearance, needle nosed, with stubby, razor-sharp wings. It was the first airplane since the Wright flyer to hold at the same time all

---

14 As it turned out, three from my class got F-104s, the others going to the colocated F-100 wing.

the most important performance marks: top speed, absolute altitude, and the various time-to-climb records from the surface to any height.

Stable and easy to fly, the F-104's tiny wing gave it a marked disadvantage in any turning fight. Worse, the horizontal stabilizer was mounted on top the tail in a "T" configuration. Hard maneuvering brought airflow from across the wing in touch with this high tail, resulting in pitch-up, an unpleasant departure from controlled flight during which the airplane sort of flopped around and you couldn't predict what it might do next. The textbook pitch-up recovery was to try to force the airplane into a spin, a recognizable and perhaps more manageable flight condition, though spin recovery could itself be a problem.[15] However, for the interceptor mission, the shortcoming in maneuverability was not so important.

Meanwhile, facing an uncertain future, Tactical Air Command was having a tough time defining requirements for a general-purpose fighter to replace the F-100. The F-105 was supported as a fighter-bomber, carrying twice the tonnage of the famous B-17 and optimized for high-speed, long-range surface attack. However, the F-105 was heavy, with a wing loading that created a severe disadvantage for any use other than nuclear strike. Hedging its bet, TAC purchased a few F-101 and F-104 interceptors and had them modified as tactical fighters. A wing of F-101Cs stood up at RAF Bentwaters, in the United Kingdom, and the 479th Tactical Fighter Wing at George converted from F-100s to operate the 77 F-104Cs bought for TAC. In addition to the Sidewinder air-to-air missile used by the interceptor, the fighter version was air refuelable, had a six-barrel 20 mm Gatling gun, and carried both conventional and nuclear explosives.

---

15 In 1963, Chuck Yeager jumped out of a highly modified F-104 that had entered a flat spin at 104,000 feet. He gave up trying to recover and ejected at 7,000 feet, surely one of the epic spins in aviation history.

I was assigned to A Flight of the 436th Fighter Squadron and began the transition from F-100 to F-104. After completing local ground school, I flew my first F-104 sortie in the backseat of a two-place trainer, the F-104D, on 17 December 1959.[16] This sortie took the form of a "dollar ride," an orientation on aircraft performance. We made an afterburner climb, apparently straight up, and ran the aircraft out to Mach 2. It was an elating experience. (In 35 more years as an Air Force pilot, I would never go faster.) The aircraft was small, the cockpit snug though comfortable even for larger pilots. It felt like clothing. You put the jet on, you *wore* it.

The Starfighter's downward ejection seat could be a problem if the engine quit on takeoff or close to the ground. Iven Kincheloe, an ace from Korea and the first human to fly over 100,000 feet, was lost in mid-1958 when he ejected downward after experiencing engine trouble shortly after takeoff from Edwards AFB.[17] At the front end of the J-79, inlet guide vanes repositioned as needed to direct airflow smoothly into the turbine compressor section. Cables controlling these guide vanes failed alarmingly often, driving them full open or closed and causing compressor stall. Apparently, this was what happened to Kincheloe. He got out, got a good chute, but was too close to the aircraft and followed it into the fireball. Losing him cost the Air Force one of its most promising officers.

To accommodate downward ejection, F-104 pilots strapped a sort of spur to each boot. The spurs hooked to cables that pulled the feet off the rudder pedals and back into seat stirrups at the start of the ejection sequence. Walking around in these spurs made a lot

---

16 Three days before, on 14 December 1959, the F-104 set the world altitude record—for aircraft, as opposed to rocket-powered flight—of 103,395 feet.

17 Kincheloe set his altitude record in the rocket-powered Bell X-2. At 126,200 feet, he climbed fully 35,000 feet higher than anyone had ever been.

of noise, a dead giveaway the wearer was an F-104 driver. I found some excuse to wear my spurs whenever possible.

———⟟———

My second sortie, on 18 December, was another in the two-seater—this time in front. I launched as second airborne spare for the annual Christmas flyby. The event, after which the two wings stood down for the holiday, was a tradition at George. The F-100 wing led it with 36 aircraft, nine four-ship flights in trail. My wing followed, also with 36 aircraft, nine flights of F-104s. In all, a parade of 72 aircraft would pass the control tower in a grand review.

These things can get a little hairy, especially at the back of the gaggle, but I didn't have much chance of getting in the act. Each wing launched two spares in case somebody dropped out for any reason. As the number two F-104 spare, I figured to have a good seat for the show and no work to do, which was OK by me since this was my first front-seat ride in the jet.

However, two F-104s did drop out, and I was obliged to fill in at the back of the formation. Settling into position, I seemed surrounded by aluminum. The gyrations got quite wild as even the gentlest corrections made at the front of the column accordioned to aircraft behind. I cycled from afterburner, to idle power and speed brakes out, then back to burner again, helpless to maintain proper position. My assistant flight commander, John McCurdy, was in the backseat as IP. He took over for a while, had no better luck, and gave the airplane back to me. On return to Earth, I swore never again to participate in a mass flyby (a promise I did not keep).

———⟟———

Putting up a Christmas flyby had almost nothing to do with training for combat, being more akin to a sheer waste of taxpayer money. However, military flying in those days was not quite the grim pursuit of readiness it later became. Squadrons were still full of World War II veterans, demobilized in the late 1940s and then recalled for Korea. Memories of those wars were fresh. Our most admired colleagues had the sort of go-to-hell attitude we associate with the fighter pilot image. Some of the best, like McCurdy, my IP that day, were products of the Aviation Cadet Program, maybe not book smart but ahead of their better-educated comrades in aviation experience and skill. They might not meet high standards of "professionalism," but they were great airmen, men who loved flying and who worked and played hard. This seemed particularly true of pilots who managed to wrangle an assignment to the F-104 wing at George or, as I would later learn, to the F-101 wing at Bentwaters, outfits that exerted extra gravitational pull because of flying something other than the fleet-standard F-100.

Shortly after joining the 436th Squadron, I picked up the additional duty of assistant maintenance officer, meaning I'd be responsible for helping prepare the aircraft to fly each day, an important job. The officer whose assistant I became, Capt. Bob Pugh, was a smart operator who taught me a lot about aircraft maintenance at squadron level. However, I didn't put much effort into it. The position was soon taken away, and I was handed a much less prestigious additional duty: squadron athletic officer. My fitness report from this period accorded me the high-sounding but comparatively inferior rating of "a very fine officer of great value to the service."

The word pictures that accompany officer evaluations are nearly always models of embellishment, relentlessly glowing descriptions thought needed to safeguard due-course promotion. But my rater could manage only: "Lt. McPeak maintains himself in top physical condition." At the time, the Air Force was having trouble with pilots who either refused to join the Officers Club or were slow to pay dues. My fitness report contained the code phrase invented to deal with this issue: "To my knowledge, Lt. McPeak has never failed to satisfy his social and financial obligations"—faint praise that was the assessment's highlight.

But I had no reason to take the report card seriously. I got the more or less automatic promotion, so my brown bar turned silver, and now I was a *first* lieutenant with a Mach 2 fighter and government-issued credit card. I entered fully into the spirit of the moment, to put it mildly, having a good time.

⊥

In early 1960 John F. Kennedy announced he would run for president; four African-American students from North Carolina A & T in Greensboro began a sit-in at Woolworth's segregated lunch counter; and Harold Macmillan canceled Britain's Blue Streak missile project, putting an end to the myth of an entirely independent British nuclear deterrent. Meanwhile, about 1,000 refugees a week were streaming into Florida from Cuba. President Eisenhower secretly authorized CIA training for Cuban exiles, with a view to overthrowing the Castro regime.

In April 1960, universal military conscription was imposed on the citizens of North Vietnam, the tour of duty set at indefinite duration. About the same time, 18 distinguished South Vietnamese nationalists sent President Diem a petition advocating reform of his family-run and increasingly corrupt government. Diem ignored the advice, instead closing opposition newspapers and arresting journalists and intellectuals, further eroding his popular support.

In May, the Food and Drug Administration approved "the pill," the first oral contraceptive.

⊥

As part of my initial F-104 checkout, I qualified in both day and night air refueling with the KB-50 tanker, an upgraded World War II vintage B-29 converted to an aerial gas station. The F-104 did probe-and-drogue refueling. The tanker reeled out a heavy-duty hose, at the end of which was the drogue, a funnel-shaped basket looking something like a large shuttlecock. Bolted to the left side of the F-104's fuselage was a pipelike probe that we had to slide into the drogue. The Starfighter's probe sat only a few inches from the pilot's eyes so (unlike the F-100) it was easy to see and plug into the drogue. Fuel transfer began when the receiver aircraft made good contact with the basket and pushed the hose in so it was taken up into its reel. The hose, maybe 35 feet long at contact, shortened to 10 feet or so, and the receiver held it in place by flying formation with the tanker. Drifting back and letting too much hose reel out during refueling would cause it to start flailing, which could get bad enough to rip the probe off the receiver aircraft. This was not good, since the F-104's left air intake was positioned just behind and below the refueling probe. The engine would surely swallow any debris coming off either the probe or drogue.

The KB-50 could deploy three drogues, two from wing pods and one from under the tail, so as many as three fighters could refuel at once. Fuel transferred slowly, about 250 gallons a minute; receivers low on fuel stayed hooked up for a while. Also, the KB-50 was basically a prop job, though some had been fitted with auxiliary jet engines. We refueled at 220 knots, well below our best cruising speed, flaps partway down so we could hang in there.

During my night checkout, I was comfortably positioned and receiving fuel under the right wing when the tanker's number four engine started belching flame. The night was moonless, and we were up over Death Valley, not many lights on the ground. The engine fire was quite spectacular and quite close—plus, we were transferring fuel. Often, the probe and drogue did not seal tightly—after all, the connection was meant to make and break easily—so fuel sometimes sprayed out from around the coupling. With all this flame so close, it seemed a good idea to discontinue refueling, so I backed away to disconnect, at the same time alerting the tanker of the engine fire. A voice responded with an offhand acknowledgment: "Yeah, we know."

Disconnected, I watched as the propeller feathered, its rotation abruptly stopping, and the fire snuffed out. Then another laconic radio call from the KB-50: "Cleared back in."

George was in the Mojave Desert, with a climate and topography we were used to from our time at Phoenix and Las Vegas. Little lawn grew on the base—only a few patches around important buildings. The wind kicked up dust devils that seemed to make deposits on only one side of the grass, making it two-tone—dun on one side, green on the other. Walking across a lawn produced little puffs of dust that squirted sideways with each step. When the wind wasn't blowing, the visibility was great—though the haze layer from Los Angeles was beginning to spill over Cajon Pass into the high desert.

We did some practice moving at George. On arrival, no quarters were available on base, so we looked in nearby Apple Valley, where some of the squadron's families had bought on speculation. There was not much there aside from a scattering of ranch-style homes; the Map Room, a bar popular with pilots; and the Roy Rogers Museum, Trigger's stuffed carcass rampant near the entrance. Apple Valley real estate looked a sure bet to appreciate, but we decided instead to rent a small three-bedroom on the side of a hill in Victorville. After only a few weeks, space opened up and we moved on base into Wherry (also known as Weary) housing, an already-dated style named for the senator who sponsored the initial appropriation. Wherry was being upgraded so we soon relocated again as part of the renovation effort. By June 1961, when I left George, we'd been in the Air Force three and a half years and had loaded furniture into a moving van eight times.

The Air Force paid an allowance that never covered the full cost of moving. I kept careful accounts, determining at the end of each pay period whether we were on track with our budget, and it was only after several months at George that we broke even. When, at last, we ended the month with a small surplus, we drove down to San Bernardino, went to a department store, and Ellie bought a new paring knife.

⏄

One bright day, I was flying very low at the bottom of Death Valley. We got a kick out of doing this, since in routine operations pilots don't often see an altimeter reading below sea level. I was going fast—just barely subsonic—when my throttle seemed to disconnect from the engine. This frightened me a little, as I quickly added up the number of bad things that would happen to me unless I could regulate engine power. So I jumped right on guard channel and declared an emergency, starting a climb to higher altitude. Almost immediately, the engine began responding to throttle movement. Now feeling silly, I continued to an uneventful landing back at George—uneventful except that all the fire engines were out to greet me and I got to shut down the aircraft after exiting the runway and ride it back to the squadron during a humiliatingly long, public towing.

Something called T2 reset had caused the problem. Up around Mach 2, airflow down the intake was hot enough to distort metal at the engine's front section, so a temperature sensor took the throttle out of the loop and wouldn't let the pilot make the aircraft go faster. Reducing the temperature of air going down the intake restored throttle control immediately. I knew about T2 reset, having experienced it at high Mach numbers, but I wasn't prepared for it to happen at subsonic speed, which Death Valley's low altitude and hot air apparently made possible. How embarrassing. I'd overreacted to a trivial problem.

In a fighter squadron, the genuine camaraderie overlays a deadly serious daily assessment as each pilot watches the others and assigns standing that is in many ways more important than military rank. I slipped a few notches that day, and recovery would take a while.

At George, we had a rather high accident rate. In February 1960, Capt. Einer "Oley" Olson, my first flight commander, was killed on a cross-country flight to Nellis. Letting down for a night landing, he ran into hills northwest of the base. His wingman, in loose spread, narrowly avoided the same fate.

Olson's replacement as my flight commander, Capt. John P. "Sam" Houston, was killed five months later when he took a ricochet down the left intake while strafing at Cuddyback, our local gunnery range. He shut it down and tried to dead-stick it onto the dry lake just at the edge of the range, coming pretty close to making it.

⬥

As with any aircraft, when you lost the engine in a Starfighter, you set up a glide toward the best-looking spot—preferably a nice long runway, though around George lots of lake beds like the one Sam Houston tried for could be put to service, at least in summertime when they were bone dry. The glider you were now flying had a maximum range defined as *half the distance to the nearest emergency field*, an axiom holding for all powered aircraft, but especially the F-104. Notwithstanding its many other virtues, the F-104's stubby wings wouldn't take you far in a glide. If the engine was windmilling, there was a chance it might restart, but it was best to assume it wouldn't, or if it did, was going to quit again. You should aim for a succession of power-off checkpoints, called keys, defined by altitude and a certain relationship to the proposed touchdown spot: high key, low key, and base key. For most airplanes, at high key, directly over the desired landing spot, you could put the wheels down and dead-stick it through a 360-degree circling turn to touchdown. If you couldn't make high key, or arrived there short on altitude, delay putting the gear down and glide around to low key, abeam the touchdown point, with 180 degrees of turn to go. If you were high enough there, put the undercarriage down and press on. If you still hadn't been able to meet the altitude requirement at low key, keep the wheels up a bit longer and glide to a final decision point at base key, only 90 degrees of turn from touchdown. If it didn't look good there, nobody would complain if you stepped overboard.

The procedure works pretty well for the general run of airplanes. Most aircraft, even jets, glide at a fairly slow speed, and the key points are at reasonable altitudes, so the pilot can judge how he's doing through the maneuver. But the glide speed of the F-104 was *240 knots*, and high key was *20,000 feet* above terrain. Even though we practiced simulated flameout patterns all the time, at high key the aircraft was nearly four miles (vertically) from the touchdown point, making eyeball judgment much tougher. Moreover, until you get used to it, a 360-degree turn to the ground from 20,000 feet is quite stimulating, a lot like straight down. But—and here's the kicker—even this 20,000-foot high key altitude assumed a *clean* configuration through the turn. The bird was already falling like a set of car keys, but putting the landing gear down would definitely invalidate the manufacturer guarantee. The entire 360-degree descending turn was made *with the wheels up*. Starting to round out for landing, you could (finally) put the landing gear handle down. With the engine stopped, it was unlikely you'd have enough residual hydraulic pressure for landing-gear extension, but the handle had to be down in order to do the next step: pulling a lever that actuated an emergency air bottle to blow the gear down. With any luck, the wheels would have time to extend before ground contact.

Then all you had to worry about was getting it stopped.

Including my first two flight commanders, the 436th Squadron lost six aircraft and four pilots during the 19 months I spent at George. Ellie came to think of memorial services as a normal squadron function, always capped by the missing-man formation coming in low over the chapel.

In part, our high loss rate at George was symptomatic of a larger problem for the Air Force. In calendar 1958, the year I spent in pilot training, we had 894 major accidents, destroyed 531 aircraft, and lost 302 pilots. This sort of result was not unusual in the post-Korean War era. In fact, it was a pretty good year, the accident rate trending down. Anybody who thought about it knew we couldn't tolerate this state of affairs for long, and we worked very hard on the problem over the years, building airplanes that were more reliable and easier to fly and introducing training that was safe while retaining its relation to combat.[18]

However, many of the 436th Squadron's safety problems were specific to our unit. Much always depends on leadership, and ours was pretty thin.

At first, Lieutenant Colonel Smith (as I'll call him), an officer showing few signs of greatness, commanded the squadron. Shortly after I became mission ready in the aircraft, our wing was put through an important test. A headquarters inspection team came to live with us for a week of demanding exercises. As a part of the drill, I launched late at night as Smith's wingman to intercept a T-33 employed as a faker target. We managed a messy but successful intercept.

The published instrument approach for recovery back to George required us to descend from the radio fix at Daggett, some miles northeast of the base, to an initial level-off altitude of 8,000 feet. Ordinarily, Edwards radar picked us up there and directed further descent. Colonel Smith departed Daggett OK but misread his altimeter and leveled at 18 instead of 8, immediately getting snotty with Edwards radar when they couldn't find us on their scope. Although flying close formation at night, I could manage an occasional peek at important cockpit dials. I noted the altitude mistake but couldn't figure out how to deliver the message without embarrassing Smith, who was by now in a spirited discussion with the radar guy. We wound up flying the published letdown track all the

---

18 By 1991, my first full year as chief of staff, we were down to 41 major accidents, in which we wrote off 38 airplanes and lost 10 pilots. Our rate for that year, 1.11 accidents per 100,000 flying hours, was a record low. At the time, I reckoned this was about as good as it would get and, in fact, the Air Force did not improve on this statistic for nearly a decade.

Accidents continued to upset me and I pressed hard to prevent them, but military flying carries built-in risks. We can get the accident rate to zero if we lock the hangar doors.

way across the top of George at 18,000 feet. Given the difficulty of landing from up there, Smith canceled our instrument clearance and proceeded VFR. On the ground during debrief, he said, "Did you see what those guys did? Leveling us 10,000-feet high?"

Here was exposed the gravest defect a combat aviator, or for that matter, any military leader, can have: inability to face facts. Sometimes you have to fool the boss. Very infrequently, it's necessary to fool the troops. But never—repeat, never—fool yourself. There's too much at stake.

Midway through my time at George, Lieutenant Colonel Smith was reassigned to Korea as an adviser to the Republic of Korea Air Force, flying F-86s. Out by himself one day, he got lost, strayed across the demilitarized zone and was shot down and killed.

Back at Victorville, the new commander of the 436th was "Major Jones," a man whose painfully obvious limits made his selection for the job quite baffling.

So, leadership played a role in our accident rate. Still, six aircraft down in 19 months was unusually bad because we were a small squadron. The 479th Wing had the standard authorization of 72 aircraft, but these were divided among four 18-aircraft squadrons, rather than the more usual configuration of three 24-aircraft squadrons. We preferred this arrangement because the wing had an overseas commitment, the squadrons in turn spending four months in Europe. Having four squadrons in the wing meant, in theory, we'd have 12 months back home before our turn to rotate overseas came up again.

———✦———

On May Day, 1960, near Sverdlovsk, deep inside the Soviet Union, the Russians shot down a CIA-operated U-2 reconnaissance aircraft, piloted by Francis Gary Powers. The White House initially mishandled the affair, issuing false denials, and Khrushchev subsequently demanded an apology from Eisenhower, putting an abrupt end to a summit conference in Paris. Tried in Moscow and sentenced to 10 years, Powers came home early, traded in a spy exchange. When asked afterward how high he was flying when he got smoked, Powers said, "Not high enough."

⊥

The F-104 could sustain flight above 50,000 feet, but we didn't go up there often. When we did, we were supposed to wear pressure suits. A number of pioneer airmen died ascending to altitude in unpressurized aircraft. Their internal body gases expanded, a high-altitude variation of the bends experienced by deep-sea divers who come up too fast. Jet engines in the 1960s were untrustworthy at high altitude, and since bleed air off the engine is what pressurizes the airplane, losing cockpit pressurization at high altitude was always a live possibility. If the engine quit above 50,000 feet, you were going to need a pressure suit. Contoured to the body, these suits were handmade for each of us and then proof-tested. I'd already spent enough time in altitude chambers to know I didn't like them much. Now I was sent to a special, *really* high altitude chamber to test my new pressure suit. We went to 70,000 feet and the suit held up. I took it back home to George and hung it in my locker.

One morning shortly after Powers was shot down, we got a call from NORAD about a radar track coming down the West Coast at altitude. Could we have someone suit up and go take a look? I was hanging around the operations counter, so heard the conversation. I raced to the locker room and started wriggling into my pressure suit. (The standard procedure called for sprinkling talcum powder all over yourself and sliding into it.) I was about halfway dressed when NORAD called again, saying they'd ID'd the contact.

⊥

At George, my designation as a distinguished graduate of flying school caught up with me in the form of a second offer of a commission in the regular Air Force. Though I still had no intention of staying in, this time I accepted. It kept the options open if I later decided to make the Air Force a career. On 15 May 1960 my

Reserve commission terminated, and the next day I was sworn in as a lieutenant in the regular US Air Force.

In the 1950s, Strategic Air Command built bases in Spain—near Zaragoza, in the north; Madrid, in the center; and Seville, in the south—then sent B-47s to pull alert at each of these places. Over time, SAC gradually abandoned forward basing as it transitioned to the longer-range B-52, which could sit alert in the continental United States, but for now we needed these Spanish bases, and needed to defend them. At Madrid and Zaragoza we had interceptor squadrons permanently assigned, but in southern Spain the base near Seville did not have family housing or other facilities to support a large, permanent population, and therefore the air defense mission was covered by my wing at George, which sent squadrons in on temporary duty.

We called this rotational duty, and many Tactical Air Command wings had it, shuffling squadrons in and out of Europe. Rotation always carried some kind of alert commitment, usually in the form of 15-minute alert with conventional or nuclear bombs. Our George-based F-104s were of course the tactical version; still, they were pretty good interceptors, so we could pull air defense rotational duty in southern Spain. The base, at Moron de la Frontera, was maybe 60 kilometers east of Seville. This was a beautiful TDY assignment: the weather good, the surroundings colorful, Spanish airspace wide open, Franco in charge, Americans welcome. If you had to pick a spot to pull alert, this would be it. My squadron flew into Moron on 10 August 1960.

The squadron kept two armed aircraft on high alert, with a round-the-clock commitment to be wheels up in five minutes or less from a standing start. Best case, sprinting to the aircraft, climbing in the cockpit, strapping in, getting it started, taxiing the short distance to the runway, doing engine checks, and getting airborne took every second of the five minutes but, in daylight hours, at least, it was just doable. At night, I slept fully clothed, including g-suit and spurs.

A support facility in the center of the pad featured phones connecting to the radar site that gave us scramble orders and attack vectoring. We had a chow hall, some bunk beds. Two large rainbow-roof hangars arched out from the central facility. The hangars were intended to hold a single interceptor, but the F-104's tiny wingspan allowed us to squeeze in two on each side. We met the alert commitment by keeping two at the ready on the ground and flying the other two, practicing scrambles to improve response time, then splitting up to run radar-directed intercepts on each other. Our practice intercepts usually ended in a little 1 v. 1 hassling—fun, of course, but the F-104 would never be a great dogfighter. Flights took the duty by turns but the flying off the pad was so good we looked forward to the weeklong alert periods.

We were also lucky the interceptor squadron permanently stationed at Torrejon was transitioning from F-86Ds to F-102s, meaning we had to keep a flight in Madrid for daytime air defense coverage during their conversion. We ferried our jets back and forth between Moron and Torrejon as required for maintenance, a competition developing to see who could get from one place to the other fastest. I caught it just right one day, taking off to the north from Moron, staying right on the deck in burner, and making a super-sonic run to Torrejon—just over 22 minutes from brake release to touchdown. I scattered a few sheep but didn't get the record.

The Air Force kept a small transport aircraft in Spain to fly spare parts and other logistic support around the country. Occasionally, the crew scheduled a run down to Gibraltar, and any of us could hop on for the ride. I overnighted in the British Officers Club there. The shower was saltwater, hard to get soap to lather. It might have been a water-conservation measure, or maybe another indication the Brits hadn't yet caught up with the Romans in the plumbing department.

From time to time, the Spanish asserted their rightful ownership of Gibraltar, but I can't say my first, short stay in the country made me sympathetic. In 1946, we joined the British and French in calling for Franco's ouster, rightly considering him a pro-Nazi dictator. With the onset of the Cold War, we got less fussy about our friends. Now, more than a decade into our strategic relationship, *El Caudillo* himself may have lost a step, but his regime wore its velvet glove stretched thin over an iron fist. Members of the much-feared *Guardia Civil*, symbol of authoritarian government, patrolled in pairs that seemed always just around the corner. Late at night, returning to Moron from an evening in the fleshpots of Seville, our headlights would pick them up along some lonely section of road, just standing there, full of menace in their distinctive *tricornio* hats.

By contrast, the citizens of Gibraltar had nothing to fear, except perhaps the return of the Spanish.

⏀

We kept a Vary pistol on the alert pad in case we had to launch and recover aircraft with flare signals in a comm-out scenario. One afternoon, four of us were upstairs in the small, windowed perch where the phones coming in from the radar site terminated, waiting for a practice scramble. I thoughtlessly began twirling the flare pistol around my trigger finger, like they do in Western films. When the gun fired, it was loud. The flair bounced off the observation window and left a smoky trail of sparks as it ricocheted around the room. The other three pilots were not happy; worse, the window everybody in the squadron looked through every day now bore a painful souvenir, the scar of a long, jagged crack in its thick glass.

I'd just recently recovered some standing following the great Death Valley T2 reset incident. This carelessness returned me to the beginning of another salvage cycle.

⏀

Following a campaign that featured the first live television debates, Senator Kennedy beat Vice President Nixon in a close contest for the White House. On security issues, Kennedy ran at Nixon from the right, citing a "missile gap" and otherwise coming across as more anticommunist than Nixon, who'd made a career of it.

In Vietnam, the National Liberation Front, a political umbrella for the Viet Cong, was set up in the South, with active support from Hanoi. President Diem jailed or executed dissidents, communist and nationalist alike. His autocratic and nepotistic regime granted government contracts, business favors and tax concessions to Catholics, increasingly alienating the Buddhist majority. The Catholic Church was the largest landowner in the country and exempt from land reform which, as administered, was anyway a mechanism for taking land from Buddhists and giving it to Catholics.

Following his inauguration, Kennedy stepped up assistance to Diem's army, including expanding the role of Special Forces. When Vice President Johnson visited Saigon in May 1961, he called Diem "the Winston Churchill of Asia."

We completed our four-month stay in Spain, another of George's F-104 squadrons flew in, and we got set to rotate home. We'd bring back only 17 aircraft, Dick Strickland having stepped out of one that quit running because a lot of fuel got trapped in one of the internal tanks. We redeployed in two waves, a day apart. I was in the second wave, seven aircraft led by Capt. Earl W. "Snake" Pitts, a good driver. The first planned stop was at the Portuguese air base at Lajes, in the Azores, where we landed on 12 December in terrible weather. Next up would be Myrtle Beach AFB, South Carolina, but we needed sky clear enough to find tankers in three refueling tracks stretching across the Atlantic from Lajes to Myrtle.

Nowadays, the jet-engined tankers we use cruise at about the same speed as receivers, and the procedure for long-distance deployment is to stay with them, flying formation and ducking in for gas as needed. However, in the early 1960s, the tanker force consisted almost entirely of prop-driven KB-50s, which of course could not cruise with jets. For long-range deployments, the tankers had to launch ahead of time and take up orbits along the planned track. The procedure was to find the first set of tankers, get gas, then press on to the next set. In our case, two three-ship formations of KB-50s would take off from Lajes and a third set would launch from Kindley Field, Bermuda, and await us in the vicinity of that island. We had to be able to see the tankers during rendezvous. We could paint them on cockpit radar and get close, but safety rules required a visual end game. Thus, in mid-December, we needed reasonably good weather in three widely separated parts of the North Atlantic.

The flight from Lajes to Myrtle would take seven and a half hours, a long time to sit strapped in a small cockpit with no powder room. Such flights call for special preparation—elaborate crew rest procedures, a controlled diet. Although the weather did not look promising for the next day, we followed the routine—early to bed, up at 3:00 a.m. for a low-residue breakfast, exhaustive briefings covering everything—all followed by cancellation for bad weather in one of the refueling orbits. Now we had nothing to do all day until another early turn-in rolled around. Naturally, we were delighted when, late afternoon, we were told there was no chance of launching the next morning. We could relax and enjoy the evening. Lajes didn't offer much in the way of nightlife, but what little it had sure beat crew rest. With Snake Pitts showing the way, we put everything on the table, getting to bed late and maybe a little the worse for wear. Sure enough, we were rudely awakened after what seemed like a nap. Weather in the refueling tracks looked OK. We were cleared to launch.

The Air Force had a rule about drinking and flying: *24 hours between bottle and throttle.* We'd made a counteroffer: *No drinking within 25 feet of the airplane.* Breakfast was steak and eggs, no coffee, then a perfunctory briefing, our prelaunch procedures not as fastidious as the morning before, but we'd been through it all just recently and knew what we were doing. We were a sad-looking bunch and some of us didn't feel so good, but we managed to get all seven birds airborne, notwithstanding crappy weather, with severe crosswinds on takeoff.

We found the first set of tankers and refueled without incident. The flight plan called for us to join the next set quickly since, if unable to refuel for any reason, we'd have to turn around and go back to Lajes with the fuel on board at the second rendezvous point. The KB-50 had a search radar with better range than the F-104's, so after a short cruise segment, the lead navigator in the second set of tankers made contact, steering us north to a routine join-up. This refueling, too, went well.

Shortly after drop-off from the second set of tankers, we were supposed to fly past a Coast Guard C-130 Duckbutt, so-called because this had been the affectionate nickname of the HU-16 Albatross, the first aircraft to do this type of work. Duckbutt had a search-and-rescue mission, but we hoped to use it today only in its secondary role of providing navigation assistance. Its crew provided weather and position reports and would track us on radar, giving steering guidance that was valued highly during over-water deployment of fighter aircraft. However, the Duckbutt navigator was having trouble with his radio, the transmissions breaking up. Maybe he was saying he'd not picked up our radar squawk, but possibly a skin paint, and if it was us he was painting, we were well north of course, the information presented in the form of a theory we had no way of testing.

Assuming the second set of tankers, with full-time navigators and good equipment on board, had left us at the planned drop-off point—maybe not, if we heard Duckbutt right—we headed west on dead reckoning, settling in for the long leg to Bermuda. It was mid-December, we were riding single-engine jets, and the North Atlantic, when I could see it, looked very chilly.

Perhaps flying over open water has its attractions for the Navy, but I could find no romance in it. Just as certain airplane sounds will be heard only at night, my engine now began to whistle and moan, running saltwater rough. I tried thinking of something else.

Pilots of the Royal Flying Corps, hurrying across the Channel to France in August 1914, wore inner tubes that served as makeshift life belts. Drowning was perhaps not their most pressing concern: they had orders to ram any zeppelins encountered en route, a disagreeable prospect, as they carried no parachutes.

We had parachutes, and Duckbutt would shadow our planned track for a while. With luck, Duckbutt just might find a downed crew and drop survival equipment, including larger and better-stocked life rafts than those we carried in our ejection-seat survival kits. But a single airman in a one-man raft in the middle of the North Atlantic is a desperately small object.

Below certain temperatures, regulations required fighter crews to wear special insulated suits that protect against exposure in cold water. Nicknamed poopie suits, they added a few minutes to survival time. We'd spent several hours in the swimming pool at George, and again at Moron, testing these suits and concluding they were worse than worthless—leaky and very uncomfortable to fly in—so we'd elected to wear normal flight suits and jackets. As we droned toward Bermuda, I hoped not to regret the decision.

I thought about Lindbergh. His flight took more than 33 hours, a show of personal toughness and a demonstration of how far single-engine reliability had come by 1927. A few years later, in the winter of 1936, Beryl Markham made the first-ever east-to-west Atlantic air crossing, by anybody, man or woman. Some lines from her book, *West with the Night*, seemed written with us in mind:

> "If you are still determined to fly the Atlantic this late in the year," the voice said, "the Air Ministry suggests that the weather it is able to forecast for tonight, and for tomorrow morning, will be about the best you can expect."

We continued west, in and out of weather, an hour, an hour fifteen, fuel not yet a concern. By now, the next tankers should be orbiting overhead Bermuda. If we were on course and could stay there, the three-ship flight of KB-50s would bloom big in our radarscopes. We should paint them at our maximum search range,

40 miles. If we were off a little to either side, we'd still get a nice, fat return but toward one edge of the scope, and at somewhat shorter range. We wouldn't have to miss by much for them to slide by, off the scope entirely. Our ace in the hole: Bermuda's radio navigation aid, a VHF omnidirectional range, called VOR, or Omni.

Most military aircraft then had avionics capable of receiving a variety of radio navaids. Not so the F-104C. We had only a VOR. The gauge in our cockpits had a needle that would eventually point at the Omni station located at Kindley Field, on the island of Bermuda. Reception was line of sight, so at our altitude the practical range was something like 200 nautical miles. We might be north of course already, and quite possibly winds would blow us farther north. If so, we wouldn't paint the tankers. But we couldn't miss Bermuda by 200 miles. We'd certainly receive Kindley VOR—and so would the tankers, which meant we could locate each other. It would be a while before we'd receive it, but with nothing else to listen to I dialed up Kindley's frequency. Out of range, the VOR needle spun in a lazy circle.

Actually, Lindbergh had a lot going for him—pretty good weather and a tailwind. His little airplane even had a wingspan more than twice ours. Also, he didn't load up the *Spirit of Saint Louis* with cheap wine, betting on a friendly customs agent at the port of entry. (Here's another wagering opportunity: who can hide the most cases of rioja in the smallish F-104?) On the other hand, we had considerably more than Lindbergh's 400 gallons of gas, plus the opportunity to get some more from the tankers. This air-refueling technology is what had made ocean crossing by whole squadrons of single-seat fighters commonplace three decades in Lindbergh's wake.

The F-104 didn't use much fuel at cruising altitude anyway. The slick little jet had great fuel specifics—that is, could get either lots of distance (specific range) or lots of time (specific endurance) out of each pound of fuel. Usually we wanted distance and got it by cruising at about .9 Mach. If instead of distance you needed time—say air traffic control wanted you to hold at a fix or you were capping a downed wingman—maximum endurance slowed you to about 75 percent of the speed for maximum range. Today, we wanted both range and time. We needed to cover the distance to the tankers, and maybe needed time to find them.

We cruise-climbed as the aircraft got lighter. With a clean aircraft, we'd climb well above 40,000 feet nearing the end of a cross-country flight. As a rule of thumb, at about 1,000 pounds of fuel remaining, we reduced power to consume 1,000 pounds per hour and started a long glide to destination. Thus, 1,000 pounds remaining gave us about an hour of flight, if we traded altitude for time.

No sign yet of a lock-on to Kindley VOR, but maybe it was still a little early to expect one.

To increase range, the F-104 could carry four external fuel tanks: two quite streamlined ones at wingtip stations and two pretty draggy ones under each wing. Unless jettisoned after they fed out, the aircraft gained only a small increment of range by carrying the under-wing tanks. Aircraft performance was nothing to brag about with four external tanks loaded, so we'd elected to redeploy in the two-tank configuration, another decision giving away a little margin.

Tip tanks long since empty, I was now burning internal fuel. Another piece of pilot wisdom: *Any attempt to stretch fuel is guaranteed to increase headwinds.* The thing about fuel: it doesn't make any difference how good a pilot you are, when you're out of gas, the engine quits. In a pinch, I could jettison the empty tip tanks and stretch it a little. However, controlling anxiety is a necessary part of the inner work of flying and, anyway, the other six guys were in the same shape. I guessed we were all dealing with something that, in aviation, has a technical name: the pucker factor.

Nothing doing with the VOR and no radio contact with the tankers—my fuel gauge showing 1,500 pounds. I asked myself, "Just how accurate are these fuel gauges, anyway?" A gallon of JP-4 weighs about 6.7 pounds, so I was down to something over

200 gallons—not much gas, even in an F-104. I wondered, "Why do we measure fuel in pounds instead of gallons?" It could have something to do with weight computations for center of gravity or takeoff roll, but I supposed it more likely related to engine performance. We rate thrust in pounds, a measure of mass, and it's really the chemical energy in fuel that matters—that is, fuel consumed per pound of thrust produced. A pound is a pound, but gallons expand and contract according to temperature, a gallon of cold fuel having more mass and thus containing more energy than a gallon of warm fuel. Anyway, foreign pilots flying our equipment must think it odd to use this English anachronism, the pound, for such a critical measurement. High above a chilly Atlantic, I formed a theory that both fuel and thrust should be measured in grams.

Down to 1,000 pounds, the welcome mat was not yet out at Bermuda Omni.

I divided my attention about evenly, now, between the fuel gauge and VOR. As a backup, a low-level warning light would illuminate at 750 pounds remaining. If the gauge failed for any reason, this light meant maybe 30 minutes to flameout.

I was not painting the tankers, although they should be close. The VOR needle spun slowly, hunting a signal at the selected frequency and taking no stake in the outcome, a buzzard wheeling carrion, or maybe a shark circling. Even if *my* receiver was bad, all seven of us were tuned to the thing. Somebody had to pick it up.

Bermuda is supposedly the model for the magical isle of Shakespeare's *Tempest*. Maybe Caliban had switched off the Omni. The Bard thoughtfully cast a character named Ariel who would be sympathetic, but just now we needed industrial-strength help, maybe Prospero's more potent sorcery. If we missed the tankers, the Naval Air Station at Kindley was the abort base, but we'd never find it if this damn VOR didn't start working.

A burst of relief as, at last, the tankers made radio contact. Their lead navigator had us on radar and gave a steer of 145 degrees, requiring a turn of more than 90 degrees—back in the direction we'd come from! It seemed improbable we could have missed by so far, but none of us had a better idea and, in any case, he sounded quite confident.

Still no signal from Kindley Omni.

The tanker navigator was right, his vector taking us to a visual sighting. We each grabbed a few pounds of gas, deferring the emergency, then settled in to fill 'er up. No doubt the tanker navigator had saved the entire flight of seven aircraft.

As I refueled, a break opened in the clouds and I saw an island— it must be Bermuda—slip beneath us. I still had no VOR lock on, so I asked the KB-50 navigator if he was pulling in Bermuda Omni. He said, "Sure, it's five square. Maybe you guys didn't get the word: it changed frequencies this morning."

Bermuda Omni had changed broadcast frequencies, the news announced in the regular way through notices to airmen posted at every air base. None of us had been awake enough—or sober enough—to read the NOTAMs, an elementary precaution. A stupid mistake, paid for with much tightening of the GI tract.

We dropped off the tanker, leaving Bermuda behind, its excellent VOR loud and clear now that I'd cranked in the right frequency. Toward the end, the Carolina coast appeared from starboard and slid effortlessly down to fill the windscreen.

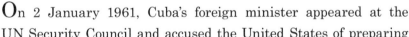

On 2 January 1961, Cuba's foreign minister appeared at the UN Security Council and accused the United States of preparing to invade his island. We formally denied any such intention and the council rejected the charge without a vote.

Three days before leaving office, Dwight Eisenhower broadcast a farewell address to the nation. He noted that we were maintaining large standing armed forces and a vast armaments industry, a first for us during putative peacetime. Pointing out that we spent more each year on defense than "the net income of all United States corporations," he warned us to keep an eye on the result, a new life form he called the military-industrial complex.

⊥

Back at George, flying the F-104 was pure as peaches. On average, each month has 21 working days. We flew about 14 sorties a month, or two days out of three. Typical sortie length was around an hour and a half, so line pilots accumulated 20 hours a month, about the right level of training to stay proficient if combined with a monthly simulator ride and incidental ground training. When not flying, we had additional duties to take care of in the squadron, so the days were full.

I spent many hours on Cuddyback range, sharpening both nuclear and conventional gunnery skills. A stable gunnery plat-form, the Starfighter featured the M-61 20 mm Gatling gun—one of the best weapons ever invented. The gun was new, introduced with the F-104C.[19] In the Korean War, our F-86s came equipped with six .50-caliber machine guns. On the other side, the MiG-15, designed to shoot down B-29s, had three cannons, two 23 mm and one 37 mm, larger-caliber guns with real killing power when they hit. We countered by moving up to 20 mm cannons in the F-100—four of them, each a separate gun with barrels that tended to flex after a few rounds, whipping bullets into a wider pattern near the end of a burst. By contrast, the F-104's M-61 Gatling was a single gun, its rotating barrels united so they became steadier and the bullet pattern tighter as the gun accelerated. Our normal load for practice strafe was 100 rounds of ball ammo, but we carried a few extra rounds to account for already-chambered bullets that would not fire as the gun wound down following trigger release. These extra rounds explained how I twice put more than 100 holes in a strafing panel, scoring above the theoretically possible 100 percent.

---

19 In 1958, the year the M-61 gun appeared, a Chinese National-ist F-86 got the first heat-seeking missile kill, using the AIM-9 (Side-winder). Of course, in 1960 the Russians achieved the first radar-guided SAM (SA-2) kill when they brought down Gary Powers. Though it wasn't obvious at the time, this trio of air-superiority weapons would dominate the air arena for a generation.

Such shooting would be unimaginable in the F-100. (In fact, it was not bad in an F-104.)

We had done a little nuclear dive-bombing in the F-100, though none of us took it seriously. The Hun was unlikely to get enough altitude to dive at a target, punch off the nuke for an airburst and still get out of Dodge. In principle, the 104 could attain sufficient altitude to establish a dive toward the target and release around 25,000 feet, go burner and beat the shock wave. Whatever your confidence level, it was fun to practice the maneuver and another opportunity to bet on scores. A 25,000-foot release was never going to be very accurate, but, as we said, "close" counts in horseshoes, hand grenades, and H-bombs.

We had other training squares to fill as well—instruments, or night, or refueling, or some other requirement to satisfy. If nothing else, we made a run down the coast, dragged contrails across Miramar and hoped the Navy would come up and play.

We were gone from George a good bit, sometimes in short bursts. The wing kept an officer at Cuddyback to supervise the range crew and perform safety functions in the scoring tower. I pulled week-long tours there when my number came up. I spent 10 days at Keesler AFB in Biloxi, Mississippi, training as a forward air controller. FACs are assigned to and live with the Army, supervising air support for ground combat formations, more or less the exact opposite of what fighter pilots want to do. What we wanted was exemplified by a three-week deployment to McChord AFB near Tacoma, Washington, as part of a field exercise the Army was conducting at the Yakima firing range. We provided close air support—great fun. We took off from McChord, crossed the Cascades into the high desert of Central Washington, let down, found the Army and made low passes simulating attack on targets. It was a license to buzz.

Counting the rotation to Spain and all the other TDY, I was away from George eight of the 19 months I was assigned there. However, I was at home for one event of real importance: the Bay of Pigs invasion. In mid-April 1961, 1,400 Cuban exiles landed on the swampy southern coast of Cuba. The CIA supported them, as did the Navy and Air Force, but it didn't go well. Within days, the Cubans had rounded up the 1,200 or so survivors and put them in jail.

This was a period of intense flying for me and, I suspect, throughout Tactical Air Command. I flew every day, sometimes twice, in the 10 days following the invasion. I saw no indication we were about to take a hand in the matter, but, for whatever reason, my combat skills were certainly being polished.

The Eisenhower administration planned the Bay of Pigs fiasco, but Kennedy authorized it. Whatever his misgivings, the new president had more or less foreclosed his options with the bellicose rhetoric of his own campaign. What we say has consequences.

Afterward, Kennedy proposed a 25 percent increase in the defense budget. Maybe he hadn't listened to Eisenhower.

By June 1961, I was nearing the end of my time at George. Concurrently, Gen. Thomas White was finishing up as the Air Force's fourth chief of staff. Tommy White had been a great chief, though I knew nothing of this. I did know his retirement flyby, scheduled for Andrews AFB outside Washington, DC, would feature every type of aircraft active in the Air Force inventory. Large aircraft would be singles; fighters would appear in four-ship. My squadron was tagged to represent the F-104.

We sent five aircraft back to Andrews, so as to have a spare. Dick Lougee led. I flew number two. Over West Virginia, number four let his attention drift and managed to collide with three. Capt. Dick Derrick, the number three man, was killed on impact. Number four bailed out and survived.

From my position on the other side of the formation, I observed the entire incident as though from a great distance. It happened quite rapidly but seemed to play out in slow motion. I remember thinking, "He's going to run into three . . . I must make a radio call to warn him . . . I will now take my thumb and mash down on the mike button . . ." I couldn't make my thumb move fast enough, so I just sat there like an idiot, watching the catastrophe unfold.

This was my first experience of being overtaken by a sort of lassitude that occurs when events have sufficient gravity to warp time and space. It's as if what's happening contains too many frames and has to be slowed down for processing. Maybe the body's greater inertia can't keep pace as adrenaline accelerates the mind. The official term, "temporal distortion," recalls Dali's floppy clocks, but it's more akin to the pointillism of Seurat—reality painstakingly built up one dab at a time as the capacity to react marshals itself. It happened repeatedly to me over the years; the worse the situation, the more deliberate my reaction. Sometimes this worked out for the best because a lot of things are self-correcting. More often, as in the case of this midair, my inability to act with dispatch disappointed me.

We three remaining aircraft circled once, reporting the location to start the rescue effort, then continued onward to Andrews. There, the wing's public affairs officer met us, saying we were to service the aircraft and depart immediately. With luck, no one would connect the loss of two frontline fighters with the chief's retirement ceremony. At this point, our concern was for our squadron mates, one or both of whom might be dead. Lougee, a blond towhead of imposing stature and a champion swimmer at the sprint distances, informed the captain we were proceeding directly and immediately to the Officers Club, where we would await news of our downed comrades and consume a quantity of hard drink disqualifying us from further flight operations this day. See you tomorrow.

By next day's early-morning light, the three of us lined up for launch back to George. This time I was number three—the element lead position for which I'd recently qualified. Weather was stinko, maybe 500 feet and a mile and a half, with drizzle. Lougee and his wingman rolled while I took a few seconds spacing, planning to punch through on instruments and join them on top. Just as I lifted off, the engine fire-warning light illuminated.

Large, bright red, and top center of the instrument panel, this light blinked to signal a fire in the engine compartment. It was a reliable, though not foolproof, sign of trouble.

Engine fire is serious in any aircraft, of course, but more so in single-engine types, where shutting down the motor is almost never an attractive option. Our procedure called for ejecting if we were actually on fire, but I could see no confirming indication, such as smoke trailing behind me or some other symptom of incipient engine failure. So I made a low circling turn back around to the runway, a tricky maneuver on account of the low ceiling and bad visibility. Just prior to touchdown, I used the emergency stores release button (the panic button) to jettison nearly full fuel tanks off my wingtips and reduce landing weight and speed. One of my wing tanks rolled up and stopped at the feet of a workman repairing approach navaids—probably not a pleasant experience for him. I logged five minutes on this flight.

It turned out the fire-warning light had given a false indication. One of the rudder cables had been rubbing on the fire-warning electrical harness and had finally worn through the insulation, shorting the circuit. The ground crew fixed the problem overnight, and I launched again next day. Now, however, I was alone in a clean F-104—no external fuel tanks, of course—with a whole continent to cross en route to George. It took four hops. At each stop, I clomped around base ops in my spurs, advertising a claim to that beautiful, single Starfighter parked outside. After each launch, I leveled at 39,000 and cruise-climbed toward 50.

Here is the aerial view, seen by even the most junior lieutenant wearing wings: how things look up, from the doorway to space, and down, from the rim of Earth's atmospheric shallows, and in, from the edge of the skin.

Craftsmanship in flying develops along two pathways. In the beginning, we fly the same way we first managed to ride a bike or drive a car, using the conscious part of the brain to process commands serially. Over time, we store results that ripen into habit patterns, memories and skills kept in the subconscious, a parallel processor solving simultaneous problems at much greater speed. When the pathways finally merge, we fly the airplane without thinking about it, our conscious mind now a sentinel—alert, keeping watch.

There's a book about Charles Lindbergh, written by his daughter Reeve. In one chapter, she describes a childhood flight in a borrowed 65-horsepower Aeronca. When the engine suddenly quits and he dead-sticks it into an impossibly small Connecticut farm field, she says of her father, he wasn't "flying the airplane, he was *being* the airplane."

My flight records for 28 June 1961 show five hours, 20 minutes and four landings on this long, solitary cross-country, my last F-104 sorties before being transferred to the 79th Fighter Squadron, at RAF Station Woodbridge in the United Kingdom.

Logbook: George

1959–61	Day	Day Weather	Night	Night Weather	Total
F-104C	353:40	18:30	28:35	2:45	403:30

Qualifications:

Combat Ready, F-104C/D

Element Lead

Forward Air Controller (Ground)

Chapter 5

Tiger Squadron

All the lonely people
Where do they all come from?
All the lonely people,
Where do they all belong?
　　　　　　　—The Beatles, *Eleanor Rigby*

Woodbridge Town consisted mostly of single-story structures, a few thatched roofs still in evidence. The village sat quietly along the right bank of the Deben, a lesser river petering out abruptly at the town's north edge, leaving a pool where tides could be shut in and used to power a small grain mill. The surrounding East Anglian countryside had a severe beauty to it—shingle beach along the North Sea shoreline, salt marsh and reed beds reaching inland, canals cutting up the Suffolk Broads. Edward Fitzgerald, translator of the *Rubaiyat*, was born here and buried in a nearby churchyard, the Omar Khayyám Society having long ago planted the rose bush decorating his grave. Benjamin Britten established his music festival at Aldeburgh, just up the coast.

A narrow country road curved northeast out of Woodbridge Town, around the tidal mill and in the direction of twin airfields— RAF stations Bentwaters and Woodbridge. My new home base, RAF Woodbridge, was a typical British air station of its day, the structures rated temporary when built during World War II. Only the airfield pavements were of high quality, a long, wide runway aimed at Berlin so Eighth Air Force bombers could climb straight ahead after takeoff, joining formation atop the abiding English cloud. Over the decade the United States had assigned air squadrons to NATO, a little money had been spent on essential support facilities, but the place retained its plainness, an air of being at the front. Most American families lived on base, in small, substandard dwellings called tobacco houses because some of the profit from the postwar sale of cigarettes had financed their construction, the money pumped in as a form of economic aid.

I had no immediate need for family housing, having come to England unaccompanied. In those days, international trade accounts were settled in gold, and our overseas partners enjoyed a short-term (one hoped) but nonetheless substantial imbalance in their favor, producing a gold flow from us to them. US gold stocks dropped below $16 billion when the books were closed at the end of 1960. To help stem the tide, President Eisenhower, wrapping up his second term, called for a substantial reduction in the number of family members accompanying military personnel abroad. Now, the new Kennedy administration's secretary of defense, Robert McNamara, had decided to implement this policy by refusing to cover the cost of transferring service families overseas. We could still bring our families, of course, but only at our own expense.

The 18-hour transoceanic crossing was by propeller-driven aircraft, a C-118. We stopped at Harmon Air Base in Newfoundland and again at Prestwick, Scotland, before landing at RAF Mildenhall, the main port of entry for military personnel coming to the United Kingdom. After a drive down to Woodbridge, I checked into bachelor quarters and began the process of getting recurrent in the F-100. It was early August 1961.

———◆———

At the end of World War II, the West could not demobilize fast enough. By contrast, Stalin preserved outsized conventional forces and raced to develop nuclear weapons. The invasion of South Korea was a rough wake-up call for the West. When the North Atlantic Council met in New York City in September 1950, the issue was how to defend Europe against what looked like an overpowering threat. At first, the answer seemed simple: rebuild the West's conventional defenses. The NATO Military Committee issued its first strategy document, known as MC 14/1, calling for an ambitious buildup. Debate drove proposed force levels down, but, by 1952, the goal for ground forces remained at 96 divisions. We expected US Air Forces in Europe (USAFE) to grow to 28 wings.[20] Thus, the conventional shield would be very strong indeed, and behind it would stand SAC's nuclear sword.

It quickly became clear we would not pick up the tab for the force levels thought required. In 1953, the incumbent Eisenhower administration's New Look policy de-emphasized conventional forces in favor of less expensive nuclear capabilities. We developed smaller, tactical nuclear munitions, tested them in 1951 and began fielding them in 1955. NATO eventually codified the strategy in MC 14/2, adopted in the spring of 1957. We would deploy forward a thin ground force—a "trip wire" in the analogy popular at the time—that would serve mostly as the trigger for staged nuclear escalation. This strategy relied first on the short-range, tactical nuclear forces of USAFE and other NATO air forces, and ultimately on SAC and the RAF's Strike Command.

However, Russia soon developed its own respectable nuclear force, capable of retaliating against mainland US targets, and the Kennedy administration moved toward a flexible-response policy. That is, in case of attack on NATO, our use of nuclear weapons would be neither automatic nor massive, but carefully controlled, an American finger staying on the nuclear trigger. It took time to

---

20 In 1994, my last year as chief of staff, the entire USAF fighter force, worldwide, amounted to just 20 wings, seven of them in the Guard and Reserve.

implement such a change, especially with Charles de Gaulle standing in the way. Indeed, it wasn't until after 1966, when de Gaulle pulled France out of NATO's military structure, that the alliance was able to adopt MC 14/3, putting more emphasis on options short of nuclear war.

Thus, in the late summer of 1961, when I reported to Europe, nuclear alert continued to be the main job of our NATO-assigned tactical squadrons. At Woodbridge, the 79th Fighter Squadron's tasking was typical: four aircraft on 24-hour alert, each carrying a single nuclear weapon, ready to launch toward Central European targets within 15 minutes of an execute order. We called this Victor Alert, or VA.

———◆———

The 20th Fighter Wing included the 79th at Woodbridge and two other flying squadrons, these units and the wing's headquarters located at RAF Wethersfield in Essex County, north of London. Over at Wethersfield, Col. Royal N. Baker, who had led the 4th Fighter Group in Korea, commanded the parent wing.

Baker's résumé illustrated an interesting point about Korea. By the summer of 1951, the front lines had pretty much stabilized, and the score of our leading MiG killer, Lt. Richard S. Becker, stood at four enemy aircraft destroyed, one probable, and three damaged. In other words, at the point when the ground fighting was essentially over, we hadn't yet produced a single ace. Roy Baker got to Korea in April 1952, well after fighting on the ground stalled and truce negotiations had begun. Flying his 127th mission in March 1953, Baker shot down the 600th MiG destroyed by allied aircraft since the Chinese entered the war. Our then-leading ace, he came home shortly thereafter with 13 kills. (Joe McConnell and others later superseded Baker's tally.)

One of the best books about Korea, Clay Blair's *Forgotten War*, has 976 pages plus notes in its paperback edition. Despite its subtitle (*America in Korea, 1950–1953*), the first 940 pages take us to July 1951, when truce talks began—still the better part of a year before Roy Baker arrived on scene. The last 36 pages deal mostly with the talks, though Blair includes some discussion of the fighting at Heartbreak Ridge, Bloody Ridge, and around the Punch Bowl, action aimed mostly at improving our negotiating position. Readers will find almost no discussion of the air war that continued for the next two years.

Talk about a forgotten war. Baker and 37 other US airmen made ace, and we stacked up literally millions of North Korean dead in those last two years of conflict. We leveled more than half the buildings in 18 of North Korea's 22 largest cities. As this is written, that benighted country has yet to recover fully from the pounding we gave it. Judging by the page count in Blair's otherwise excellent book, this air combat was of little significance.

Fighting on the ground has a history that predates our existence as a species. Some understanding of it is instinctive, built into our genetic makeup. But in 1961, as I arrived in England, we had only half a century's exposure to combat involving aircraft. Clay Blair's worldview was typical and makes sense if we bear in mind the radical newness of air warfare, a not yet well understood part of the human experience.

The commander of the 79th Squadron's B Flight, Capt. Cece LeFevers, whom I had known at George, very kindly asked that I be assigned to his flight. For morning meetings, each of the squadron's four flights sat in rows, eight pilots lined up by rank. A junior birdman, I took a seat near the end in B Flight's row. Next to me, Lt. Mike Dugan occupied the last chair.

Unit cohesion is a factor much prized in operational outfits. The 79th had it. It begins with good people, but we had good people at George, so this is a necessary but not sufficient condition. Here at Woodbridge, we also had good leadership. Our squadron commander, Lt. Col. Bill Georgi (later a brigadier general), was first rate, just the guy you want in charge of an operation detached from its parent headquarters. During the time I was at Woody, Georgi was succeeded by Lt. Col. John Bartholf, another fine officer and future general. Good people plus good leadership equals unit cohesion.

———◆———

We pulled Victor Alert by flights, with a flight on for a week at a time. B Flight divided the week into three segments of two, two, and three days each. Having four aircraft on alert and eight guys in the flight meant we often got relief, but we could pull any length of shift, including up to seven days. In fact, seven-day tours came around often, because some of the guys in the flight might be on leave or TDY. Four of us disappeared into a high-security alert pad, living, eating, and sleeping next to the aircraft, each attached to a nuclear weapon with a yield higher than the one used on Hiroshima.

The food was good, we had an exercise and weightlifting room, and plenty of time to work on additional duties. Evenings, we showed films touring the BX circuit and watched enough TV to begin teasing the English out of regional accents. Sports broadcasts were particularly good. The BBC simply pointed a camera at the action and some guy, obviously an expert, provided understated commentary. The contest got reported, not the back story, the human interest pathos increasingly clogging the arteries of our own television coverage.

Higher authority exercised us continuously to verify reaction time. When the bell rang—usually in the dead of night—we sprang out of bed; hustled into flight suit, boots, g-suit, pistol, and water wings; grabbed our target folder; raced to the jet; scrambled up the ladder into the cockpit; strapped in; got our helmet screwed on; turned on the radio; and checked in with a duty officer. If it was real, he'd read a launch order, giving us an authentication code we could compare with a counterpart we carried in a sealed envelope. For an exercise, we got a time hack at check-in. The requirement was to go from deep sleep to finger on the engine start button in 10 minutes, which assumed we could get airborne in 15.

Before achieving combat-ready status and being assigned to

pull Victor Alert, we went through extended ground training. We had to understand the inner workings of the nuclear weapon we might employ. Written tests concentrated on the fail-safe procedures used to authenticate a launch order, but we also had to memorize the particulars of a specific target—what interceptor and ground defenses protected it, emergency airfields along the route of flight, escape-and-evasion procedures. Getting safely back into the United Kingdom during a nuclear exchange would take some doing; specific identification and recovery procedures were committed to memory. We practiced flying our assigned mission profile on instruments, in the F-100 simulator located over at Wethersfield. We appeared for examination before a board chaired by the squadron commander, during which we rattled off headings, altitudes, and airspeeds for each leg of the mission and described what the target would look like in different seasons, and in varied weather and lighting conditions. The embarrassment of failing this certification procedure, as tough a test as any I'd taken, meant many more hours of study before another try.

We kept a bulky target folder, including all these details, locked in a safe at the VA facility, but at night or in bad weather, an F-100 pilot would find it quite impossible to give much attention to the maps, target photographs, checklists, and the like, that were in this folder. Incapable of sustaining anything longer than momentary hands-off flight, the jet required constant attention. Maybe if you'd memorized every detail of the planned flight, you could concentrate on flying the aircraft and just might find the target. At least, that was the premise.

The target folder also contained a Moshe Dayan–style eye patch. As we strapped in and cranked up the airplane, we were supposed to put the patch on under our crash helmet, covering one eye. It would be tough enough navigating with both eyes, but inbound to the target nuclear bombs would be going off around us, with a real risk of flash blindness. Using the patch, we'd protect one eye, giving us two shots at getting there.

My first VA target was the airfield at Peenemünde, on the Baltic, the site of Germany's rocket-development effort during World War II and just then home station for an East German fighter regiment. I got through the certification process and rapidly forgot the details of attacking Peenemünde. We pulled VA for days at a time, so I always brushed up by doing a little target study at the beginning of each alert period. In any case, our targets changed periodically, as NATO headquarters juggled the nuclear-attack plan, and we were put through a full-blown certification only for our first target.

—◆—

Woodbridge base also housed the 78th Fighter Squadron, a unit of the 81st Fighter Wing. The headquarters of the 81st and its two other flying squadrons were a few road miles away at the twin base, RAF Bentwaters. The only F-101 wing in the tactical force, the 81st was full of famous and colorful people, like the F-104 wing at George. For some of the time I was at Woodbridge, Robin Olds, who'd notched 12 kills in World War II, commanded the wing. He was married to the film actress Ella Raines. Chappie James, his deputy for operations, would become the Air Force's first black four-star general. Both men were large, commanding presences—headstrong, assertive types. They'd serve together again in Southeast Asia, where they would be known as "Blackman and Robin," and where Olds would get four more kills.

—◆—

The quality of 20th Wing aircrews was measured in various ways: gunnery scores, written exams, flight evaluations. The top 20 percent were accorded the title Select Crew and got to wear a special patch on their flight jackets. A new Select Crew list was published every six months, so you could achieve this much-desired status and subsequently lose it, at which point you had to peel off the patch. With luck, I got a patch to wear immediately and never had to remove it.

Pilots also participated in the Human Reliability Program, a documentation nightmare with enough tricky paperwork to guarantee technical noncompliance. It was supposed to ensure the mental and psychological fitness of anyone with access to nuclear weapons. Voluminous files were prepared supporting this thesis for each of us. We all drank too much, and many were uncivilized to the point of clinical certifiability. None of this was disqualifying under the program. Paradoxically, were we to admit to any (quite sensible) reservations about the benefits of launching an F-100 into the gloom to make one-eyed, vertical weapon delivery maneuvers, we'd be debarred and removed from the rolls.

—◆—

October 1961 was a high-water mark of anti-Stalinist criticism. Uncle Joe's embalmed body was removed from a resting place beside Lenin and buried in the Kremlin Wall. Khrushchev launched a severe verbal attack on Albania, a surrogate for China, as the full dimensions of the Sino-Soviet split became apparent.

—◆—

After six months, I'd had enough of the single life, sipping bachelor beer and listening to the Beatles. When, at length, *Eleanor Rigby* waited at her window, I understood completely. I wrote a check for precisely $1,000 and brought Ellie and Mark to England. Since they were not "authorized," we couldn't occupy base housing and so had to live on the economy. We rented what villagers called a modern cottage in Woodbridge Town. For earthly possessions, we had only the contents of hand luggage, so we rented furnished. In the small kitchen, Ellie couldn't cook and do laundry at the same time because the wringer-washer hooked up to the sink, taking all the space. We entered Mark in the neighborhood primary school. At length, a second son, Brian, was delivered at RAF Bentwaters Hospital, arguably establishing his right to dual citizenship.

In Woodbridge Town, our English neighbors at first maintained a careful distance. In time, though, we got acquainted, a process accelerated during the legendary winter of 1962. The cold wasn't quite Siberian, but temperatures fell below freezing and stayed there. Railway switching points locked up, so coal deliveries couldn't reach electric power stations, producing brownouts. Local distribution of coal and paraffin, on which home heating depended, was intermittent. In later years, survivors of the winter of '62 would trade stories and congratulate one another.

Our small house was detached and not well insulated. We accumulated ice on the *inside* of windows; I taped sheets of clear plastic over interior frames to create an air gap. On the plus side, our plumbing was inside the walls, one of the features making the cottage "modern." Houses around us all had lagged water pipes outside the walls, the Brits still a bit behind in this department. These exterior pipes froze, so neighbors were reduced to knocking on our door, buckets at the ready.

The Brits imagined they played Athens to our Sparta. The magnificent contribution they'd made to language and the arts provided firm footings for the view. In addition they somehow managed to *seem* more literate, a good example being their use of "as if," a much sturdier frame for comparison than our overworked "like." They certainly had advanced social skills, elevating conversation as a team sport to Olympic levels. They drew you in, almost against your will, adding an unnecessary interrogative to the end of each assertion: "It's the government, isn't it?" "The Germans *are* a bit pushy, aren't they?" When it was your turn at bat, they emitted a descending "Mmmm" or the little puff of a "Yes" each time you paused for punctuation or to inhale. Still, they hadn't gotten past every grammar and pronunciation issue (how to deal with the word "issue" being one example). They often called men "blokes," used "hoover" as a verb, and there was a certain prolixity to their road signs. You'd be a ways past "Keep to the nearside lane except when overtaking" before its meaning hit home. Still, their invention of the zebra crossing nearly made up for it.

In the end, we liked our English friends and missed having them for neighbors when, eventually, Brother McNamara relaxed his gold-flow rules, tolerating our relocation into base housing.

Calendar 1962 was tough year for the 79th Squadron. Ken Kerwin and Fred Ogle were bringing a two-seater back from Getafe, Spain, in March, the jet having been down there at a maintenance depot for upgrades. It came apart on them near Poitiers: a muffled explosion, engine instruments went nuts, the airplane started burning. They stepped overboard and were not hurt.

In July, the same thing happened to Jerry Farrell, except all the above occurred on takeoff at Woody. He jumped out at low altitude and was recovered OK.

Bob Zender got zapped in September, down at Wheelus. He was on the gunnery range when the fire-warning light came on. Trying to get the bird back to base, there was a progressive deterioration in electrics, hydraulics, and engine readings. His wingman caught up with him and reported flame a foot and a half wide and four feet long coming out the left side of his fuselage. Zender ejected and dislocated his right shoulder.

In November, we lost Denny Counce. Shortly after takeoff, he got the fire-warning light, followed by the usual string of system failures. Barely feet wet over the North Sea, he turned back and made it to dry ground, but by then was pretty low. He probably should have punched out anyway, but rode it in.

———◆———

A depot team showed up to modify our F-100s to carry chemicals. New switches, allowing for control of external tanks that carried and sprayed the stuff, appeared in the cockpit. These munitions need careful handling, so a few pilots and a handful of crew chiefs got special training. For the pilots, it didn't amount to much. There were several types of chemical munitions, targeted against various body parts, though by far the most important were the nerve agents, including sarin and VX. We took the same precautions and used the same delivery tactics with any of them. The pilot stepped to the jet with his mask on, carrying an oxygen bottle. Cockpit switches were safety wired, enabled just before spraying. You had to be careful which way the wind was blowing. With some chemicals, sunlight makes a big difference. But, basically, it's crop dusting, except the harvest is enemy troops.

Ground crewmen underwent much more elaborate training. We'd use chemicals only in retaliation, and any accident on friendly soil would create a catastrophe more than offsetting the hypothetical gains. Hence, we followed special procedures for storing, transporting, and loading the tanks, ensuring the integrity of seals and so forth. Crew chiefs had to be officially certified.

The Air Force is a learning environment, one of the things I liked about it. Maybe instruction on the use of nuclear weapons was not the high point of my service so far, but for disillusionment, nothing beat training to employ chemicals.

—▲—

Rachel Carson published *Silent Spring* in October 1962, kicking off the modern environmental movement. Spokesmen for the chemicals industry, especially DuPont, the main manufacturer of DDT, pounded Carson in public and private. Former secretary of agriculture Ezra Taft Benson concluded she was "probably a Communist."

I made captain that same October, at the five-year service point. The Air Force advanced a few promising lieutenants early—from "below the zone"—but my promotion came in due course, at the normal time for officers with satisfactory performance ratings, neither better nor worse than expected.

—▲—

Because we were in the same flight, Mike Dugan and I often pulled VA together. We were on alert the evening of 22 October 1962, when a grim-faced John Kennedy turned up on the telly, broadcasting live from Chicago. The Cuban missile crisis was approaching its culmination and the young president announced a decision to quarantine the island, warning the Russians that their Caribbean adventure risked nuclear war with us. (Here also, at last, was a climax for the Berlin crisis, left unresolved from the year before.) It was a sobering speech, especially if you were sitting alert with nuclear bullets as you listened. This particular evening, the president made us wonder whether we might not actually have to do our duty. Dugan and I glanced at each other, then sauntered back to the safe to retrieve target folders.

As it turned out, both Washington and Moscow blinked, more or less simultaneously, after which there was tacit agreement not to do this again. The Washington-Moscow hotline, inaugurated in August 1963, symbolized a more predictable, if still fluctuating, relationship. The Cold War entered a new phase, not altogether a bad thing, even if that particular Monday evening featured a little extra target study.

———◆———

A marvelous officer, Mike Dugan combined a capacity for hard work with the knack the Irish have for success in a bureaucracy. He always found a way to make things better. For example, the 79th's squadron symbol was the tiger. Over the years, we'd formed a relationship with the RAF's Number 74 Squadron, at Coltishall, which also made emblematic use of the tiger. Mike parlayed this association into something he called the NATO Tiger Meet, inviting squadrons from all over Europe to Woodbridge for a couple of days of flying and fun. I was Mike's helper in putting together the first such meeting, which proved a grand success. Everybody wanted in the act. The Luftwaffe didn't even have a tiger squadron but sent a unit whose patch featured a fox, with an improvised slogan stitched around it: "Believe it or not, this is a tiger." The overseas newspaper *Stars and Stripes* quoted a Luftwaffe lieutenant: "Ach so, of course, these are Bavarian tigers."

Over the years, the NATO Tiger Meet grew bigger and bigger. Eventually, the site was moved around, with countries as far away as Italy and Portugal hosting the event.

———◆———

J. R. R. Tolkien said he detested French cooking, much preferring plain, British fare. As far as I could see, most of the natives hereabouts agreed with him. That being the case, when couples from the squadron went out together, it was often for ethnic food.

The Dugans introduced us to a Chinese restaurant in Ipswich. The upstairs dining room had a small space heater with a three-position switch: Off, Light, and Heat. With Light selected, a red bulb rotated behind simulated heat waves, making you think you were warm.

⟊

Watching and learning from Mike Dugan, I began acting as if the Air Force was a career. How could I separate myself from the others? The angle I came up with was to rewrite the squadron's standard operating procedures.

At worst—which is to say, normally—military writing is nearly impenetrable, despite much attention given at staff colleges to reducing fog count. (There must be an opposing, clandestine school where military authors master the stealthy art of circumlocution.) Of course, one can point to examples of clear military writing. U. S. Grant penciled simple, direct orders that, supposedly, no one could misread. His *Personal Memoirs* is a model of lucid, declaratory prose.[21] However, there aren't many Grants around. Clear writing requires thought, hard work most of us would sooner transfer to the reader. Wherever I went in the Air Force, I found a rewriting job to do, a resource I mined right up to retirement. While my pages were no match for Grant's, I could with effort produce decipherable sentences. Best of all (for me), technical writing cannot be done without learning something in the process.

Pulling VA provided lots of time for rewriting the squadron's copious procedures manual, as well as for other self-improvement efforts. I had no wish to attend in person the first rung of professional military education, Squadron Officer School at Maxwell AFB, Alabama, so I signed up for the correspondence course, mailing in lessons to get it out of the way. The University of Maryland

---

21 Years later, I would prescribe the *Memoirs* for staff officers who brought me particularly turgid stuff, a mistake, since reading them is pleasure rather than punishment.

had a European division that offered courses at military bases, including Bentwaters. I drove over there for evening classes. Chris Cviic, a brilliant Yugoslav émigré and fellow of St. Antony's College, taught one of my subjects, History of the Soviet Union. One evening he told the class he'd brought his mum over from Croatia to get her teeth fixed on the National Health Service.[22]

—◆—

Returning from a spell at Wheelus, Mike Dugan and I diverted a two-ship into Pisa, Italy, because of weather. Next morning we stopped at base ops to file a clearance and get a weather briefing. An Italian Air Force NCO produced a box of crayons and drew a color profile of our proposed route. He tossed it off casually enough but rendered the production to scale, quite detailed and as graphic as the illustrations in a children's book. The Mediterranean was a wavy purple, the Alps a white-crested, granite gray; rolling France was green, the choppy Channel, ice blue. Layered on this picture, he sketched the forecast weather—en route cloud cover and precipitation, a representation of ceiling and visibility at destination. Finished, it was suitable for framing.

In those days, pilots considered weather forecasting soft science, persuaded you must always check with the forecaster and never believe what he said. However, the Italian who invented these pictures was more than a weatherman and could not have been content with mere data.

—◆—

Before 1800, clouds were not differentiated and had no names. People thought of clouds as "essences" floating in the sky. The English, with a monopoly position in amateur science and plenty of

---

22 Christopher Cviic went on to achieve celebrity as a BBC commentator on the Balkans. In the New Year's Honours List announced 30 December 2000, he was made a member of the Order of the British Empire (OBE), for "services to the promotion of democracy in Central Europe."

clouds to look at, corrected this. Luke Howard, a young pharmacist working in London, published a paper in 1803 that remains a classic in the history of meteorology. Howard saw three basic cloud shapes: (1) lumpy, separated clouds with flat bottoms and cauliflower ears, which he called *cumulus* (Latin for "lump" or "heap"); (2) layered cloud, usually much wider than thick, like a blanket or mattress, which he called *stratus* (Latin for "layer"); and (3) wispy curls, resembling a child's hair, which he called *cirrus* (Latin for "wisp" or "curl"). For clouds giving up precipitation, he suggested adding the term *nimbus* (Latin for "rain"). With some refinement, we continue to use Howard's system.

East Anglia's weather presented its share of flying problems, but it was mostly the stable, solid stratus of low ceilings, bad visibility, fog, or steady rain. I could deal with this sort of weather. The other kind worried me—the violent, high-energy cumulus of thunderstorms—but English weather was fun to fly in because it challenged your instrument skills without scaring you silly.

—◆—

Our most common training sortie had us taking off with a wingman in chase, climbing to altitude and heading southwest. The BBC's powerful London transmitter gave us a positive fix, after which we turned all navaids off and proceeded by dead reckoning toward France. We let down into Normandy, often dodging weather to stay legal, and flew a low-level route of several legs to a hard-to-find target, usually a characteristic feature of the transportation network, maybe a bridge or rail tunnel. This was supposed to simulate the mission we would fly against Pact targets. It could be a test because every little French town looked the same at low level and high speed. Once off course, it was hard to find yourself— or maybe better said, it was easy to convince yourself you knew exactly where you were when you were more or less completely lost.

Following the target run, we'd head back for an instrument recovery at Woody, calling en route to make sure we still had weather minimums for an approach. We flew these training sorties with external tanks, and the changeable weather often forced us to return early so we'd have enough fuel to divert to an alternate, if we needed to. Occasionally I did divert, mostly for the fun of going somewhere else.

The 79th could spend days without turning a wheel in the lowering, foul weather along the North Sea coast. Ceiling and viz would improve to just above operating minimums and stall there, daring us to fly. We kept phone lines to the weather station hot, pleading for a constructive reading that would make it legal to launch. A terminal forecast was a horoscope with numbers anyway, and we figured we could handle it. More than once, I did get airborne, only to be recalled immediately as the weather deteriorated behind me. Way too heavy to land, I'd shoot one instrument approach after another to burn off fuel, breaking out time after time right over the numbers, acquiring an instrument proficiency and confidence that would last a lifetime.

It was interesting to watch the operations of the 78th Squadron, at the other end of the tarmac. Like the rest of the 81st Wing, this squadron was full of vivid characters. In general, their pilots were somewhat older, more experienced than us. They flew the twin-engine F-101, with ground-mapping radar and other avionics a notch better than ours. For whatever reason, they often flew in weather that stopped us, which I couldn't understand, owing to a conviction that I was as good as anybody who ever strapped on an airplane when it came to flying instruments. Anyway, they roared by our operations building, those two big engines cooking, already out of sight in cloud, while we stood around the ops counter hoping for a weather dispensation.

The 78th Squadron symbol was the bushmaster, a large snake. They kept one in a glass case in their ops building and fed it on Tuesdays, providing local color. The 79th did not have a live tiger, but we had a couple of stuffed heads, one mounted behind the bar in the Nissen hut that served as our Officers Club. Rusty, the Brit who tended bar, protected the trophy as best he could, but our tiger came in for a good bit of punishment, a magnet for thrown glasses, the object of periodic theft.

—◆—

Weather and our accident rate aside, it was a marvelous time to be living in England. The economy had recovered from the period of wartime austerity and the disastrous postwar experiment with socialism. The countryside remained pastoral and tidy. Shopping was good to great, the dollar strong against the pound. It was also a richly creative period. A social and sexual revolution was racing through the Western democracies, England in the lead. The Beatles had ignited an extravagant new chapter in the history of rock 'n' roll. The National Theatre had been organized in London, Laurence Olivier at its head. Ellie and I were season ticket holders, there to watch his quirky, magnificent Othello, his wife, Joan Plowright, a dazzling Desdemona.

—◆—

In the aftermath of the Cuban missile crisis, the Kennedy administration looked for alternatives to massive retaliation. The binary outcomes, either conventional defeat or all-out, mutually devastating nuclear war, were bleak. The search for a flexible response raised again the question of whether we might do better in conventional war. From the beginning, airpower advocates, our own Billy Mitchell included, argued that the airplane was a decisive instrument in combat. Actual results so far, aside from the two nuclear attacks on Japan, were at best inconclusive. Those (like me) who believed in the central importance of conventional airpower understood what a huge difference it makes if you actually hit what you're aiming at, not least because friendly losses abate so quickly when you don't have to revisit defended targets. Achieving airpower's promise was therefore closely connected to the accuracy with which we delivered conventional weaponry. We'd long had guided air-to-air missiles, showing we understood the principle. Now we began to introduce guided air-to-ground munitions.

At Woodbridge, our F-100s were modified again, this time to carry one of the early air-to-ground guided missiles, the Bullpup. We fired the missile from a wing station. After coming off the wing, its rocket motor ignited flares on its aft fins, providing a bright light source the pilot superimposed on the target using up/down, left/right commands transmitted from a small joystick mounted just behind the throttle. Because of gravity and changes in target aspect resulting from forward motion of the aircraft, we needed to make continuous corrections to keep the Bullpup on a line-of-sight trajectory to the target. Thus, the pilot had to let go of the throttle and manipulate the joystick during the missile's entire time of flight.

Hitting anything with the Bullpup required finesse, so we weren't allowed near a live round until we got 350 runs in a special Bullpup simulator. Following this, I fired the missile at Wheelus and scored a gross miss, cratering empty desert so far from the intended target the range safety observer couldn't give me a score. The problem: as the Bullpup came off the launch rail, a plume of sparks and smoke blossomed in front of me, much of it funneled down the intake, causing compressor stall, something the J-57 engine liked to do anyway. I had not been prepared for this, a nice example of the limits of simulation, and by the time I woke up, the missile had fallen well below line of sight to the target. I couldn't recover it, even with maximum continuous up commands.

After landing, I signed the hand receipt that officially removes high-value property from government inventory. The advertised price—$5,200—equaled the retail cost of a luxury automobile. I'd just buried a brand-new Cadillac, unscorable at six o'clock. No matter. Mark me qualified. We couldn't afford to let anybody shoot two.

———◆———

When I first arrived at Woody, we had an L-20 (later designated the U-6), a military version of the deHavilland Beaver that we used for administrative flights, mostly back and forth to the headquarters at Wethersfield. A handful of 79th pilots checked out in the

L-20 and logged a little extra flying time. I immediately asked to become part of the group flying it and did get a few hours, including some of the dreaded copilot time, before one of the guys ran the aircraft off the runway and totaled it. After that, if we had business at Wethersfield, we drove back and forth on those interesting English country roads.

————◆————

On average, we spent maybe two months a year at Wheelus—more than enough to maintain gunnery qualifications. In the winter months, we flew local there, filling training squares, mostly low-level navigation routes over spectacular Libyan desert. We lived in dormitories, laundry and room-cleaning service provided by gangs of young men, all called "*sadik*" by us. This marked the extent of our Arabic. If you can pick only one word, *sadik* ("friend") is not a bad choice. Still, we should have done better than this. Libya was an Italian colony for a long time, so, in addition to Arabic, most of these guys spoke fluent Italian—and some English. We were still a little raw at this world-power business, but we needed to get moving on languages.

The Mediterranean formed a boundary for Wheelus Air Base, though to reach the beach we had to cross the coastal highway running out of Tripoli east through the impressive Roman ruins at Leptis Magna and on to Benghazi. We made much use of the beachfront, staging parties that scored high on the Richter scale.

Wheelus had a desert survival school we attended, followed by annual refresher training. Our UK flying usually took us over the North Sea, and hops to and from Wheelus overflew the Med, so we also did water survival training at Wheelus. Our semiannual ejection training always included a review of the survival gear built into the seat, and how to use it.[23] It was all good stuff, and you never knew when it might come in handy. Hank Higgins, a

---

23 At three-year intervals we also went for a ride in the altitude chamber, a survival school for thin air.

pilot stationed at Soesterberg, in the Netherlands, and a fraternity brother of mine at San Diego State, ran out of gas and jettisoned an F-100 while en route to Wheelus, spending an amazing three days and four nights in a one-man raft before being picked up.

What with Victor Alert, Wheelus, and other TDY, I was away from the family quite a lot.

———

By the summer of 1963, I'd accumulated 1,000 hours of single-engine jet and more than 500 in the F-100. Several nice things happened. First, my instrument card changed color. We all carried a wallet-sized card certifying our instrument rating. Relatively inexperienced pilots had a white card and had to be cleared for instrument flight by someone with a green card. This was no problem in a squadron because there was always a supervisor on duty during flying periods. On cross-countries, however, junior pilots had to find the so-called aerodrome officer, who in turn would satisfy himself we were ready to go by asking questions, finding out if we'd checked the weather and so forth. Having a green card allowed us to clear ourselves for cross-country flight. Second, orders were cut making me a flight lead, so now I could brief and lead flights of three or more aircraft. Finally, I became a squadron IP, checking out newly arrived pilots in local transition, flying the front seat during hooded training, and helping others prepare for check rides. Though not the same as being a real IP in Air Training Command or at a formal combat crew schoolhouse such as Luke, it was still pretty good.

———

Things were heating up in Southeast Asia. The North Vietnamese had expropriated a big chunk of Laos as right-of-way for the Ho Chi Minh Trail. The Laotian government had its hands full in what amounted to civil war with the communist Pathet Lao. In Vientiane, an uneasy coalition fell apart and fighting intensified, Hanoi giving substantial help to the Pathet Lao. We propped up loyalist forces, beginning a bombing effort that would last nearly a decade.

In South Vietnam, unsuccessful attempts to remove Diem were made by paratroops in 1960 and air force pilots in 1962. Seeming to have no good alternative, President Kennedy doubled the number of military advisers and involved us directly in combat by sending helicopter units to transport South Vietnamese troops in battle. Nonetheless, VC guerrillas controlled much of the countryside, frequently engaging and defeating government forces. We upgraded our Military Assistance Advisory Group to a larger, more senior headquarters, the Military Assistance Command for Vietnam, or MACV. In Saigon in May 1962 on fact-finding visit, Secretary of Defense McNamara declared, "We are winning the war."

However, South Vietnamese Army officers, chosen for loyalty to Diem instead of competence, were told to avoid casualties and above all else block any coup attempt. In *A Bright Shining Lie*, Neil Sheehan shows how this policy led to the Viet Cong's first big combat success. In January 1963, at Ap Bac, in the Mekong Delta southwest of Saigon, 350 lightly armed insurgents, outnumbered at least five-to-one, decisively defeated a formidably equipped force of regular South Vietnamese troops, advised as ably as could be by John Paul Vann.

In June 1963 the Buddhist monk Thich Quang Duc burned himself to death at a busy Saigon intersection, a particularly impressive protest against the Diem regime, witnessed and tellingly described by *New York Times* reporter David Halberstam. A photograph of the event showed up on President Kennedy's desk the next day. Madame Nhu, President Diem's sister-in-law but regarded as the South's first lady, said she would "clap hands at seeing another monk barbecue."

Back in the States, August 1963 saw a quarter of a million people demonstrate for civil rights in Washington, DC. Martin Luther King Jr. gave his "I Have a Dream" speech. The next month, four young African-American girls died in the bombing of the Sixteenth Street Baptist Church in Birmingham.

At Bracknell, the RAF Staff College staged a North America Week every year. A sprinkling of US and Canadian officers were invited to attend, me included in the 1963 event. The week featured classroom lectures, sports, and a Friday night dining-in. I pitched for North America in a humiliating softball effort and also played in the cricket match, an even more lopsided defeat, but one carrying less embarrassment.

The RAF invented the dining-in. We copied many of their structures and procedures, but the Brits remain unmatched in its execution. It is a black-tie event. The Royal Army, Navy, and Marines sent exchange students to Bracknell, so the evening featured a rainbow of uniforms, the Highland Regiments particularly splendid—kilted up, knives sticking out of stocking tops.

The RAF regimental band was present for duty, neatly turned out, a program of musical selections left at dinner places. They got through maybe three numbers before the fruit barrage. The tuba was thought an excellent aim point for the plums and bananas that began as an offering at each table. The band hung in there, stoically, through half the program, then decamped with instruments.

Midway through the meal we formed a conspiracy, knotting napkins to fashion a sort of drag line that was in turn attached surreptitiously to a corner of the linen covering the head table, where the air vice-marshal and his guests sat deep in conversation. At a signal, we whipped away the tablecloth, the trick not quite succeeding in leaving the place settings intact.

As an after-dinner highlight, we held a contest to see how many people could get on top of a folding table before it collapsed.

The beauty of these games was their simplicity.

———◆———

As the winter of 1963 approached, I went to Germany for jump school. The Air Force assigned some pilots for duty with Army battalions, where they served as forward air controllers. The FAC's job was to call in and direct Air Force fighters providing close air support to engaged ground units, a good FAC being the

infantry battalion commander's best friend. While at George I'd
gone through the course taught at Keesler AFB, Mississippi, and
accordingly had the entry-level qualification to serve as a ground
FAC. A few FACs needed to be jump qualified so they could be
assigned to Army airborne units. I was asked whether I had any
interest in this. I'd have to pass a fitness test, but it looked easy
enough on paper, so I volunteered.

In those years, the Army offered airborne training at several
locations, including in Europe, where the Eighth Infantry Division
ran a school at Wiesbaden. The course was three weeks long, two
weeks of ground training and a week of jumping. Students reported
for screening on the Saturday before ground training began. As
advertised, the test included push-ups, pull-ups, sit-ups, and a
short run. But jump school had its own standards regarding, for
instance, what a push-up is supposed to look like. About 300 of us,
mostly private soldiers recently graduated from Army basic training, showed up for the test; more than half failed it. The rest of us
lined up in formation, and the rejects were paraded by, a departing
tribute and an interesting demonstration of Army-style motivation.

The 130 or so of us who had made it through the fitness test
turned out for ground school Monday morning. That's when the
yelling started. Naturally, we could do nothing right. The first
week, every miscue evoked a demand for push-ups. The second
week, we carried reserve parachutes attached our chests, making
push-ups either too hard or too easy, so we did squats or deep knee
bends instead. Shouts of "Airborne!" punctuated every activity.

Our instructors showed us, then we practiced at considerable
length, every possible way to fall down. A surprisingly large number of mistakes can be made when performing this modest task.
We dropped into sawdust pits from four-foot-high platforms, per-
fecting the "PLF" (parachute landing fall), a twisting maneuver
meant to distribute the landing force into muscular body parts—
thigh, butt, and shoulder. (Too often, I absorbed the shock in bony

parts—knees, elbows, and chin.) We sprang through simulated aircraft doors, flexing into the rigid, semi-fetal body position that must be held while awaiting canopy deployment, this maneuver, too, terminating in quick impact with the ground. We hung at length in suspended parachute harness, releasing into the dirt. We leapt from a tall tower, sliding down long cables to yet another potentially bruising ground contact.

A few in the class were officers, all fighter pilots. The Army issued me a helmet with "4" taped on it, meaning I was the fourth-ranking student. Over the next two weeks, the Air Force contingent attracted its share of attention from the Army NCOs who ran the school. My platoon sergeant, a large man, claimed to be the Army's heavyweight boxing champion, an assertion I did not contest. When he yelled at me, he always began with respectful use of my number—"Captain Four, *sir* . . ."—followed by sharp corrections aimed at improving my attitude. (I sometimes mistakenly yelled, "Air Force!" instead of "Airborne!") As miserable as jump school was for officers, it was far worse for other ranks. We went home at night to bachelor officers' quarters, relaxing and resting for the next day; they went to barracks, enduring round-the-clock harassment.

People washed out during the two weeks of ground training, some through injury but most because they hadn't passed the fitness test with enough margin. Jump school was more like work than sport, and gymnasium tough didn't hack it. Washouts who could still walk made a daily parade past the holdouts, the ritual becoming part of our airborne folkways.

Nietzsche said, "What does not destroy me, makes me stronger," which is nonsense and proves he never went to jump school. In the film *Apocalypse Now*, Willard has it right. He recalls that Kurtz was 38 years old when he went through airborne training: "The next youngest guy was half his age . . . I did it when I was 19, and it damn near wasted me."

I just gradually wore down, eating into reserves. No doubt I could do more push-ups the day I arrived than at the end. On the other hand, I hardened, falling to earth so often I wondered, half seriously, whether I'd need a parachute.

The graduation run was seven and a half miles, in jump boots. Piece o' cake.

In Saigon, on 1 November 1963, a military junta backed by the United States removed Diem, executing him and his brother. Twenty-one days later, President Kennedy was assassinated.

Everyone then alive remembers where they were the day Oswald shot Kennedy, or so they say. I was in jump school. Saturday morning, 23 November 1963, as we fell in for morning formation, the president's death was announced and we were dismissed.

Jump Week, and we needed to leap out of an airplane five times. I can't say I liked it much. With the side doors open, an ominous wind whistled through the airplane. Had I been able to do so without embarrassment, I would have returned to ground with the flight crew. I made it through by putting my brain in neutral and stepping through procedures the instructors had drilled into us. Stand up, hook up, check the parachute of the man ahead of you, shuffle to the door, spring out, assume the position. There were some other niceties after parachute opening, but I always felt slightly giddy seeing the canopy blossom above, confident I no longer faced death but merely the prospect of serious injury. On one jump, a trooper near me in the stick somehow got tangled *inside* my shroud lines. This was a dangerous situation—both our canopies might collapse—but I was lethargic, my euphoria complete.

"Slip!" he shouted, demanding I steer my parachute away from his.

I reckoned it was his fault. "Slip, yourself!" I called back, the dispassionate observer of his eventually successful effort to wriggle free.

Germany's oncoming winter stretched Jump Week to 10 days, giving me a protracted, outsider's look at the Air Force. My Army classmates and I showed up on the tarmac every morning well before dawn and waited in full combat gear while the aviators decided whether the weather was good enough. The Army's T-10 main parachute, meant for serious, repeat use, was much heavier than the emergency types worn by pilots. You didn't stand around long wearing a T-10, your reserve chute, a rifle, and the rest of your combat gear without noticing the load.

One dark morning, we huddled under a C-130 wing for at least an hour and a half, trying to keep our equipment and ourselves dry. As the sky showed the first streaky signs of a miserable day, a crew vehicle appeared. On the dashboard, paper cups ran steam up the windshield. The passenger-side window cranked down and an anonymous message issued: "Won't jump today. Weather." The pickup sped away. One can imagine the reaction of these Army privates. Among other things, it seems some would have liked a cup of coffee.

Of the 101 of us left at the beginning of Jump Week, 100 finished. The young soldier we lost was our strongest man, outdoing the rest of us in the pure physical stuff—push-ups, pull-ups, squats, running—that had become our measure of merit. After we already had a couple of jumps under our belt, he got into a scuffle with a waitress at the enlisted club. The Army couldn't stomach this. He was the last man we watched pass in review, tears streaming down his face. All the kid wanted was a set of jump wings.

———◆———

Back at Woodbridge and sporting my own new jump wings, the authorities offered to extend my overseas tour for a fourth year. Normal tour length was three years, but at about the two-year point we could opt for the extra year. I did so.

Mike Dugan also completed a tour but made a different choice, leaving to volunteer for the Air Commandos. Stationed at Hurlburt

Field in Florida's Panhandle, this outfit flew older, prop-driven airplanes, a big backward step for jet jockeys. But the Air Commandos were already at work in Southeast Asia, among the 16,300 military advisers we had there by the end of 1963, and Mike was a warrior who understood the importance of moving to the sound of guns.

Shortly afterward I was reassigned to headquarters Third Air Force, located at South Ruislip, on London's northern edge.

Logbook: Woodbridge

1961–64	Day	Day Weather	Night	Night Weather	First Pilot	IP	Total
F-100D	610:30	69:20	44:25	3:50	643:50	84:15	728:05

Rating:

Parachutist

Qualifications:

Combat Ready, F-100D/F (Select Crew)

Instruments (Green Card)

Flight Lead

Squadron Instructor Pilot (IP)

Forward Air Controller (Jump Qualified)

Gunnery Qualifications:

Bullpup, AGM-83

Chapter 6

South Ruislip

It's pretty dreary living in the American age—unless of course you're American.
                    —John Osborne, *Look Back in Anger*

Third Air Force's Tactical Evaluation (Tac Eval) Team traveled to the various Air Force bases in the United Kingdom and tested their readiness for combat. Being part of this team was fine duty, giving me many insights into the organization and leadership of wings and squadrons. Because my recent service with the 20th Wing presumably gave me an understanding of its strengths and weaknesses, I was attached to fly at RAF Lakenheath, with the other F-100 wing stationed in the United Kingdom.

The Air Force of the Cold War was lucky in many ways, maybe the most important being that normal, peacetime operations closely approximated the real thing. We had no need to march out of the fort or sail away from the pier. We lived and flew at bases from which we might fight. Combat would be riskier, of course, but the difference was of degree rather than kind. We launched, flew and recovered in much the same way. Though we dropped live munitions only occasionally, we handled them all the time. It took only a little imagination to design exercises that were a realistic approximation of combat. In this regard, we were the envy of the other services, which would undergo a much more radical transition to a war footing and therefore could not so easily measure unit readiness in peacetime.

Our evaluations usually started with a practice scramble of the alert aircraft. We followed up with several days of simulated combat. Units did a lot of flying, especially practice runs on targets we picked so that aircrews would not have seen them before. My designation as a flight examiner authorized me to administer proficiency flight checks to the unit's pilots during this flying phase. We simulated mass-casualty exercises, bomb-dump explosions, fuel-tank fires, and so forth. We checked how the base would deal with attack by chemical or biological weapons. Combat is a round-the-clock proposition, and we wanted to know how strong the night crew, the B team, was, so we put the unit being examined on a 24-hour duty cycle.

In large measure, our exercises were meant to test unit commanders. We devised problems for commanders to solve—not difficult, but aimed at showing whether they had paid attention, day to day, to the war mission, it being pretty easy to get caught up in routine peacetime administration. If he wished, the Third Air Force commander, a major general (two-star) and our big boss, could use our reports as a factor in grading the performance of subordinate commanders. We therefore created a certain amount of anxiety. All Third Air Force wings covertly tracked our location. As long as we were in the South Ruislip headquarters or out flying with units to which we were attached, they felt secure. In a game of cat and mouse, we employed a variety of ruses, often bringing the Tac Eval Team together quietly in the countryside near a base, then pouncing.

We had to be businesslike, absolutely incorruptible, even though we were testing our friends. During the wrap-up phase of an exercise at Bentwaters, Robin Olds asked the team over to his quarters for cocktails, something no other wing commander would have had the nerve to do. Our team chief, Colonel Anderson, should not have accepted the invitation, but he reasoned (I suppose) that the exercise was nearly over and the 81st Wing had done well. In any event, I was glad we went. Ella Raines took us back to their sleeping quarters to show off a bedspread she'd had made from the remnants of discarded mink coats.

———◆———

We moved onto the economy again, renting in Uxbridge, on London's northwest side. Our detached house was nicer than the one we'd had in Woodbridge Town, in part because of what the estate agent called "central heating." Actually, it was a centrally *located*, coal-fired boiler that heated the water used for cooking and bathing. The boiler's chimney ran through an airing cupboard, where Ellie could spread laundry to dry, and enough warmth seeped through interior walls to create a gradient between ambient, outside temperature and what we felt inside the house. The boiler produced a clinker I removed at intervals, but we figured we'd be OK as long as there was no repeat of the winter of '62.

Ellie had started work on a master's degree in economics when I rotated to Spain from George and continued the project during the time I'd been away at the beginning of this UK tour. She now pressed on with her research, using the library at London's famed School of Economics. At one pound sterling a day, we could afford to hire household help. Mark entered second grade at the local comprehensive, his teacher rendering a quick verdict: a known criminal, it was unlikely he could be salvaged.

There was much to like about life on the edge of London. We read the *Daily Telegraph* and watched BBC, these media a notch above US comparables. We walked often into Uxbridge Town and back, window-shopping and telling ourselves we already had everything we wanted. Though the Tac Eval Team stayed on the road a good bit, it was still a staff job, one of the great anxieties of the fighter pilot. Not flying as much as I liked, I sought partial solace in a new, bright-red MGB.

Again, we made lasting friendships with English neighbors. Russ March lived across the street. Ex-RAF and a cricket fan, he was an expert on *Vanity Fair* cartoons. Cricketers were his personal specialty, but the magazine published, between 1907 and 1912, cartoons of pioneer aviators, including Frank Hedges Butler (Spy) and Alberto Santos-Dumont (Geo. Hum). With Russ's help, I gradually acquired all six of these early-aviator cartoons, perhaps the only complete set in existence.

On 10 March 1964, along the inner German border, Soviet MiGs shot down an RB-66 reconnaissance aircraft. Its planned profile called for a turn to the west, but it didn't make the turn for reasons that were never clear. The wreckage came to ground 16 miles inside East Germany, right in the middle of an exercise area seething with Russian troops on maneuver.

Losing the RB-66 was an embarrassment, a small-scale replay of the Gary Powers incident four years earlier. A few months after the RB-66 was shot down, USAFE, the senior Air Force command in Europe, called me to Germany to help write procedures aimed at preventing a recurrence. We established a buffer zone along the border and made up a code word to be broadcast when any of our people showed up on radar about to penetrate to the east. No matter where a pilot *thought* he was, if he heard "brass monkey" on guard channel, he should take up a westerly heading until the situation sorted itself out.

Early in 1964, the Beatles hit it big with "I Want To Hold Your Hand." In February, they made their first American tour, and by April, Beatles tracks held the top five spots on the Billboard charts.

In the States, this was the later-famous Freedom Summer, with hundreds of white students going south to spearhead a voter-registration effort. Ku Klux Klansmen murdered civil rights workers Andrew Goodman, Michael Schwerner, and James Chaney near Philadelphia, Mississippi. The Mississippi Freedom Democratic

Party challenged a segregationist delegation at the Democratic
National Convention in Atlantic City and was rebuffed by white
politicians, including Hubert Humphrey, with long and distinguished records in support of civil rights. A political realignment
was underway that would eventually remove the "solid South" to
the Republican column.

Meanwhile, President Johnson ordered 5,000 additional military advisers into the deteriorating Vietnam situation, bringing
our troop strength there to 21,000, and sent in Gen. William Westmoreland to command the effort. He also appointed Gen. Maxwell
Taylor, chairman of the Joint Chiefs of Staff, to be our ambassador to Saigon. During his one-year tenure, Taylor dealt with five
successive governments in the unstable political environment we'd
helped create.

Early in August, Johnson claimed the North Vietnamese had
fired on two US destroyers in the Gulf of Tonkin and asked Congress for a free hand in using armed force without a formal decla-
ration of war. The Gulf of Tonkin Resolution passed unanimously
in the House and with only two dissenting votes in the Senate. The
wave of student protest grew, symbolized by Berkeley's free speech
movement. Somehow the cause of civil rights and the peace protests fused into aspects of the same thing, with incidental music
provided first by folk singers like Joan Baez and Bob Dylan, then
increasingly by rock 'n' roll groups.

In October, Leonid Brezhnev replaced Khrushchev as first
secretary, a gray face moving to the top of a gray Soviet bureaucracy. China exploded an atomic bomb. Martin Luther King Jr.
won the Nobel Peace Prize. In November elections, Lyndon Johnson swamped Barry Goldwater, a major general in the Air Force
Reserve.

———◆———

During this period, one or our best outfits was the 48th Fighter
Wing, located at Lakenheath. It was full of talented pilots, among
them Jay Closner (later, a major general and head of the Air Force

Reserve). Jay was one of several bachelor pilots who rented a stately home in the Norfolk countryside, the scene of legendary social activity. The 48th Wing staked out a section of beach down at Wheelus, its members coming together there as required to produce and distribute a virulent punch known as Blabbermouth. Chuck Horner, later the brilliant air commander of Operation Desert Storm, held a spot near the top of the beach party all-star lineup. He rotated home out of the 48th Wing just as I was attached, but I knew him from Wheelus and admired his hardiness.

Unfortunately, the 48th was in the middle of a string of accidents, planting an aircraft a month in the English countryside. We didn't have anybody better than some of the guys involved in these accidents—Jim Chestnut, D. H. Williams, Skip Scott, Ron Clements, Tom Allbee, Ken Staten. A couple of wing commanders were replaced; nothing seemed to help.

Wings usually established boards to investigate their accidents and recommend corrective action but, on the theory that they needed some outside supervision, I was brought in to help with a particularly nasty one. The leader of a three-ship flight had put his wingmen in trail to do aerobatics along Omaha Beach in Normandy. During an aileron roll, the number three man, seeing he was too low, aborted the maneuver, but number two tried to follow lead and impacted at about the waterline, killing himself. In a bit of bad luck, parts of his aircraft hit and decapitated a Frenchman fishing from the beach.

The flight lead's last name was Malone, and even before this incident his nickname had been Mayday Malone. A natural pilot, he was a consistent winner of the wing's top gun competition, a tough adversary in simulated aerial combat. But he'd jumped out of an F-100 down at Wheelus under suspicious circumstances. The airplane might have been OK; some thought he just wanted to test the ejection seat. On another occasion, he'd aborted a takeoff at high speed, also at Wheelus, and ended up with the nose gear collapsed and the engine intake wrapped around a palm tree. And now he'd lost a wingman, in the process not improving our relationship with the French, who were anyway unhappy about the low flying we did down there.

The accident board found Malone at fault. He eventually left the Air Force for a job with the airlines.

———◆———

In March 1965, we began the sustained (as opposed to reprisal) bombing of North Vietnam, an operation called Rolling Thunder. Three thousand five hundred Marines splashed ashore at China Beach, near Da Nang, our first commitment of ground combat units. At a July press conference, President Johnson announced he would send 44 combat battalions to Vietnam, raising our presence there to 125,000 troops. Monthly draft calls doubled to 35,000, and Congress passed a law making draft-card burning a crime.

———◆———

As time drew near to leave the United Kingdom, I applied to join the Air Force's aerial demonstration team, the Thunderbirds. Every year about 100 pilots volunteered for the team, so the odds were against me. I made it to the finals, coming back to Nellis, the team's home base, for a flying tryout. But I was not selected and soon got orders to report to Luke Field, where the Luftwaffe had set up a training program for its version of the Starfighter, the F-104G.

*Ellie and I prepare a response during
one of our intercollegiate debates, 1957.*

Husband-Wife Debate Team To Compete At West Point

Tony and Elynor McPeak, husband-and-wife debate team, last week earned the right to compete in the National College Debate tournament at West Point, N. Y., April 24 through 27.

The two placed among the top three teams in last weekend's District One finals at Reno, Nevada.

First Married Couple

The appearance of McPeak and his wife will mark the first time a married couple has competed. McPeak will be attending his third West Point tournament.

San Diego State's Daily Aztec *reports, 12 April 1957, that we are the first husband and wife team to compete for the national debate title.*

Student pilot, Hondo Air Base, 1958, in the earmuff headset worn before the era of jet helmets.

Mr. Robinson and the students at my table at primary flying training, Hondo Air Base, Texas. At front, the aviation cadet who was especially helpful with suggestions.

Ken Thomas and students, basic flying training, Vance AFB, December 1958.

Starfighter pilot, George AFB, January 1960.
I found some excuse to wear my spurs whenever possible.

*John McCurdy, Earl "Snake" Pitts and I have been in
Spain long enough to buy hats. Ed Rock, maybe not.*

*Pulling alert
with, behind us,
the window I
tried to kill with
a flare gun.*

Scramble from the Moron alert pad, fall 1960. If you kept your g-suit and spurs on, you could just about get airborne in five minutes.

Thanksgiving 1961, in San Diego. Ellie, Mark, and I with Fern and Asher Moskowitz. I got to know Ellie's family perhaps better than my own.

Mike and Grace Dugan, with their children. Mike always found a way to improve things at the squadron.

79th Fighter Squadron, RAF Woodbridge, 1962. Two future Air Force chiefs of staff: front row left, Tony McPeak; front row right, Mike Dugan. Front row without hat, Lt. Col. Bill Georgi, an outstanding squadron commander.

*Christmas 1964. Ellie, Mark, and Brian in the
backyard of our Uxbridge, England, semi-detached.
We told ourselves we had everything we needed.*

With Ellie, Mark, and Brian, Luke AFB, 1966.

Logbook: South Ruislip

1964–65	Day	Day Weather	Night	Night Weather	First Pilot	IP	Total
F-100D	110:05	14:10	4:25	0:55	67:40	61:55	129:35

Qualifications:

Flight Examiner, F-100D/F

Chapter 7

Luke Luftwaffe

The Congress shall have Power To . . . raise and support
Armies . . . To provide and maintain a Navy . . .
   —Article I, Section 8, *US Constitution*

Gunnery instructors at Luke had personal call signs. Mine was
Wolfgang, honoring a favorite composer. My German students gave
it a Continental pronunciation, making a *v* of the *w* and flattening
the *a,* so it sounded like "Vulfgong." In the haiku of fighter pilot
communication, this often shortened to "Vulf." About half the students were sergeant pilots who had seen action in World War II.
Some had not been dazzling successes as civilians in postwar Germany, and when the Luftwaffe began to revive in the late 1950s,
they welcomed the chance for steady employment and a pension.
Germany switched to an all-officer pilot force as fast as it could,
but building an air force takes time, and these combat-hardened
NCOs helped bridge the gap to a fully rehabilitated Luftwaffe.
Older, more seasoned, and perhaps a tad less trainable, these sergeant pilots could pose a special problem.

One morning I led a flight to the gunnery range. My number
four man, one of these NCO pilots, wouldn't do anything right.
Watching in my rearview mirrors, I saw his taxi spacing was much
too loose. In the arming area just before takeoff, he didn't align the

aircraft canopies properly. He was out of formation on the way to the range. His bombing and strafing scores were awful and his flying sloppy on the return leg, as was his performance in the traffic pattern, through the de-arming pits, and back to parking. During debriefing, I started through the list of misdemeanors and saw him get more and more fidgety. Finally, he asked, "Vulf, how many kills do you have?"

Sometimes a mediocre pilot can be a wonderful instructor. If anything, I was the opposite, better at flying than teaching. But this sergeant pilot's rhetorical question stayed with me over the years, not so much because it underscored a lack of sophistication in my instructing skills, but because it raised indirectly a much larger issue: how do you rebuild an air force? Formerly one of the world's premier fighting outfits, the proud Luftwaffe was now experiencing a troubled rebirth, in large part because of F-104 accidents.

To a degree, the jet itself was to blame. In the F-104A, the Air Force had produced a pure interceptor, designed for speed and climb rate. The F-104C I'd flown at George was a fighter version, a waypoint developed during the period when tactical forces were grabbing for a life preserver. The Luftwaffe's model, the F-104G, was missionized for theater nuclear strike. Accordingly, it had radar that could paint ground returns as well as airborne targets and an onboard inertial navigation system. These avionics made the G heavier than earlier versions of the F-104, but in theory they freed the pilot from dependence on ground-based navaids. The trade-off was a reduction in (already poor) maneuverability and what some asserted was an unforgiving disposition.

West Germany counted on the F-104G as the backbone of its air contribution to NATO. In 1960, Lockheed delivered the first of what would eventually be 900 jets. By the mid-1960s, 61 had crashed, with the loss of 35 pilots, generating plenty of criticism for the Bonn government, including charges of a tainted decision to buy the airplane. At the height of the crisis, the F-104G accident rate peaked at 139 per 100,000 flying hours. Gen. Wernher

Panitzki, the Luftwaffe chief, had to resign.[24] In the end, 292 German Starfighter accidents killed 115 pilots. (Their nickname for the airplane: *Witwenmacher*, or "Widowmaker.") As a consequence, the Luftwaffe lost much public standing in Germany.

Perhaps too hardened by experience with high accident rates, my view was the F-104G gave rather good service. The overall loss rate for Luftwaffe Starfighters—about 30 percent—was certainly no worse than that racked up by the Republic F-84F, the aircraft the F-104 replaced. A deeper, structural problem was the struggle by the Luftwaffe to get reestablished, exemplified by the recall of NCO pilots. Air forces are complicated mechanisms that can be expected to work only if all the many moving parts somehow mesh.

At beer call one Friday evening, a young German officer illustrated the point: America shipped high-octane fuel to the RAF during the Battle of Britain, increasing the speed and climb rate of Spitfires and Hurricanes. By contrast, the Luftwaffe had to rely on lower, 87-octane fuel, which compromised their performance. They nearly won anyway.

Germans invented the jet engine and produced the first operational jet fighter. Now, 20 years after the war, here they were in Arizona, taking instruction from Americans on how to fly American airplanes.

Regarding armed forces, our Constitution gives Congress the power to "raise and support Armies" and "provide and maintain

---

24 His successor, the legendary Johannes Steinhoff, served in combat from the opening days of World War II until April 1945, when an accident in the first operational jet, the Me-262, ended his combat flying and left him badly scarred. By then, he had 176 confirmed kills and had been shot down himself a dozen times, nearly always riding the aircraft in. (He didn't trust parachutes.) A thinking-man's pilot, he also risked much at the forefront of the "fighter pilot's revolt," which, in 1945, opposed the air-employment strategies of Hitler and Göring. Following his service as Luftwaffe chief, Steinhoff became a four-star general and served as chairman of NATO's Military Committee.

a Navy." The drafters chose this language carefully, the young republic leery of a standing army, but they must have reckoned the citizenry could be relied on to possess the basic skills of soldiering, marching and shooting, so if the nation needed an army, it could "raise" it quickly, more or less from scratch. By contrast, a navy takes time to build; a country wanting a navy must put it in place and "maintain" it.

We can forgive the Founding Fathers the omission of any reference to an air force, but even more than a navy it's a construction that takes decades, with the briefest interruption forfeiting the accumulated understanding and experience that makes the thing possible at all. The Luftwaffe had barely survived just such an interruption. We'd cut down the tree and dynamited the stump, and now we were trying to make it grow again.

In the fall of 1965 we had our first real fight with North Vietnamese regulars, the Battle of Ia Drang Valley. We won a victory of arithmetic, establishing a four-to-one casualty ratio. The war would go on for many years but, finally, 17 November 1965 would be one of our bloodiest days: 155 Americans killed.

By December, the US force level in-country reached 185,000, helping make good the loss of 90,000 or so South Vietnamese soldiers who had deserted in the past year. Up to 50 percent of the Vietnamese countryside was now under some degree of Viet Cong control. *Time* magazine chose General Westmoreland as 1965's Man of the Year.

At home, draft calls approached 40,000 a month. In early February 1966, Lt. Gen. Lewis B. Hershey, longtime head of the Selective Service System, announced that local draft boards could take students who ranked low in class standing, meaning middle class families were no longer insulated from military service. In May, students seized the University of Chicago's administrative building in the largest of many protests against providing class rank to draft boards.

———◆———

Family housing always seemed to be scarce when going to a new posting, so at Luke we once again looked for and rented something in the community, this time a ranch-style house in suburban Glendale. We always put a clause in the lease giving us an out when base housing became available; still, it was no fun unloading stuff, then packing it up and moving again in short order.

We spent Christmas of 1965 in the Glendale rental, inviting Ellie's parents over from San Diego for the holiday. They were with us when Ellie's gift turned out to be an automatic dishwasher. She was happy about this, and Fern and Asher Moskowitz decided it was possible (though still a long shot) I would make the grade as a son-in-law. The machine was a portable model, so we took it along to the base when we were allotted a nice new set of Capehart quarters, the type replacing Wherry housing.

Ellie attended classes at Arizona State, across town in Tempe, finishing the last few credits she needed for a master's degree in economics.

———◆———

I had lots of F-104 time, of course, but here at Luke I would be a real instructor in a formal training course, something different from the squadron IP duties I'd previously pulled. First, I went through the normal transition to a new aircraft, the Luftwaffe's G model being considerably different from the F-104C I had flown. With inertial navigation equipment and a reliable autopilot, we actually could fly a low-level profile to and attack a target in bad weather or darkness. We trained to do this by getting in the backseat under the hood and flying blind combat mission profiles. What we wanted was a sort of stealthy approach to the target. Were we to allow the radar to transmit continuously, the enemy would likely detect us inbound. So our tactic was to turn on the radar a couple of minutes out from each checkpoint, allow two or three sweeps to verify our location, update the inertial nav system and put the radar back to sleep. Approaching the target, we'd wake up the radar, paint the target, and either toss the bomb to get an airburst or fly over and lay it down for a surface burst. Not easy, some were better at it than others, but in marked contrast with the F-100, tactical nuclear strike was just possibly doable.

After getting current and qualified in the G, I went through a formal course of instruction on how to instruct. Much of this involved academics, but I also got a lot more sorties in the TF, the designation of the two-place F-104G, giving pretend instruction to pretend students (other IPs). My flight records show I was at Luke four months and had 42 F-104G sorties before I logged my first minute of IP time, which I finally did on 18 February 1966.

About the same time, I met the requirements for and was granted the rating of senior pilot, so I bought new wings—with a star above the shield. By this time, I'd accumulated 1,854 hours total flying time, with 1,614 first pilot and 1,586 single-engine jet, both these latter categories excluding student time. If I lasted to 15 years service and 3,000 hours flying time, I'd become a command pilot, at which time a wreath of oak leaves would sprout around the star.[25]

The F-104Gs at Luke belonged to the Germans, but they didn't send over their own maintenance people to take care of them. Lockheed performed all maintenance, under contract. Therefore, a civilian met me at the airplane as I prepared for flight. This was OK, I suppose, in the training environment. In any case, these civilians were all ex-military, probably better qualified to do flight line maintenance than the airmen and NCOs we had in regular Air Force squadrons. Still, it broke up the team I'd learned to count on. A pilot and his crew chief are the tailback and pulling guard of modern air war. In a well-run squadron, both names will be painted on the airplane.

---

25 A popular version holds that pilots earned the star over their wings by flying a general, and the wreath by killing one.

After spending a brief period as a line IP in an F-104G training squadron, I was pulled up to wing headquarters and given duties as staff weapons officer. This was interesting work, involving supervision of all phases of the wing's weapon training program. I also helped manage Luke's gunnery range complex, 2.7 million acres stretching south from the main Yuma-to-Phoenix highway to the Mexican border. This vast desert area was dotted with manned ranges, where practice bombing and gunnery could be observed and scored, and unmanned target arrays, where pilots could practice free-form combat tactics. Generally speaking, civilians weren't allowed to enter the range, though some parts were opened during hunting season. My responsibilities included publishing range procedures, reporting on use, planning future improvements, and inspecting periodically to monitor target construction and maintenance.

A small crew headed by a midgrade NCO manned one of the scored ranges, near Ajo, Arizona. When I visited, I was impressed by the way the crew kept up the facility. The sergeant in charge, a real desert rat married to a local woman, had been in the job for 11 years. His was not a sought-after assignment, but he did it well. As a bonus, hardly a season went by that he didn't rescue some hunters. Unfortunately, his military bearing did not match his performance. He knew I was coming to inspect but didn't bother to shave or get a haircut. Shirtless, he met me in old khaki trousers, cut off as shorts. In the Air Force vernacular, he'd gone native. Soon, the personnel system would try to recapture him by reassignment.

After looking around, I decided nobody else would be dumb enough to want his job, let alone turn in such an excellent performance. He was happy here. Why make someone else unhappy by creating a requirement to replace him? Nevertheless, I knew he was ripe for reassignment. I asked him where he wanted to go. He said he'd applied for Korea, a one-year remote tour that would give him a choice of return assignments. He wanted to come right back to Ajo, figuring he could serve out 20 years to retirement.

I resolved to help him get to Korea. I also made sure none of my superiors visited the range and got a look at him.

In Vietnam, Westmoreland settled on a maneuver scheme: fly troops by helicopter into a hostile zone, engage in heavy fighting (unless the Viet Cong chose to melt away into the jungle), then withdraw by helicopter, after which the VC returned and retook control. The newspapers called these tactics "search and destroy."

Vietnam's air force commander, Nguyen Cao Ky, became prime minister in mid-1965, after which he and Gen. Nguyen Van Thieu of the army ended the corrosive cycle of military coups that had made governing impossible following Diem's assassination. But Ky and Thieu didn't trust each other, and Thieu eventually out-maneuvered and marginalized Ky to centralize power. Like Diem, Thieu was Catholic, appointed close friends to key ministerial and military posts and ruled autocratically. If possible, his regime was more corrupt than Diem's had been. In November, the *New York Times* reported that 40 percent of US economic aid sent to Saigon ended up on the black market.

By year-end, the US troop-strength level reached 385,000. More than 5,000 American troops had been killed and 30,000 wounded.

I continued to instruct students, but this became a less important part of my duties. At Luke, for the first time, I was designated a functional check flight pilot, testing aircraft returning to the flight line after periodic maintenance. At stated intervals, a wing's maintenance organization takes each airplane apart and puts it back together again. A check flight then makes sure the ground crew has reinstalled everything properly and that the aircraft can operate safely throughout its envelope, including, for the F-104, a run out to Mach 2. The test hops I flew did not, of course, belong in the same league with the experimental test work done at Edwards and elsewhere in the Air Force. They could nonetheless be quite inter-esting if the bird had not been buttoned up properly. I accumulated many such flights in the F-104G.

In October 1966, Betty Friedan founded the National Organiza-tion for Women. In Oakland, California, Huey Newton and Bobby Seale organized the Black Panther Party.

I wanted to attend the Fighter Weapons School at Nellis, the Air Force's postgraduate school for fighter pilots. Only a few pilots got to attend the four months or so of intensive training in both air-to-air and air-to-ground employment. Graduates carried a special identifier in their personnel records and were entitled to wear a dis-tinctive shoulder patch, a stylized dartboard—hence the unofficial nickname for weapons school graduates: "Target Arms." When my wing at Luke was assigned a slot in the upcoming class, I went to my boss with a pitch that I should go. After all, I was his weapons officer and needed the schooling to do my job properly. The wing's director of operations was a grizzled colonel named Chanault, nor-mally a good guy.

"How long will you be gone?"

"Four months, sir."

"When you get back, what will you be?"

"Your weapons officer, sir."

"What are you now?"

I never attended Fighter Weapons School, one of the few regrets in a 37-year Air Force career.

In the fall of 1966, I applied again for the Thunderbirds and this time was selected.

Logbook: Luke

1965–66	Day	Day Weather	Night	First Pilot	IP	Total
F-104G	241:20	9:50	19:25	137:25	133:10	270:35

Rating:

Senior Pilot

Qualifications:

Instructor Pilot, F/TF-104G

Functional Check Flight Pilot, F/TF-104G

Gunnery Qualifications (Nuclear):

Visual Toss

Visual Laydown

Radar Toss

Radar Laydown

Chapter 8

Thunderbird!

That which is currently happening is not impossible.
— McAdam's Second Law

"**W**e'll be doing the Opposing Inverted at 50 feet"—this from the current Thunderbird Five, Capt. Bob Beckel. It was January 1967, and Bobby Beckel was beginning my training to be his wingman.

Robert Duane Beckel was a remarkable young man. A member of the first class graduated from the Air Force Academy, Bob had been cadet wing commander, the ranking student. Tall, slender, and fair, he'd captained the academy baseball team and been a basketball All-American, establishing scoring records that stood for many years. A Germanic commitment to excellence, balanced by a sense of humor, made him a standout performer in early fighter assignments. He applied successfully for the Thunderbirds in 1965 (beating me out in the process) and spent most of his first year on the team as wingman to Bob Morgan.

Morgan, a good friend who'd served with me in the 79th Squadron at Woodbridge, was killed during a training sortie late in the 1966 show season when he and Beckel collided at the top of an Opposing Loop. Unsurpassed in sheer flying ability, Bobby Morgan was nothing if not aggressive. Responsible for clearing Beckel at the top of the loop, he always missed close in order to give the crowd a pleasing collision effect. This time, he didn't miss. Beckel managed to get his jet back on the ground in a nice display of airmanship and flew single solo for what remained of the 1966 show season.

———▼———

In the numbering scheme, Thunderbird One was the leader, Two flew left wing, and Three, right wing. Four positioned himself directly behind and underneath lead in the slot. These four made up the Diamond, fastened together in various formations for nearly the entire air show. The remaining two Thunderbirds, Five and Six, were the solos—Five the solo leader and Six the solo wingman. During parts of the show, the solos joined with the Diamond to do six-ship (called Wedge) aerobatics, but most of the time they operated separately, performing maneuvers that added color and contrast. Typically, solo figures were somewhat more difficult technically, often performed symmetrically, head-on, and fairly close to the ground.

Pro forma, the Thunderbirds picked three replacement pilots each year from a large pool of volunteers. With a tour length of two years, the rotation scheme was meant to produce a team of three veterans and three rookies. For 1967, numbers Three, Four, and Six—right wing, slot, and me—were the new guys, with lead, left wing, and lead solo being holdovers from the '66 team. Diamond pilots typically flew the same position for their two-year tour, but Six graduated to Five, becoming the lead solo as a new solo wingman came aboard. All the wingmen were junior officers, usually captains, but lead was a field grader, normally a lieutenant colonel. For most of the team's history, Thunderbird One had served not only as formation leader but also as squadron commander, picking up the substantial administrative responsibilities of this role.

Except for a new leader, replacement pilots joined the team in December, making the move to Nellis before Christmas. Training started after New Year's, with the first official air show scheduled around the beginning of March. However, the team tried to get a new leader on board the summer before he was to take charge. He'd spend six months or so as executive officer, flying cross-country with the team, usually in a spare jet. This routine was meant to familiarize him with all aspects of the operation while gradually preparing him to step into the lead aircraft when formal training began in January. In fact, when Morgan and Beckel had their mid-air, Maj. Frank Latham, the new exec slated to take over as leader in 1967, was getting an orientation hop in the back of a two-seater flown by Morgan. Like Morgan, Latham was killed on impact.

The loss of Bob Morgan showed why rotation of team personnel was not always orderly. From its beginnings through the mid-1960s, the team lost fully one-third of its solo pilots through accidents, creating much bumpiness in the theoretically smooth progression from Six to Five. Incidentally, all the losses had occurred in training flights. As I came aboard, the team had not yet had an accident in front of a crowd during an official air show.

The Thunderbirds were formed in May 1953, at Luke Field. The pilots, all Korean War veterans, were instructors in the F-84 combat crew training school. At the start, the Thunderbirds were only one of several Air Force aerobatic teams, but they quickly established a monopoly. In 1956, they transitioned to the F-100 and moved to Nellis. Initially, it was a four-ship show—no solos—but the team traveled with spare pilots and aircraft that over time were fitted into the act, first as single, and later as dual, or opposing solos.

From the beginning, the team performed both at home and overseas. They first toured Central and South America in 1954. During a second trip south in 1957, the presidents of Argentina and Brazil became the first heads of state to exceed the speed of sound when they flew in the Thunderbirds's two-seat F-100F. Deployment to the Far East came in 1959, a spectacular tour that won the Mackay Trophy. The team went to Europe in 1963, flying the Paris Air Show for the first time. As I joined, the Thunderbirds had flown 1,141 aerial demonstrations in front of 62 million people in 45 countries.

———◆———

Arriving at Nellis in December, Ellie, the boys, and I moved into base housing. Once again, this was the older style, Wherry housing. I bought some plywood and enclosed the water heater, which otherwise sat in plain view next to the kitchen door. I gave the new structure a coat of paint—avocado, a color matching the period's dubious taste. Brian turned the backyard sandbox into a neighborhood youth center. Here at Nellis, he would enter kindergarten.

Ellie managed to wrangle a full-time job at UNLV, teaching freshman economics. This was quite an achievement, since being what was called a Thunderbride was a full-time job. She showed a lot of talent on both fronts. The university salary was her money. We were about to enter the age of two-income families, but I never liked the idea. I provided for the family; any money she made went into her own account, to be spent as she wished.

———◆———

I'd now been back and forth a few times between the F-100 and F-104 and had to get recurrent in the Hun. In the last days of 1966, I flew a couple of sorties in the two-seater with Hank Canterbury, the departing slot pilot, as my IP.

Hank was the first Air Force Academy graduate to join the team. A gymnast, he had unnatural body control, falling off barstools or down flights of stairs, impressing girls without doing much damage to himself. He would be a finalist in the category Strongest Pilot I Ever Flew With, making the aircraft part of his tumbling act. As for courage, he didn't need it. He was half man, half airplane and did not believe one half would hurt the other.

Hank had tested the limits of what a slot pilot could do and still spend almost all his time looking up lead's tailpipe. In the Diamond four-ship takeoff that opened the show, the slot man rolled down the runway outside the right wingman until the formation broke ground, then crossed under the right wingman into his position below lead. Hank made this move early and assertively. More than once he'd banked hard immediately at liftoff and dragged his wingtip along the concrete in a shower of sparks. He was convinced he could do this safely and had to be talked out of adding the feature to the normal show sequence.

The slot man's formation position forced his vertical stabilizer up into lead's engine exhaust. It was a little silly to ask the ground crew to scrub the soot off after every flight, so the tail was allowed to blacken over time. How quickly and thoroughly the tail got black was a matter of pride for slot pilots. Nobody ever did it faster or better than Hank.

During my recurrency checkout, Hank showed me some things I'd not seen before from inside an F-100. What he did with the airplane was a form of magic.

The Thunderbirds trained in phases. For most of January, the Diamond and solos flew separately. Toward the end the month, while continuing to practice individual maneuvers, the solos occasionally joined the Diamond for six-ship work. Around the first of February, the team began flying the show sequence; that is, the six aircraft flew together, doing maneuvers in the order planned for the air show. Initial training took place at Thunderbird Lake, well away from eavesdroppers. When lead judged the team ready, he moved training sessions from the lake to Indian Springs Air Base, an auxiliary field north of Nellis. The Springs had a small Air Force population and was located along the main highway from Reno to Las Vegas, so there was some opportunity for embarrassment, but it was a better spot for show sequence drills—an actual airfield, the environment we'd see often during the show season. Thereafter until we hit the road in March, the team alternated between show-sequence training at Indian Springs and returning to Thunderbird Lake as necessary to revise maneuvers causing particular difficulty.

Now, in the first week of January 1967, I embarked on phase one of the training program, during which Beckel and I would work alone at Thunderbird Lake. Bob made it clear our first few sorties would concentrate on standard operating procedures, formation flying, and inverted flight.

———◆———

All squadrons have distinctive operating procedures, but the Thunderbirds pushed the concept to its boundaries. That was because the team's success depended on doing all the routine things exactly the same way every time—the action automatic, based on a rigid pattern from start to finish. We had a certain way of walking to the airplane, greeting the crew chief, climbing in the cockpit. There was a way to check in on the radio, to do after-start checks, to taxi. Radio calls during the show were not exactly scripted, but a pattern evolved in training, then hardened as lead talked when he needed to and left gaps so solos had the airtime they required. There was absolutely no extraneous radio chatter during the show; eventually, even the slightest deviation would set off buzzers, warning the whole team something was amiss.

As much as possible, we settled on options before the first practice flight and never changed them. For instance, instead of flying the convenient wing, either left or right, as was done in normal squadrons, I'd always and ever fly the right side, either on Bob's right wing when we were in two-ship together, or outside right when we were with the Diamond in Wedge formation. Bob knew where to look: I could be found to starboard. Making the small stuff automatic let us give full attention to excursions when weather or the physical characteristics of a show site meant improvisation had to be married to system.

It would take some practice to get the many special Thunderbird procedures in hand. There was, for instance, the matter of the smoke switch. Except for the paint job, Thunderbird F-100s were virtually identical to regular line fighters flown in combat squadrons. The team wanted to represent the operational fleet—first, so we could quickly reconfigure for combat in an emergency, and second, so we could tell the audience they were seeing true combat potential, not some tricked-up circus act. We made a small concession for the smoke system, modifying one fuel tank to carry oil and installing a special smoke switch among the other knobs and buttons on the throttle. Activating this switch pumped oil into the jet exhaust, producing white smoke at normal power settings.

Turning the highly visible smoke on or off at the wrong time was impossible to conceal. Especially mortifying, accidental activation on the ground produced an oily plume that fouled everything it touched, causing much extra work for the maintenance guys, who had to keep all of the ground equipment sparkling. The presence on the throttle of other switches that controlled much-used functions such as the radio and speed brakes created ample opportunity for error, but I somehow managed never to squirt smoke while on the ground, one of the few mistakes I avoided.

As for formation flying, fighter pilots of course do a lot of this in line squadrons, but doing aerobatics in formation was forbidden, except for the Thunderbirds. The solo wingman spent a lot of time in formation with Five and, when joined up with the Diamond, the solos flew the outside left (Bobby) and outside right (me) wings. It was arguably more difficult to fly these outside positions. Because of their location inside, next to lead, Diamond wingmen needed to compensate for less movement. The solos took pride in the handicap and argued it showed they were stronger formation flyers than Diamond pilots, who did it for a living. Of course, the assertion was frivolous because the Diamond wingmen were so good they made it easy to fly the outside positions, but jumping their claim provided additional fodder for the perpetual struggle between Diamond and solos. At any rate, Bobby wanted to make certain I didn't smell up the place when we joined the Diamond. The early emphasis on formation flying suited me, as I considered it one of my strengths. However, I was not fully prepared for the examination Bobby had in mind.

In operational squadrons, the rulebook requires wingmen to

hold at least wingtip clearance during a formation takeoff. If something bad happens early in the takeoff roll, both aircraft can safely abort at low speed, but if the leader aborts at high speed, having wingtip clearance allows the wingman to roll on by, continuing the takeoff, much safer than trying to stop both aircraft on what little may remain of the runway. After liftoff, a good lead looks to see that his wingman is safely airborne before signaling (a backward nod of the head) to retract the landing gear. After wheels up, wingmen can safely drop into the slightly low position commonly used in close formation.

As Bob and I taxied out for that first sortie on a crisp January morning, these procedures would not apply. Breaking to a stop on the runway, I established six feet of wing overlap, the solo standard. Showmanship played no part here because, under normal circumstances, the crowd would not see the early stages of our takeoff well enough to be impressed by how tight I was. However, as noted, closer is in a sense easier because relative movement shows up quicker and can be corrected for with smaller adjustments. (Also, since the Diamond overlapped wings only three feet, some solo-pilot macho was at work here.) In any case, for a year's worth of takeoffs, I'd keep Bob's right wingtip in my lap, betting he wouldn't abort.

Bob gave me the run-up signal, an index finger spun in a circle. Following engine checks, he looked at me, I nodded, and he hoisted a thumbs-up, meaning, "Let's have a good one, buddy." In a couple of weeks, we'd be doing the solo Roll on Takeoff, something I was not yet ready for, but Bob would make our departure representative in every other respect. He nodded his head for brake release, then again to signal lighting the burner, then throttled back slightly in the afterburner range to give me a little power to play with as I modulated position fore and aft. At about 135 knots, he started the stick back; I followed suit to keep our fuselage pitch attitudes exactly aligned as our nose wheels elevated for takeoff. Seconds later I saw him and felt myself break ground. This was the critical moment. On the takeoff roll, I'd been making delicate throttle adjustments for exact station keeping. Now I had to take my hand off the throttle, find the landing-gear handle without looking for it—I don't dare look away from Bob—move it to the up position, and get my hand back on the throttle. (Jostling the throttle out of afterburner while fumbling to find the landing-gear handle would be a potentially fatal mistake.) These moves had to be done the instant we broke ground or Bob would get his wheels up before I did and accelerate away from me.

On this, my first training sortie, everybody in the squadron was out on the flight line watching. I was on Bob like a saddle blanket as we broke ground. In a flash, his landing-gear doors dropped open, indicating he'd already initiated the wheels-up sequence. He'd said he would do this quickly, without a signal or so much as a glance in my direction to make sure I was airborne. He was off the ground, so I should be, as indeed I was. I yanked the landing-gear handle up, swearing to myself, just barely able to stay in place with full afterburner as his wheels retracted a microsecond before mine. Take a note: when he says he'll get the gear up quickly, he means *quickly*.

Following gear retraction and just barely off the ground, Bob *lowered* the nose to reduce pitch attitude. Again, I knew this was coming. Still, the actuality took some getting used to. Bob had to prevent any altitude gain because he wanted to do the Roll on Take-off nice and low. It was a simple maneuver, basically a slow-speed, lazy Aileron Roll. The trick was to do it low. We had to accelerate to sufficient airspeed to pull the nose up to a safe pitch attitude for roll entry, and stay close to the ground while doing this—hence, the rather uncomfortable lowering of the nose immediately after we broke ground, so that we skimmed along inches above the surface while gaining speed. He knew he could do this safely only because I was level with him, not lower. "Level" meant I had his head on the horizon and was looking down at the top of his wing, not a natural feeling when flying with six feet of wing overlap. I made another note to be *at least* level during this part of the takeoff sequence. I didn't want Bob worrying about me as he worked the ground. For the air show, his job (the hard one) would be to set us up properly for the low-speed roll. He had to get this right. If he did the roll with too little nose up at entry or too slow an airspeed, we'd both be toast. I sure didn't want him worrying about where I was or what I was doing. Assuming he got the entry right, I'd have the relatively simple job of performing a mirror-image roll away from him.

We did no such roll this day, much training standing between me and the maneuver. Instead, right on the deck, we accelerated away from Nellis toward the Sheepheads, a line of hills rising between the base and Thunderbird Lake, 50 miles north.

I wondered what we must look like to the guys in the control tower. At Nellis, the Thunderbirds had a license to steal, but we were sucking pollen off the sagebrush, low enough to make my fanny hurt. I was just a bit antsy, I suppose, but I trusted Bob completely and, anyway, formation flying is always a question of character. (Also, I was in so tight, if I bounced off the ground, the fireball would get him, too.) I saw only his aircraft, kept the reference points lined up, tried to ignore the ground rushing by in peripheral vision as we drilled into a canyon I'd get to know by heart in the coming days.

At length, we crested the Sheepheads, putting some air under us, and turned a few degrees to align with a valley running north toward the lake. At this point, the training routine called for the solos to spread out and do a few individual warm-up maneuvers, so I moved off a short distance, did some rolls, made a stab at a few seconds of inverted flight. Mostly, I watched Bob as he performed advanced figures like the Eight Point or the Inverted to Inverted, maneuvers the lead solo did by himself in the show sequence.

Soon Bob turned on smoke, signaling for rejoin. Back together, we popped over low hills south of Thunderbird Lake. Small, dry, pancake flat, the lake had a dirt road running north-south along its eastern edge that we used as a practice show line.

Then the fun started. This was my first experience doing rolls and loops in formation and no doubt about it, it was hard work. But there was no physical reason I couldn't stay with him, no matter what he did. His airplane was the same make and model as mine, had the same engine, would dive, stall, go straight up, spin, or whatever else, the same way mine did. So I said to myself, "Bobby, my friend, you have got me stuck to your wing. Period." That will usually work.

After a little formation practice, Bob gave me the lead, dropped back to an observer position, and started my introduction to solo aerobatics.

The word "aerobatics" has, so far as I know, no trustworthy definition. We're all familiar with air transportation, the straight-and-level flight and gentle turns and changes in altitude that bring us from one place to another. By contrast, most of us have at least some notion of the abrupt maneuvering that typifies crop dusting, barnstorming, or dogfighting. But where exactly do we cross the threshold from one kind of flying to the other? Pilots have no need to think deeply about this, a rhetorical question. However, to make better use of the word, let's say aerobatics is the *intentional* departure from straight-and-level flight in order to perform maneuvers involving extremes of bank, pitch, and acceleration.

Aerobatics started *unintentionally* when, in 1913, a young Frenchman named Adolphe Pegoud tried parachuting out of his airplane. Already people had parachuted from tethered balloons, but no one had yet jumped successfully from an airplane. Luckily for Pegoud, his parachute opened, but what his fragile Blériot monoplane did after he abandoned it was even more remarkable. Until that day, pilots mostly flew straight and level, making timid turns as needed for course adjustment. Aircraft were expected to come apart if subjected to anything more demanding. But after he left it, Pegoud's aircraft twisted and tumbled, rolled and turned, soared and dived, apparently none the worse for wear, until finally crashing into the French landscape. Watching in his parachute and from the ground, Pegoud resolved to duplicate the maneuvers in manned flight, and aerobatics was born.

Amazingly rapid progress was made in expanding the aerobatic repertoire. In the beginning, spins were little understood, the spin thought to be a death sentence. A Brit, Wilfred Parke, managed purely by chance to recover from one, afterward remembering what he'd done and writing it down. Pegoud approached aerobatics in a more systematic way. He was the first to perform many maneuvers, including inverted flight, for which he trained by suspending his aircraft upside down in a hangar. This experiment led him to invent the modern style of lap belt and shoulder harness.[26] However, the honor of being the first to do a loop probably belongs (by a few weeks) to Peter Nesterov, a pilot of the Russian Imperial Air Service. Near the city of Kiev, Nesterov climbed to 3,300 feet in a Nieuport monoplane, cut the engine to prevent overrevving the prop, dived a thousand feet or so to build some speed, pulled up sharply into the beginning of the loop, restarted the engine and kept pulling until he went completely over the top. Then he shut the engine down again and glided to a landing. He was arrested and held 10 days for taking undue risk with government property.[27]

It was well into 1904—the better part of a year after their first flight—before the Wrights could horse their flyer around a level 360-degree turn and land back at the takeoff point. It's hard to believe that by January 1914, less than a decade later, enough aerobatic pilots existed in the world that a dinner could be held in London of the Upside Down Club. Courses were served backward, starting with dessert, and a singing waiter entertained while standing on his head.

---

26 Pegoud became a national hero. French newspapers described him as an "ace," perhaps the first use of the term, though it's not clear he shot down any aircraft. He was lost in aerial combat during World War I.

27 The Nesterov Cup is given to the winning men's team in world aerobatic competition.

All aerobatics consist of variations on four basic figures: the roll, loop, hammerhead, and spin. Each of these figures will be seen in civilian competition. However, competition aerobatics involves a series of well-defined, precise maneuvers performed single-ship under the skeptical eyes of certified judges. By contrast, air shows are largely sound and sensation meant to please an uncritical audience, with much concealed by cape work, as different from competition aerobatics as professional wrestling is from the amateur kind.

Certainly, the military flying teams, the Thunderbirds and the Navy's Blue Angels, stray rather far from the purity of competition aerobatics. In general, the Thunderbirds believed the show sequence should be representative of maneuvers Air Force pilots actually perform, an approach ruling out many competition figures. For instance, in combat, fighter pilots are loath to slow down. As a practical matter, both the hammerhead—a 180-degree pivot turn performed in the vertical, just as the aircraft runs out of speed—and the spin—a stall condition in which one wing stalls more fully than the other, producing downward auto rotation—are low-speed phenomena and, therefore, liabilities in combat. My generation of pilots did not practice hammerheads at all and learned spins at flying school mainly to get out of one in case of inadvertent entry. The intentional spin was a prohibited maneuver in every fighter I ever flew. Accordingly, the Thunderbirds did nothing (intentionally) resembling a hammerhead or spin. With one exception, the air show I'd be part of was a sequence of figures based entirely on the roll and the loop. The exception: inverted flight.

Pilots pass through upside down—inverted—during some portion of any roll or loop, but the term "inverted flight" applies to sustained upside-down flying. Operational squadrons do not practice inverted flight, again because it has little combat value. So it was with this problem of inverted flight that Bobby Beckel began my education in solo air-show aerobatics.

As Bob explained, sustained inverted flight was not very complicated. We would begin the maneuver by pulling the nose up just slightly, then neutralizing the controls to more or less "unload" the aircraft.[28] The roll to inverted would be started promptly, before the airplane could climb. The idea was to get from upright to inverted without delay, so the nose couldn't drop much as you were rolling in. As a practical matter, we used maximum obtainable roll rate—in other words, full aileron deflection—a sharp, sudden control input banging the stick against the control stop, sort of jerking the aircraft around to inverted.

Inverted, we'd push the stick forward to hold the nose up, though at our normal entry airspeed not much forward stick would be required. Just as we experience the one positive g of everyday gravity, sustained inverted flight subjected the aircraft to one negative g. The pilot and anything loose in the cockpit *dropped* to the top of the canopy. It was essential to tighten the seat belt until it couldn't get any tighter. The crew chief would help with this as you strapped in. He must also be meticulous about loose objects in the cockpit, cleaning house regularly with a high-powered vacuum and inventorying tools in and out when doing maintenance work.

Of course, the jet fuel also dropped to the top of the tanks. Civilian aerobatic aircraft usually have special fuel and oil systems that continue to pump fluids to the engine during inverted flight. Our jets could have been modified in the same way, but this would not be in keeping with the team's concept of using operationally representative aircraft. Inverted maneuvers would not last long

---

28 When pilots speak of "unloading," they mean pushing the stick forward to produce a light-in-the-seat feeling of weightlessness, usually for purposes of rapid acceleration. (At least in short bursts, engine power pushes this "weightless" object to higher speed quickly.) But Bob and I were doing something else. Unloading put us in a low lift, low drag condition that allowed for safe use of abrupt control inputs. If done symmetrically, it also produced mirror-image ballistic arcs for the opposing figures.

enough for lubrication to be a problem, but fuel was another matter. Fuel in the plumbing lines and in a small inverted flight tank designed to buffer momentary negative-g excursions was all that would keep the F-100's engine running. We figured maybe 15 seconds to flameout. Accordingly, to reduce fuel consumption, we flew inverted maneuvers at idle power. Even so, our rule of thumb was to hold inverted flight for no more than 12 seconds before rolling upright and putting the fuel back on the bottom of the tanks, where the boost pumps were located. It didn't take much imagination to figure out how it would feel to flame out from fuel starvation while flying upside down at 50 feet.

Because we used idle power, the aircraft decelerated and we lost lift unless the control stick was eased forward gradually to increase the wing's negative angle of attack as the aircraft slowed.

All this was pretty straightforward. What made inverted flight difficult at first was the altitude. As Bob had said, during the show season, he'd set this maneuver as close to 50 feet as he could get. Until you're used to it, even upright high-speed flight at 50 feet can be quite stimulating. In training, he would start me at a comfortable altitude, perhaps a couple of hundred feet, then step it down as my proficiency increased.

With Bob chasing me, I established myself on the show line. He called the maneuver, using the language and rhythm of the air show.

"Power idle . . . Nose coming up . . . INverting."

I responded by chopping the throttle, allowing the nose to rise just a tad, then popping the aircraft upside down on the "IN" of "INverting." The roll-in was surprisingly abrupt—it would knock your head against the canopy if you weren't braced for it—and so rapid it took some touch to stop the wings exactly level, upside down. It was easy to over- or undershoot, mistakes that would be painfully obvious to the crowd. Inverted flight itself was no real problem at 200 feet. At 12 seconds, Bob called, "Rolling out . . .

Ready . . . NOW." Rolling right side up to complete the figure was also a no-brainer at initial training altitudes but, during the air show, we would put a bottom on the maneuver.

With Bob in chase, I did Inverted after Inverted after Inverted. In the days ahead, the sequence—power idle, nose up just a bit, flip upside down, hold for 12 seconds while gradually easing forward on the stick, recover, bottom out—was ingrained. It became fairly easy at 200, even 100 feet. At this altitude I could work on proper roll-in technique, countering the deceleration caused by idle power and holding for 12 seconds. Bob left it to me to work the altitude down consistent with comfort level, and I did so, progressively getting lower until the ground started to look awfully close. After several training sorties, I asked Bob whether I was (I hope, I hope!) down to 50 feet yet. "Nope, still a little high"—this with the tight, tough-guy grin real cowboys save for city slickers.

It's the dirt you watch when upside down at low altitude, not your altimeter or airspeed indicator or *g* meter or, for that matter, anything inside the airplane. It's the dirt that will get you.

Formation aerobatics, a little inverted practice, and we headed back to Nellis for an exhilarating, if unconventional, traffic pattern. Tucked in close, I watched as Bob blew dust off the runway. He pitched up to downwind, and I followed at a four-second interval. A tight base turn and routine landing brought an end to my first sortie as a Thunderbird.

Chapter 9

Opposing Solo

Any activity becomes creative when the doer cares about doing it right, or better.

—John Updike

Bobby and I settled into a routine: Monday, Tuesday, and Thursday, a sortie in the morning and another in the afternoon; Wednesday and Friday, a single sortie planned each day, an add-on if required. We conducted very long briefings and debriefings. When I stumbled, we discussed each discrepancy at length. Patient at first, Bob eventually assessed the usual price for buffoonery: I bought the beer on Friday. I logged 30 hours and 50 minutes on 26 sorties in January, double the sorties and half again as many hours as fighter pilots get in normal squadron service. Moreover, there was not a moment's relaxation in the air. The training was *intense,* and my proficiency simply skyrocketed. Every one of the early sorties cemented the building blocks of solo flying: working at low altitude, close formation, inverted flight.

Gradually, Bob added other aerobatic figures to our repertoire, starting with maneuvers we would do in formation, such as the Calypso. In Calypso, Bobby was upside down, with me flying upright on his wing. This was both a figure in the show sequence and the way we entered the traffic pattern for landing. It required technique, but little in the way of judgment from the wingman.

For Four Point Rolls, the idea was to hesitate at intervals, striving for uniform, 90-degree roll segments. A fair amount of aileron was used, slapping the airplane around to each of the points, so it took coordination to hit the points precisely and prevent the wings from bobbling. Bob chased me through many single-ship Four Points, all to the right, calling count and getting me used to the rhythm of the maneuver.

At length, we joined in formation. Bob began the maneuver from a low entry. By this time, I could ignore the altitude and work on the main job: matching his pitch change as he pulled up slightly to initiate the figure: "Nose coming up . . . and ONE . . . and TWO . . . and THREE . . . and FOUR."

On "ONE," we rolled smartly away from each other, stopping at the knife-edge point. We were belly to belly, so I couldn't see him, but in any case I focused on the horizon, to dress the point. On the count of "TWO," we were inverted, still quite close, with only the separation induced by the maneuver. "THREE" brought us again to knife-edge, this time canopy to canopy. Finally, at "FOUR," back upright, I could shoot a quick glance at Bob to make sure we didn't rub together as we played the bottom.

Doing the figure properly required both aircraft to fly the same arc, hit the points in sync, be inverted right at show center, and make symmetrical bottoms—the hard parts. The figure itself was fairly straightforward.

———◆———

By contrast, the solo wingman was on his own for the vertical rolls. Nearing the end of the air show, the Diamond performed its signature maneuver—the Bomb Burst. Lead pulled the formation into the vertical, calling a break when going straight up. The Diamond split, its pilots tracking away from one another for a few seconds before diving back to a crossover near show center, approaching on collision courses from compass points. Shortly after they split, the solo wingman was supposed to climb through the Diamond break and do vertical rolls that would cause the smoke to corkscrew, putting what looked like a pigtail on the Bomb Burst.

To do more than two or three rolls, the aircraft had to be dead vertical. If I misjudged vertical, the aircraft wouldn't stand on its tail, but rather would wobble and fall over like a child's top running out of momentum. Of course, going straight up caused the F-100 to lose speed rapidly, the more so as I couldn't use afterburner. (With the afterburner on there would be no pigtails, since the afterburner reignited and vaporized the oil we pumped into engine exhaust to cause smoke.) So, I needed to arrive at the Bomb Burst break point with plenty of speed. The technique was to have the burner cooking and the smoke switch already on while pulling up into the vertical. Then, as I popped through the exact center of the Bomb Burst, I'd simultaneously come out of burner, showing smoke, and begin max-rate vertical rolls. If truly vertical, and if fast enough when I came out of afterburner, it would be no problem to get six or seven rolls.

The recovery could be tricky. Running out of airspeed, I would typically begin to wobble a bit. What I wanted to do was stop the roll, turn off the smoke, and let the nose drift down through the shortest arc to the horizon for an uneventful, if low-speed recovery. I began the recovery at about 150 knots—pretty slow, close to the $1 g$ stall speed of the F-100. At this speed it paid to be gentle with the airplane. I got anxious once or twice and tried a brute force recovery, accumulating experience. On the other hand, if I left it alone, even zero airspeed was not a bad problem. Running out of energy, the jet might come to a momentary standstill or even tail slide backward toward the ground. Eventually, it could be relied on to pivot around its center of gravity, flop over, weathervane a little and start building the speed needed for return to controlled flight.

With Bob chasing me, I did countless vertical rolls at Thunderbird Lake. When we started working with the Diamond, I'd have to deal with a delicate timing problem, but out here by ourselves, there was not much to the maneuver. Soon I was doing enough vertical rolls to please any crowd.

———◆———

Next, we began working on figures we would do head-on: Slow Roll, Aileron Roll, Loop, and Cuban Eight. During the show, each of these maneuvers would start with the two of us flying at each other, seemingly on a collision course. But to begin training, Bob chased me through many, many repetitions of each of these figures, making sure I had the techniques down pat before we tried doing them head-on.

For the Opposing Slow Roll we pulled the nose up a few degrees to establish a very brief climb, unloaded the aircraft—that is, relaxed stick pressure to produce light-in-the-seat, zero *g* weightlessness—then rolled slowly through 360 degrees. We made no attempt to hold the nose on a point, as would be done in a proper Slow Roll, instead flying a curved, ballistic arc. We wanted to leave symmetrical smoke trails, so my initial training concentrated on developing a feel for the entry attitude and roll rate that Bobby would use.

Bob called the shots: "Nose coming up . . . and . . . ROLLing."

I followed his commands, trying to keep the roll rate lethargic and uniform. The key was getting the nose up just the right amount, then judging the roll rate correctly as the aircraft floated through the maneuver from entry to exit. If the nose was too high or the roll rate too rapid, I would finish well above entry altitude for an unimpressive exit. Not getting the nose up enough or rolling too slowly obliged me to hurry the maneuver at the end to avoid the ground. More than once I did speed it up because of concern about terrain clearance, a matter that became more worrisome as we worked our way down to show altitude.

Another rolling maneuver, Opposing Aileron Rolls, resembled the Slow Roll except, instead of one languid roll, we did several at the maximum rate the jet could produce, about 180 degrees per second. Generating this roll rate required banging the control stick hard against the aileron stop and holding it there, after which you hung on for the ride. Inside the cockpit, the horizon whirled in a kaleidoscopic blur. But it was a simple maneuver, if you were exactly unloaded at the start of the rolls. The slightest positive or negative *g* on the aircraft would show up immediately as coupling. That is, the roll would induce a response in the pitch axis that caused the aircraft to rock along its lateral axis, sort of like see-sawing, rather than revolving cleanly. This could be quite disorienting and difficult to correct because lags in reaction time meant control inputs were likely to augment rather than dampen the coupling. With its inherent stability shortcomings, the F-100 was especially bad in this respect. Even if you did nothing, once started, the coupling quickly became divergent; it got worse if you insisted on continuing the roll. Thus, maximum rate Aileron Rolls could be semi-dangerous at low altitude.

The real killer was overconfidence. Solos wanted to do a lot of Aileron Rolls because more is, of course, better. Nobody ever got in trouble for doing too few, but just the year before, the Blues had lost Dick Oliver, a classy solo pilot, at Toronto, Canada. According to Beckel, he'd done one too many Aileron Rolls and ended up in Lake Ontario. At this point, overconfidence was an issue for neither of us. I wasn't even entry-level confident, and Bob had a healthy respect for the maneuver because once or twice his jet had tried to couple on him. Anyway, he worked me down slowly to lower altitude and gradually increased the number of rolls until we got up to four—the number we'd use in the air show.

I did about a million sets of low-altitude, four-revolution, maximum-rate Aileron Rolls.

Over-the-top maneuvers in the solo show sequence included the Loop and Half Cuban Eight. The Half Cuban was identical to the Loop, except after crossing at the top, the two aircraft rolled upright when headed down 45 degrees on the backside, and flew away from each other into the bottom of the maneuver.

Bob followed me through many Loops and Half Cubans, wanting me to make nice, round figures and be consistent. From the beginning, he made the radio calls we would use in the show sequence:

"Nose coming UP . . . right in to FIVE."

I started the pull on the word "UP," aiming to hit 5 g's on the word "FIVE" and concentrating on a wings-level, 5 g pull. At the vertical—"Now, LOOK"—I relaxed to 2 g's and threw my head back, picking up the horizon visually and correcting to the show line as needed. After floating over the top, airspeed built up again down the backside. At about 225 knots, hearing "Back in with the PULL," I gradually fed in stick forces, building to 5 g's during recovery, then playing the pull as needed to make a good bottom. This transition from 5 to 2 g's, to a float, then back in with the pull, made for round loops because the turn rate stayed about the same as airspeed and g varied through the maneuver.[29]

In mid-January, I took a break from solo training and flew down to Luke with Lt. Col. Ralph Maglione, Thunderbird leader. The Germans had gotten permission from the Old Country to give me honorary Luftwaffe wings. This was a big deal, the occasion calling for a special dinner. Maggie and I left Nellis as a two-ship. En route, he tested me by doing a few Bon Tons.

The Diamond did a figure called the Bon Ton Roulle. Approaching low and level, the four aircraft spread out slightly on lead's command. A moment later, at show center, each aircraft performed an in-place, max-rate Aileron Roll. Lead and right wing rolled right, left wing and slot rolled left. Then, quickly, they came back together in tight formation. Not much to the maneuver, but even a few seconds out of close formation boosted wingie morale. And all

---

29 For most aircraft, the turn radius, and thus the shape of a loop, can be kept constant only by varying the amount of g. A constant g loop would be more egg shaped than round because constant g produces variable turn rates as airspeed changes in the maneuver.

those polished aluminum wings flashing like swordplay in bright sunlight would impress the crowd. Like it said in the narrator's script, "Let the good times roll!"

Maggie liked doing the Bon Ton, so he kicked me out to spread and we did a few, both of us rolling in place to the right. For the cruise down to Luke, we flew at medium altitude, maybe 10 or 12,000. By this time, I'd done a lot of max-rate rolls with Bob, so there was nothing much to the Bon Ton. Anyway, Maggie admired how well we did it together, our timing and recovery altitudes conforming nicely. He said, "We should have put you in the Diamond."

No thanks.

———◆———

The air show's opening sequence was meant to contrast the elegance of Diamond formation flying with the thrill of solo work. The Diamond would take off and make a steep, graceful climb to get a few thousand feet of maneuver altitude. Once they were a little away from the airfield, Bob and I would run up engines, release brakes, and do our Roll on Takeoff.

For this figure, basically an unloaded, Slow Aileron Roll, Bob needed to establish an entry trajectory that would keep us climbing during the first half of the roll. Immediately after liftoff, we'd raise the gear, accelerate to 180 knots, pull up briskly to a slightly nose-high attitude, and slowly roll our aircraft in opposite directions. During the air show, we'd bottom out and continue away from each other to opposite ends of the show line, where we'd set up for the first of the opposing maneuvers.

Our formation takeoffs in early January were high fidelity in every respect, except we didn't do the roll. We began working on this figure at Thunderbird Lake, near the end of our second week together. With Bobby in chase, I lined up on the practice show line. Slowing to near-takeoff speed, I lit the burner, simulating liftoff and acceleration to 180 knots. On Bob's call, I pulled up, unloaded the jet and rolled 360 degrees to the right.

Like most fighter pilots, I'd roll left, given a choice. I can't say why. The airplane doesn't care which way it rolls. Maybe we just feel better rolling left, into the throttle hand. For whatever reason, the Diamond always rolled left. When Bob and I were with them for the six-ship Wedge Roll, we'd do it to the left. I did pigtails to the left. For opposing maneuvers, Bob and I passed to each other's right, allowing both of us to roll left. However, for both the Four Point and the Roll on Takeoff, I had no choice but to roll right because I'd be on Bobby's right wing and had to displace away from him.

The Roll on Takeoff I rehearsed at the Lake didn't go well. It just felt squirrelly, hard to do without scaring myself. The aircraft handled sluggishly at slow speed; there seemed little margin for error. Once committed past the inverted, there was no alternative to completing the maneuver, which made me uncomfortable because I like options. Bobby did his best by starting me with a good altitude cushion, but the figure just didn't work at the lake. At length, we decided I'd simply have to try it on an actual takeoff from Nellis.

We briefed for a normal training sortie except I'd lead the takeoff, with Bob in chase. I was to do the roll whenever it felt good to me. We'd overcome the mental barrier, after which we could work on getting it right.

To this point, I'd done nearly all of my training at Thunderbird Lake. Others in the squadron had seen nothing except our formation takeoffs and Calypso landing patterns, figures that, after the first couple, became routine—not real tests of pilot skill or courage, like the Roll on Takeoff could be. So, again, the squadron turned out to watch my maiden effort. We did a normal Thunderbird startup and taxi, then I lined up to lead the takeoff. I accelerated down the runway in afterburner, lifted off, sucked the gear up, lowered the nose to gather speed, pulled up firmly to a nose-high attitude, began the roll, and—stopped, when it looked to me as though I was too low to get through the maneuver.

Dropping back, I joined Bob's wing for the flight out to the lake and another dose of solo training.

How humiliating! I could read the headline now: "Thunderbird Solo (Refuses to) Roll on Takeoff." I felt like an idiot, having spun everybody up for a nonevent. Somehow, I got though the sortie. After landing, my crew chief and the other ground support people acted natural but avoided eye contact.

During debriefing, Bobby was charitable: aborting the maneuver was the right decision because I hadn't pulled the nose up enough, good judgment on my part, or so he said. It was no help. Next time, I'd either get through the roll or leave a smoking hole in the ground. I said, "Just put me on your wing and let's go do it."

Which is what we did. I can't say the first couple were much fun, but I survived and was soon slowing the roll at completion to make perhaps too aggressive a bottom. We needed to mirror image one another, so Bob told me to knock it off. Though intent on watching the ground as we completed the figure, I could see him out of the corner of my eye and adjust to finish at his altitude, which was manly enough.

Nearing the end of January, I'd become familiar with the maneuvers we'd perform and was making fewer mistakes. As I gained proficiency, we began making opposing passes, flying at each other to perform the figures symmetrically, head-on. The artistic success of opposing work required collision effects; we meant to miss each other, but without too obvious a margin. Thus, for the solos, "missing" had a quite specific meaning. Anybody could miss; we wanted to miss close, to appear (and, in fact, to be) at substantial risk of collision.

Inbound, each of us put his right wing over the show line—easy to do when there was an actual line on the ground, like a runway centerline or the edge of a taxiway. We just laid the right wing over the line, and it was easy to tell it was there at 50 feet altitude. (If the sun was right, you could fly the wing's shadow up the show line.) In concept, if we did nothing, our right wings would clang together at show center. Then Bob called a figure—say a roll—as we approached each other and we got our spacing in the maneuver. We passed to each other's right, like English traffic, rolling left as we went by, displacing a little away from each other. If we got it right, I could feel Bobby go by, a sort of thump of air overpressure telling me we'd missed, but not by a lot. We wouldn't be perfect every time, and within reasonable limits the crowd couldn't tell if we had a little too much spacing, the preferred mistake.

On every opposing pass, one of us would fly on the inside with respect to the audience—just a tad closer to the crowd. Watching from grandstands, the public would look through the closest solo, so we had to compensate for grazing angle. In other words, if we were at precisely the same altitude, customers would see the inside solo as just slightly high—a geometry problem, the amount of correction needed depending on the length of the hypotenuse (that is, eyeball distance from the crowd to the solos). The FAA mandated that we stay at least 1,500 feet laterally away from the crowd, so for consistency we tried always to rope the audience at this distance. Then, I needed to be just a little off Bobby's altitude as we went by each other—either higher or lower, depending on the maneuver. For our opening figure, the Opposing Slow Roll, I'd be on the outside from the crowd's perspective, so I needed to be slightly higher than him as I went by to produce a perfect collision effect.

We flashed past each other, head-on, eight times in the high show sequence. One of us—me in most cases—had to make sure we missed. But creating the collision effect on top an Opposing Loop or Half Cuban was so hard that responsibility for missing transferred to the lead solo.

For looping maneuvers, solos approached each other on the deck, at the standard 425-knot entry airspeed. Bob called the start of a 5 g wings-level pull into the vertical. I matched his pitch change and, headed up, tried to pass him, close. At vertical, on Bob's radio call, "Now, LOOK," we relaxed to 2 g's and craned our heads back to find the other guy, who should be about level on the horizon, a mile or so away. Best case, we'd see each other in rough alignment at about the same altitude and I could continue a nice, fat loop, with Bob maneuvering to pass over the top of my aircraft. As we approached each other, we could have as much as 200 knots airspeed, but usually it was closer to 150 and occasionally even less. This wasn't enough energy for anything except last-second fine-tuning, which is why producing collision effects on top was a difficult and potentially dangerous job, one that could not be delegated to the solo wingman.

At the top, a little light in our seats, we floated toward each other. Bob must cross right over me, passing under my belly so I'd lose sight of him at the very end. From the crowd's point of view, I'd be the close aircraft, so he needed to offset just a bit to the outside to achieve a true collision effect. If we got it right, the centerline of his aircraft would cross just inside my wing root—exactly where Morgan hit Beckel in 1966.

Tops were hard. If solo events were graded like springboard diving, this was where we earned degree-of-difficulty points. We'd never fly a perfect air show, but when we got the tops right, it pretty well made up for other mistakes.

———◆———

As our training progressed, I began to understand collision effects and could at least perceive the outlines of the next problem we'd have to solve: centering the opposing maneuvers. Much hard work remained, but Bob could take a little time away from training me to practice the figures he would do alone—the Eight Point, Wing Rock and Roll, and Inverted to Inverted. I chased him through these as a safety observer and debriefed him afterward, but there wasn't much I could do or say to improve Bob's airmanship. His hands, in themselves, seemed to contain the laws relating to flight, so the jet did whatever he wanted, each move in total harmony with the subtleties of solo work.

It was time to join the Diamond for a little six-ship work.

Chapter 10

With the Diamond

To create we need both technique and freedom from technique.

—Stephen Nachmanovitch,
Free Play: Improvisation in Life and Art

The 1967 show season opened with Lt. Col. Ralph Maglione as formation leader and squadron commander. As a young lieutenant, Maggie had won the Silver Star in Korea while working with the Army as a ground forward air controller, no doubt a hard assignment for him. Ordinarily nothing could keep him on the ground and, once aloft, he was fearless up to the boundary of recklessness. As for leadership qualities, most people look but don't actually see things. Maggie had the capacity for close observation and when something needed fixing, fixed it. This will do as a short summary of what it takes to be a good officer.

In the mid-1960s, the team experienced a spate of accidents, resulting in separation of the leader and commander positions on the theory that some additional supervision might help. Maggie came in as squadron commander, and Paul Kauttu, an ex-slot man, moved up to lead. The loss of Frank Latham, 1967's incumbent formation leader, gave Maggie an opening to convince authorities they should reunite the jobs. So, at the start of the 1967 show season,

Maggie was only technically a veteran. Although he'd commanded the squadron for a year, he'd yet to fly an air show.

Capt. Chris Patterakis was Thunderbird Two, left wingman and one of the holdovers from the 1966 team. From California's Central Valley, Chris began his flying career in F-86s with the Fresno Guard. He'd later integrated into the regular Air Force and was instructing at one of the basic flying schools when he applied for the team. His selection from Air Training Command was unprecedented—the first pilot not serving in a fighter unit when picked for the team. Chris was in great shape, a gym rat and weight lifter. He was also a much better than average guitar player, and his wife, Vicki, a talented contralto. They entertained when the team spent evenings together at Nellis.

Thunderbird Three, Capt. Stan Musser, had come to the team from Vietnam, where he'd flown hundreds of sorties as a forward air controller in the slow, prop-driven O-2. A gifted athlete, he'd been a nationally recognized wide receiver at Gettysburg College. One day I watched him catching a football—a pickup game, Stan in flying suit and boots. He staged the event: move to the ball, reach for it, gather it in, the three separate things done effortlessly, not quite too slowly, and stitched together so the seams didn't show.

Stan was the team doctor, by custom the right wingman's job. We put a premium on staying healthy because we had no spare demo pilots. However, except for overseas trips, we didn't take a flight surgeon on the road with us. Stan had great natural talent for the work, becoming quite knowledgeable. Something of a health freak, I never dipped into the black bag Stan carried, though I'd have trusted him in a pinch. What I liked best about Stan: he flew formation with the economy of a panther—lucky for me, as I'd spend a big part of the next two years looking at his right wingtip.

The slot man, Capt. Jack Dickey, was a slender towhead from Minnesota. His compact size and fluid movement suggested he might be a first-class infielder and, in fact, he'd played a little semi-pro ball. One of the most knowledgeable guys in our business, Jack came to the team from a post as instructor at the Fighter Weapons School, the Air Force's elite graduate course for fighter jocks.

A year or so before we joined the team, our respective organizations had picked Jack and me to be part of a committee tasked to rewrite the Air Force regulation on gunnery qualification, a lengthy document about as simple as the tax code. The group gathered at Nellis, Jack chairing the session, but it was typical committee work, the conference degenerating into random motion. Nearing the end of our allotted time, Jack and I agreed to meet at his place and do it ourselves. We made a fair-sized dent in his whisky supply in the process of producing a draft the Air Force subsequently adopted.

Some months later, when I learned we'd been selected for the team, I telephoned congratulations. After discussion, we agreed I should be the new slot man and he'd fly solo. Both of us knew we faced daunting comparisons in replacing Hank Canterbury and Bobby Morgan—from a pure hands standpoint, as good a slot man and solo pilot, respectively, as ever flew for the team. But when we reported for duty, Maggie put Jack in the slot and handed me over to Beckel for solo training, a decision I soon learned to appreciate.

Before going to Indian Springs to practice show sequence, Bob and I linked up with the Diamond at Thunderbird Lake for some six-ship aerobatics. When Bobby joined at outside left, on Patterakis' wing, and I came aboard at outside right, on Musser's wing, we matched their use of three-foot wing overlap to create a symmetrical, wedge-shaped formation.

The Diamond had been together for a month and was already quite solid, in part because the wingmen used full nose-down trim to counter the excessive band of free play in the F-100's flight controls. Free play exists when flight controls can be moved some distance before the airplane reacts. It occurs at or near the stick's trimmed, or hands-free position, and is described as a band because pilots cannot know precisely where in the range of stick movement the control system will become effective. With conventional flight controls, once you get a control surface deflected, free play disappears because you're pushing the stick in one direction and air loads on the deflected control surface push back, providing the feel pilots rely on for precise control.[30]

Some free play is OK, even a good thing. We prefer an aircraft that's not twitchy, not jumping around with every small control input. But an appreciable band of free play like the F-100 had makes precision formation flying difficult. The usual remedy is to apply some nose-down trim, moving the stick's free-play band and making the airplane feel heavy in the hand. Thus trimmed, the pilot makes small pitch corrections either by relaxing the right bicep very slightly or tightening it just a bit against the steady back pressure of the stick, all without traversing the free-play band.

Of course, the purpose of the trim system is to take the work out of flying, a splendid aerodynamic advance now discarded in the name of formation cosmetics. I used lots of nose-down trim when flying Bobby's wing, and both of us cranked in all we could get when with the Diamond in Wedge. But (happily) we spent most of the show doing solo work that let us take out the trim and give our arms a rest. Diamond wingmen used full nose-down trim through nearly the entire show sequence, developing strong right arms. Even so, they looked for opportunities, however brief, to roll out a little of the trim—for instance, at the top of loops, when low dynamic air pressures make precise formation flying somewhat less difficult.

From the beginning, the six-ship rolls and loops we did were beautiful and a pure pleasure to ride through. The Wedge Loop was a particular favorite. Maggie made a 4 g pull. Once into the

---

30 The F-100's hydraulic flight controls were irreversible and thus immune to wind pressure, but the aircraft had a built-in artificial-feel system that produced virtual pressures that could be trimmed out in the conventional way.

maneuver, speed dissipated rapidly, the airplanes becoming progressively easier to fly. Smoke streaming behind us, we cut a wide, handsome arc through the sky.

The first time we did a Wedge Loop, Stan Musser found a way at the top of the figure to flash a rude gesture in my direction. Staring hard at him, keeping his head superimposed on lead's, I could not avoid seeing it.

Stan was making a statement here. First, in a tactless display of flying skill, he showed he could roll out the nose-down trim, let go of the throttle, fly the airplane left-handed, and hoist a disrespectful visual signal, all while I was working my tail off to maintain position as the six of us curled around the top of a loop. I marveled at how he could do this. Second, he gave expression to the Diamond's professed low regard for solo pilots. Their nickname for us, the "Dummies," reflected a semi-affectionate assessment of the IQ it took to do some of the stuff we did. Stan went further, calling us "Fillers," meaning we'd been made part of the show to fill gaps while the Diamond repositioned for its next maneuver. (The solo attitude was a reciprocal: the Diamond's entire purpose was to gather a crowd for the solos to impress.) Anyway, I admired Stan's attitude, knowing we'd do many six-ship loops together. From the very first one, he began establishing the world record for consecutive uncouth signals to a solo pilot.

After the first of February, the team moved its practice sessions from the lake to Indian Springs and started flying the show sequence. Now the real difficulties of the air show, especially timing, were exposed.

Solo figures could be tricky, mostly because of the altitudes we flew. Doing the figures while creating legitimate collision effects was much more difficult. Putting collision effects at show center was hardest of all, the final layer in the buildup of these cultured pearls.

As we approached each other at 425 knots, Bob and I covered

the ground at 720 feet per second, the closure rate double that, 1,440 feet per second. If I was five seconds early and he was five seconds late—not hard to do—we'd pass each other two-thirds of a mile from show center, a gross miss, a yawner for the crowd. But say I was *one* second early and Bob *one* second late—something really easy to do—we'd cross about 700 feet away from show center, a disappointing result. So the essential first step in getting solo timing right was to overcome a natural indifference to the value of single seconds. The clock's sweep-second hand was an implacable, hanging judge. We wanted to arrive *exactly* at show center, at *exactly* the same time.

How to do this? The problem couldn't be swallowed whole, so we bit it off in chunks. Each year, reconnaissance aircraft took photos of our scheduled show sites. Bob penciled a show line on these photos and tried to find easily identifiable ground checkpoints at each end, ideally 14,400 feet equidistant from show center. At our approach speed, if we flew past these checkpoints at the same instant, in 20 seconds we'd go by each other right in front of the VIP seats.

Now the problem backed up to arriving at the checkpoint precisely 20 seconds from the time we wanted to cross at show center. For this purpose, we imagined a "perch," a set of relationships in space and time putting us 20 seconds from the checkpoint. Best case, the perch was at an angle to the show line and along the ground track of a diving turn into it. However, any location 20 seconds from the checkpoint was considered a perch. Within wide limits, we could trade position over the ground, airspeed and altitude, for time. I had to learn the trick of visualizing the perch— in other words, judging when I was 20 seconds from the checkpoint—and already in early January, as Bob chased me through our first training sorties, he made timing calls that helped me develop a feel for it.

Once I could visualize the perch, I had to get to it. Bottoming out at the completion of an opposing figure, the solos made hard

90-degree turns off the line to get behind the audience, leaving the stage to the Diamond. We followed with a repositioning maneuver called a whifferdill. The whifferdill was too dynamic and multi-dimensional to be described easily, and no two were ever the same, but in vertical cross section it was a climbing turn toward the perch and could be counted on to be aggressive because we wanted to get to the general vicinity of a perch quickly.

At some point during the whifferdill, taking his cue from the Diamond leader's commands, Bobby would make a radio call:

"Solos, take one minute . . . Ready . . . NOW."

Assuming I'd been sufficiently forceful with the whifferdill, I should be about 20 seconds from a perch when this call came. I hacked the clock on "NOW" and played the turn to the perch, getting there as the sweep-second hand passed 20, then continuing a descending turn to the checkpoint, passing it with 40 seconds of elapsed time showing on the clock. On each of these 20-second legs, I adjusted my timing using variations of angle and altitude, energy and distance, speed and position.

Inbound from respective checkpoints, solos fine-tuned timing in choreography of moves and radio calls. If luck was with us, we would arrive at checkpoints on time, with 425 knots showing on the gauge. One of us would make a cryptic radio call: "On time." The other would answer, "Samo." We kept radio calls succinct; everybody knew what to expect; and the Diamond stayed quiet when the solos needed the airwaves. "On time," followed by "Samo," was a nice relief for the solos, because we could then concentrate on tracking toward each other, missing close, and doing a nice figure, knowing the maneuver would center itself—assuming, of course, we'd made these calls precisely at the checkpoint and exactly as the sweep-second hand passed through 40 seconds. There was zero tolerance here; wishful thinking wouldn't cut it.

Of course, Bob was already quite skilled at solving the timing problem. As I developed a feel for it, I started to arrive at the 20-second checkpoint nearer the right time, but my standards also become more exacting so, early in the show season at least, the radio call "on time" remained elusive, and the issue was how to adjust, how to correct the timing and preserve good collision effects at show center.

At the checkpoint, solos turned on smoke and made the definitive timing call. Suppose I arrived directly over the checkpoint one second too soon. I said, "One early." If Bob said, "Samo," we were in business. Each of us would need to speed up to 425, since we'd have slowed to keep from getting to the checkpoint even sooner, but we'd just accelerate toward each other, stabilize at 425, and perform the maneuver. Thus, if both of us were on time, or early or late by the same amount, there was no timing problem.

But one of us arriving early and the other late meant trouble. In response to my call of, say, "One early," Bob might radio, "One late." We now must make speed adjustments during the run at each other. For every second off, we added or subtracted 25 knots. My arrival at the checkpoint one second early meant I'd reduce approach airspeed to 400 knots, covering the 14,400 feet to show center in 21 seconds to make up for being early at the checkpoint. If I was one late, I'd set my speed 450, covering the distance in 19 seconds. The adjustments would get our aircraft to show center at the same time, and we could salvage a well-placed collision effect.

Notwithstanding much practice, the plain vanilla timing problem was never mastered, and there were lots of other flavors. At some sites, no easily identifiable checkpoints existed at 14,400 feet from show center. It would be nice if the checkpoints stood out—a nice church steeple or a major highway intersection—but they were no use at all unless fairly close to the right distance. More often than not, we were left with nothing in particular—a tree that seemed to stand a little apart, or the corner of a field planted in a different crop, perhaps offset some distance from the extended show line so that we passed abeam rather than right over it. Depending on seasonal variation and lighting conditions, the checkpoint could look a lot different than the picture of it taken by the reconnaissance guys. The lead solo made a preshow survey flight with the leader and got a look at the proposed checkpoints at each end. Although Bobby briefed me at length beforehand, I'd actually see the checkpoints for the first time at the start of the show, and maybe not see them quickly enough to avoid moments of high anxiety trying to find them.

The worst checkpoint problem was not to have one. At Myrtle Beach, for instance, the show line—an extension of the east-west runway—ran out into the Atlantic. To get a checkpoint, we'd need to row a boat out there and drop anchor. We hoped to fly show lines like Myrtle's late in the year, when the solo wingman had enough experience he could sort of fake it.

Or consider the routine business of hacking the clock. We hacked our clocks on Five's call, "Solos, take one minute . . . Ready . . . NOW." We had a standard aircraft clock with the usual features. It had to be wound, but not overwound. Each punch of the hack button stepped through start, stop, and reset-to-zero functions. Somewhere early in the whifferdill, I'd better have hit "stop" and "reset." This would seem easily remembered, and it did become automatic but was just another little thing I could miss. Certainly, a sinking feeling came with hacking the clock at "NOW," and watching it reset to zero, a mistake I made more than once. Also, since the government had purchased this clock from the lowest bidder, you'd better make sure the sweep-second hand started running when you hacked it.

Something as simple as reading the airspeed indicator presented difficulties. We needed 425 knots—not 430 or 420—but the markings on the instrument's face and even the width of the indicator needle itself made it a challenge to judge graduations of such small size.

Then, too, there were limits to how much could be done to salvage timing. For instance, we would apply only so much early correction when doing the Opposing Inverted. Because we did the figure at idle power, the aircraft decelerated, and forward stick pressure had to be increased through the maneuver to keep the nose from falling. However, at about 300 knots, there was not enough stabilator authority to stop downward nose moment. An uncontrollable nose drop, upside down at 50 feet, would be an attention getter, so our rule of thumb was not to enter an Inverted with less than 375 knots—meaning that, for Inverteds, the maximum early error we could correct for was two seconds.[31]

This discussion does not exhaust variations on the theme of timing for opposing solo work in the late 1960s. It was metaphysically difficult, a knotty, four-dimensional problem with many subtleties not discussed here, including those specific to various wind conditions and individual show sites and so requiring ad hoc adjustment, principally by the lead solo. What made it doable at all was taking the problems in sequence. First, get the timing right; next, work on the collision effect; finally, perform the maneuver itself. Immediately after recovering from any figure, go to work on timing for the next.[32]

Buried in the haystack of variables was a single constant: closure rate. Always, Bob and I would close on each other at

---

31 Large disparities in approach airspeed also affected opposing over-the-top figures. Say I was "two early" at the checkpoint, and Bob "two late." Approaching the entry for the Opposing Loop, I'd be holding 375 knots, and Bob 475, in order to center the figure properly. As we started up into the vertical with the standard 5 g pull, the hundred-knot difference in airspeeds would make it just about impossible to do symmetrical loops. In practice, we compensated by varying the g load, but this added texture to an already layered problem.

32 The Thunderbird air show has gotten progressively safer over the years. At this writing, solo figures are no longer put so low, and there is little in the way of true opposing work. Avionics now available, especially head-up displays and better clocks, make solo timing somewhat more manageable. Still, how the timing problem is solved remains a good test of air show quality.

850 knots—1,000 miles an hour, or near enough. There was something oddly comforting in this. Whatever other adjustments we made to solve the simultaneous equations of solo timing, I could count on Bobby getting bigger in my windscreen at exactly the same rate, every time.

At Indian Springs, the runway centerline stood out well, the usual white stripe down the middle, and we used it for a reference as we approached each other for the Opposing Slow Roll. From the checkpoint, I looked up the line and saw Bobby at his end, smoke on, and began to fly formation.

It seems odd to speak of flying formation with someone five miles away, but that's the feeling I wanted. I paid no attention to my own ground clearance—which, I noted out the corner of my eye, was nonexistent—matching his altitude, aiming right at him. As he grew in size, I could refine the altitude. I wanted the fuselages of our aircraft to superimpose, but for the Opposing Slow Roll I would be on the outside from the crowd's perspective, so my head should be very slightly higher than his. Flashing by each other, we made the aircraft float through the roll in wide, symmetrical arcs into a bottom that bounced smoke off the ground. It was a nice warm-up, the opening solo figure in the high-show sequence, fun and as easy as anything we had to do. Nonetheless, it was possible to make plenty of mistakes, and in the coming days, I'd make them all. The miscues were noted by Thunderbird Seven, our maintenance officer, Maj. Robert Earl Haney.

Bob Haney was the boss of our maintenance operation. A former enlisted man, he'd come up through the Aviation Cadet Program. After service in a couple of fighter squadrons, he'd gone to aircraft maintenance school and subsequently acquired a lot of experience in flight test and quality control. During the show season, he ferried aircraft to and from Nellis for required repairs and test hopped them when they came out of the barn. Otherwise, Bob stayed with the team. As we moved from show site to show site, Haney flew a position at the back of the Wedge in the slot man's slot, creating a formation we called Stinger.

Haney was a great maintenance officer, a fine aviator, and best of all a trustworthy critic. He'd seen plenty of air shows, knew exactly what we were after and picked up every error. Bob watched us at Indian Springs during February and made notes we used during debriefing. He did a lot more than just record mistakes, offering constructive suggestions that did not, in my case, push me faster than my already stretched capabilities would tolerate. Working with Beckel and Haney, I continued to improve.

Except for the Opposing Inverted. This maneuver came second, following the Slow Roll. From the crowd's point of view, I'd be right-to-left, so the collision effect required that I be just a little below Bob as we crossed at show center. Intent on flying formation during the run-in from the checkpoint, I'd get my first real look at the ground after rolling inverted. It seemed breathtakingly close, the terrain filling my windscreen. I saw paint peeling on runway stripes; imagined individual grains of sand in sharp relief; pictured ants crawling around, the size of cocker spaniels. I had to push the stick forward a little anyway to maintain height as the jet slowed, and I couldn't stop myself from easing in just slightly too much forward stick, producing a shallow climb instead of a level inverted pass. Haney caught it every time. "Six, slight climb in the Inverted," the criticism noted again and again. I got sick of hearing it. At every afternoon debriefing, "Six, slight climb in the Inverted." No trick, no technique, no expert advice could fix this. It was a straight guts deal, and I wasn't hacking it. It didn't make it any better that Bob was keeping it high (he said)—still above our 50 feet objective—out of concern for my altitude sensibilities.

As for the other solo figures, and Wedge work done with the Diamond, I was doing OK.

By mid-February, our new narrator had memorized the script. He too needed to work on timing, so he joined Haney on the ground at Indian Springs for rehearsal with the team.

From Columbia, South Carolina, Capt. Mike Miller started his aviation career with the South Carolina Guard, flying F-102s and F-104s. Completing college, he volunteered for integration into the active Air Force. Before joining the team, he served a particularly distinguished combat tour as an A-1 pilot and adviser to South Vietnam's air force. Mike was very bright, had great personal charm and a nicely warped sense of humor. He liked both kinds of music—country and western—and could, if he started with E major, play three chords on a guitar and sing like a low-octane version of Ray Charles.

Mike invented nicknames for everyone. Chris Patterakis was "Greek." Stan Musser was "Tanny," a corruption of his childhood nickname, "Stanny." Jack Dickey was "Mannlein," a reference to his size, Aryan looks, and German frau, Lore. Bob Beckel was "Duane," his (not greatly liked) middle name. Beckel was from Walla Walla, Washington, so occasionally Mike would ask, "Well, which is it, Duane, Walla or Walla?" I was "Marvelous Merrill," or sometimes "Marv," neither of which stuck, leaving me with "Tony," the standard contraction of my middle name. Haney's middle name was Earl, so he became "Speedo" or "Mr. Earl," his "real name" according to the 1955 R & B classic by the Cadillacs.

Our nickname for Mike was "Mike." By nature combative, fiercely loyal, a die-hard, he was a walking reminder that two-thirds of South Carolina's male population either died or was wounded in the Civil War. Once, over a few beers, he told me other Americans couldn't understand Southerners because the rest of us hadn't experienced the humiliation of losing, the jury still out on Vietnam. This surprised me a bit. How could the Civil War be so deeply embedded in the gene pool as to surface in casual conversation a century later? Mike would say, sure, any war is easy for the winner to get over. He reminded me a little of the TV version of Doc Holliday. Like Wyatt Earp's buddy, indeed, like the South itself, the core defiance was wrapped in a cellophane of melancholy.

Mike flew Thunderbird Eight, the two-seater, usually taking a support NCO with him and flying ahead of us to the next show site to meet with officials and prepare for our arrival. He might also take some local dignitary for a short orientation hop in the back-seat of the family model. We would arrive exactly on schedule, this being one of the tests for lead. (We said you could set your watch by our arrival pass over the control tower.) After the low pass, lead typically kicked Seven (Haney) out of Stinger and we did six-ship arrival maneuvers—a Wedge Roll and Loop, spit out the solos, and a couple of Diamond figures mixed in with a Calypso and solo Four Point—then landed. When Miller didn't have to precede us to a show site and could tag along with the team, Mr. Earl moved Seven over to the slot behind left wing (Chris), and Mike fell in under right wing (Stan) to create the Outhouse formation.

———◆———

We worked hard at Thunderbird Lake and Indian Springs in Nevada's clear, bracing February, polishing the six-ship show sequence. Near the end of the month, it started to jell. We invited friends and family to a dress rehearsal at Nellis, then hit the road.

Chapter 11

On the Road

. . . that second summer we went all over the British Isles,
staying a day in each place and giving two shows each
day. There was never a whole day off; in an air circus like
that you take your weekends in the winter.
> —Nevil Shute, *Round the Bend*

We flew our first official show at Malmstrom AFB, Montana, on 11 March 1967, the crowd small at this out-of-the-way spot, as we intended. Opening away from the bright lights would put stage fright behind us before hitting the big time. The show went well, and we headed south toward better weather, wanting to get in a groove before the most important shows, scheduled for summer. From March until the Christmas break, we would be on the road nearly continuously. The 1965 team had flown a season record 121 shows, so we were looking to do at least 122.

We settled into a routine. Fly to the site. Land. Make local PR rounds. Dress for the evening social. Return to motel. Sleep. Get up. Have breakfast. Report to the show site. Walk around. Sign autographs. Often we shared the stage with others. We didn't see much of the Navy's Blue Angels (our name for them: Brand X). The Pentagon public affairs Gestapo, in charge of scheduling military demo teams, didn't like us flying together. They worried we'd try to upstage each other, adding risk to impress the crowd. But we saw a lot of the Army's great free-fall parachute team, the Golden Knights, and often appeared with notable civilian aerobatic acts.

At one of our early stops, Davis-Monthan AFB, near Tucson, Arizona, Bob Hoover was on the playbill with us. Hoover was a legend in the business, having done every kind of flying—combat in World War II and test work during the period of exciting aeronautical progress after the war. In 1947, he chased Chuck Yeager in a P-80 as Yeager broke the sound barrier in the Bell X-1. Hoover subsequently left the Air Force, went to work for North American as a test pilot and, starting as a sideline, flew air shows in North American products, principally the P-51, F-86, and F-100. I saw him do a show in the F-100 at George when I was stationed there. He did things with the airplane that were flat impossible. He was good, but also lucky, having walked away from more wreckage than anybody I knew.

At Tucson, I cornered Hoover in a bar and started talking F-100 aerobatics. We got around to vertical rolls and I modestly mentioned that a couple of times I'd gotten the airplane into a tail slide, falling short distances backward through my own smoke. Hoover said, "Sure, and you can control that, if you know how. Here's what you do." He proceeded to explain how to work the controls and check all this in the mirrors. I kept my council, but the guy was talking about flying the thing backward. Anybody else, I smell baloney; with Hoover, maybe you believe it.

Following the air show at D-M, the wing put on a black-tie dinner. I sat next to Madeline Smith, widow of Col. Lowell Smith, World War II commander of Davis-Monthan and a brilliant and colorful early airman.

Lowell Smith's military career began as a pilot with Pancho Villa's revolutionary forces. He switched to our side in 1917. He may have dropped the first real bomb from an airplane. He and another pilot certainly did the first air-to-air refueling, then made a flight in which they accomplished numerous air refuelings and set 16 world records for distance, speed, and endurance. In 1924, Lieutenant Smith led a flight of Douglas World Cruisers, single-engine, open-cockpit biplanes, on a 175-day adventure that took them 27,553 miles, circumnavigating the globe. Only two of the aircraft, including Smith's *Chicago,* now hanging in the Smithsonian Air and Space Museum, made it to Bolling Field to be greeted by President Coolidge. One of aviation's great accomplishments, this round-the-world flight was in many ways a coming of age for American airpower.

Smith died in 1945 of injuries suffered when he fell off a horse, and thus Madeline Smith was many years a widow when I met her. A lovely woman of patrician background, she lived on top a small bluff at the end of a dirt road, some miles west of Tucson. She fed desert animals that visited regularly, including some supposed to be semi-dangerous. We hit it off at dinner, and she adopted me as her honorary grandson. Ellie and I visited her many times over the years and corresponded with her regularly until her death.

———◆———

In late January 1967, Sen. J. William Fulbright published *The Arrogance of Power,* a book critical of the war in Vietnam. President Johnson described Fulbright, Robert Kennedy, and other prominent critics as "nervous Nellies" and "sunshine patriots."

In April 1967, Muhammad Ali refused induction into the Army, saying, "I ain't got no quarrel with them Viet Congs." He went to jail, stripped of the heavyweight title.

———◆———

Like the officers, Thunderbird enlisted troops were handpicked, each a volunteer who had beaten stiff competition for his position. We had 45 enlisted men in the squadron, 28 who traveled, including my crew chief, Tech Sgt. C. D. James. C. D. was what we called an aircraft general mechanic, and a pretty good one. His assistant was S. Sgt. Vernon "Red" Lichtenberg, an avionics specialist. Between them, these two guys could fix anything, but if they needed help they got it from a full range of other specialists—engine, air conditioning, egress, etc.—assigned as assistant crew chiefs to the other aircraft.

Air Force regulations required pilots to check aircraft condition prior to flight. This was done by reviewing the "forms," a bulky record of the aircraft's history written in Sanskrit, and by physically checking certain key items during a walk-around of the airplane. (The tires probably did not need to be kicked.) After flight, the pilot signed off the forms, making an entry for any discrepancy found. The maintenance empire then had to deal with this write-up before the aircraft could be cleared for further flight. By this point in my career, I had much experience with the procedure, which I now forgot for the next two years. As long as I was on the team, I never looked at the aircraft forms, never filled them out at the end of a flight. C.D. James took care of all this. I relied on his skill as a mechanic to keep me alive for a couple of years, so I figured I could trust him with the paperwork. I did a walk-around inspection only on those rare occasions when we made an en route stop and none of our ground crewmen had been pre-positioned.

Our early shows went well, except for "Six, climbing in the Inverted." It seemed I'd never do a level Inverted, but Beckel was patient with me. Maggie, who had not been impressed by my refused Roll on Takeoff back in January, was exasperated, but he was sort of stuck with me.

The weather was crummy at one of our stops, and we did what we called a flat show, mostly level passes with a lot of smoke and noise. One of the maneuvers called for the Diamond to fly by the crowd slowed, configured for landing. I was supposed to catch them and race by, my high velocity a contrast to their measured pace. I would pass them on the inside with respect to the audience, but the collision effect would be impressive only if I caught them at show center. On this occasion, I got there a little late. Of course, this was mentioned during debrief, and I wrongly offered a weak excuse: the wind had drifted their smoke toward the crowd and into me, making it tough to see them. Maggie said, "Just follow the smoke up to the end. That's where we'll be."

With Maggie, you'd be advised to avoid one-on-one repartee, where he was lethal. But he was a talented emcee, and when he introduced the team at public events, his remarks were peppered with gentler, ingratiating wit.

At Key West, we stood in for the Blue Angels, who had been grounded after an accident. During a dinner with local dignitaries, I sat next to the mayor's wife. People born in Key West called themselves "Conchs" and were a little cliquish. When His Honor gave each of us a certificate making us honorary Conchs, Mrs. Mayor was miffed. A native New Englander, she'd lived down there 25 years, and the locals still treated her as an outsider. Maggie was at his usual best, wowing the crowd, but nothing he said could mollify her.

I was senior by date of rank to the other wingmen, so at the beginning I pulled additional duty as squadron operations officer, a great job, involving me in the routine of squadron administration as number two to the boss on the operations side. Unhappily for me, Stan Musser had been selected for early promotion to major and I had not—my lieutenant days catching up with me—so I wouldn't be senior long. As soon as Stan pinned on his new rank, he took over as ops officer, and I swapped jobs with him to become navigation officer, doing the flight planning for our cross-country legs. This was fun, though I had to get to base ops an hour or so before the other guys to check the weather, do final paperwork and file a clearance with air traffic control.

In the cross-country mode, we used a formation called "spread"— a three-foot gap separating the wingtips of our aircraft. This was the normal close formation used in line squadrons, and it cut us enough slack so we could look around. The team had a discrete radio frequency that we went to after takeoff, the right wingman staying with air traffic control to receive advisories and give position reports as needed. The rest of us could relax. There was a certain amount of radio chatter that would not be advisable except on a private channel.

Seeing and calling traffic was a major preoccupation. Normally, I looked through Stan and Maggie out to the horizon on the formation's left side and had better see traffic in the sector from eleven back to six o'clock—see it and call it first. If anybody else called it, Maggie would have pointed questions about my dimming eyesight. Naturally, I liked nothing better than to call traffic at twelve, where Maggie and Jack had the best look, or in the area from one to five o'clock, where Bob and Chris had sector responsibility.

We played a complex game here, slightly different from standard squadron operations. In combat, a call describes the tactical situation. Threats don't come at you one at a time, so your first thought is, "Where's the wingman? Where's the other element?" Here, the priority was to make the call, to establish "ownership" of the traffic.

I learned many tricks to seeing and calling traffic. Along high-altitude airways, keep a sharp lookout nearing major navaids, where traffic converges. Overflying runways, watch for aircraft on takeoff, but wait until they actually break ground before calling them. (Nothing still on the ground was a threat.) It was an unpardonable lapse to make the second call of traffic someone already owned. Perhaps the gravest error was to think something was there, call it, and have it turn to fairy dust. This could happen, for instance, with level, head-on contrails. When first seen, these appear as tiny white specks. On the other hand, as with scientific discovery, if you wait for absolute certainty, someone else will publish first.

Often, we met tankers for air refueling, greatly reducing time spent on long deployments. During the join-up with tankers, we split into two flights—Red (the Diamond, which went to the lead tanker) and Blue (everybody else). When tanking, we usually had Haney and Miller with us, and they become Blue Three and Four.

The game then began: could we cycle through the tanker and fill up faster than the Diamond? Beckel, Blue lead, didn't like to lose, and we never did.

By then, all the KB-50s had retired to the boneyard. We did a couple of refuelings with the KC-97, still flown by Guard units, but most of our support came from the much-improved KC-135, which could off-load five or six times the amount of fuel the KB-50 did and, maybe more important, operated at about our speed and altitude. For long deployments, we just got on the tanker's wing. He did all the work, navigating and communicating with air traffic control, and we ducked in from time to time to fill 'er up. Piece o' cake.

In May 1967, Egypt's President Nasser ordered the UN Emergency Force that had been put in place after the Suez Crisis of 1956 to withdraw from the Sinai and began moving Egyptian forces toward the Israeli frontier. He also closed the Gulf of Aqaba to all ships flying the Israeli flag. Following much bellicose talk and a full measure of international hand-wringing, the Israelis mounted the Six-Day War, a lightning victory enabled by the superb performance of their air force.

Periodically, we returned to Nellis for a break, to see our families and get some laundry done. If we came back the southern route, Maggie liked to duck into the Grand Canyon, not at one of the popular tourist spots, which even then were off limits to aircraft, but well down the canyon, where the Colorado gets ready to empty into Lake Mead. There was a final, rather narrow constriction where the canyon walls came close together, and Maggie enjoyed taking the team through this gap. It wasn't much fun for me, and Bob, on the other side of the formation, didn't like it a lot either. On the outside of the formation, it really looked possible to get dragged off on a wall if Maggie was not dead center as he threaded the needle.

Running the canyon turned out to be a standard event so, in

addition to crowding Stan Musser as much as I could, I had a quiet chat with him about how I'd appreciate his staying nice and tight on Maggie during this portion of the homecoming.

Late in the spring, Maj. Neil Eddins joined the team. He was a former slot man who'd been selected to replace Maggie as team leader starting in January 1968. Neil would serve as exec, understudying Maggie for a while longer than normal, but he'd just returned from Southeast Asia and had no better place to go. He became Thunderbird Nine. We had only nine F-100s, including the F model, and one of these was usually back home for phase maintenance. This meant we almost never had the opportunity to fly nine-ship formation. When we did, Seven and Eight went to Outhouse and Neil flew Stinger, a slot behind the slot, forming a nine-ship Diamond. The more normal cross-country formation was for Maggie to fly the F, with Neil in the backseat.

Our 1967 schedule took us to Le Bourget in May for the Paris Air Show. We planned to deploy to Europe two weeks early to fly demos in England, Spain, and Germany. So many acts were scheduled at Paris that they had allotted us only 15 minutes on stage, so we were obliged to design a shortened show sequence especially for Le Bourget.

The team departed Nellis as an eight-ship on 3 May, Maggie flying the F, with Neil in the backseat. We intended to proceed non-stop to Wethersfield, England, headquarters of my old wing, the 20th. We met tankers over Kansas for our first refueling. Bobby took Blue Flight to the second tanker, joining the tanker's right wing in echelon (a formation with the aircraft strung out on one side of the leader). We cycled through in order: Five, Six, Seven, and Eight, ending up in left echelon off the tanker's left wing. We finished before Red Flight, as usual, and dropped away from the tanker to rejoin the Diamond, a mile ahead.

Now Blue Flight began a slow evolution from left echelon to an alignment in harmony with the requirement to join the Diamond in Outhouse. On his signal, I crossed under Bobby and went to my normal right-wing position. Closing on the Diamond, Beckel kicked me out to spread so Haney, Number Seven, and Miller, Number Eight, could get between us. I divided my attention, bringing Musser into my cross-check as I joined his wing at outside right, staying more or less line abreast with Beckel, so we came aboard symmetrically, and watching Haney and Miller as they maneuvered into Outhouse.

From left echelon, Miller had to cross under Haney to get to his slot, behind and below Stan. He made the cross under OK, but as he drove for position beneath Stan, he somehow made contact with Haney's aircraft. Instantly, both jets came apart. I watched it unfold in slow motion, teleported into that sluggish, parallel universe of the immobilized. The aircraft merged and exploded, a metal confetti erupting into the relative wind, then the whole thing was gone. Stan Musser caught the commotion out of the corner of his eye and had the presence of mind to yell, "Bail out! Bail out!" over the radio. We circled the scene, squawking "Mayday," then landed at McConnell AFB to regroup.

Bob Haney punched out of his airplane OK, unhurt. After the collision, Miller's aircraft went out of control, but he was able to jettison the canopy, undo his lap belt and kick himself free of the airplane. He was a little banged up.

The next day, the commander of Tactical Air Command, Gen. Gabe Disosway, told Maggie he was finished as leader. The Thunderbirds had had too many accidents lately. Neil would take over. Maggie could tag along to Europe. We'd practice extensively there anyway and Maggie could train Neil by riding around behind him in the F. Come summer, Maggie would be reassigned to Washington for a year at the National War College, a sought-after assignment, so he was not hurt professionally. Still, leaving the team at midseason was a blow to him.

Behind schedule now, the six of us took off at dawn the next day.

The flight was uneventful. After several air refuelings we touched down at Wethersfield in late afternoon and checked into bachelor officers' quarters. Scheduled shows crowded the coming days, plus we needed some time to practice the shortened Paris sequence. And now we had to figure out how to squeeze in training a new leader.

———◆———

This was a team of self-made men, none more so than Neil Eddins. He was from Afton, Wyoming, the spot they called Grafton when using the neighborhood as scenery for the film *Shane*. His mom once won the church bingo jackpot. On the way home, the family stopped for gas. "Fill 'er up," Neil's dad told the attendant, "and run a little out on the ground." As far as I knew, Neil authored the old joke about underwear size: "I wear a 32, but a 34 feels so good, I buy a 36."

On a previous tour with the team, Neil was a capable, gritty slot man. During a training sortie in 1959, he made a nylon letdown when his bird flamed out during a formation loop. Just over a year later, his right main landing gear collapsed on the runway and again he had to dismount and fight on foot. Since then, among other things, he'd made 100 trips North in an F-105, doing some damage on each visit. A Code of the West kind of guy, Neil didn't eat before the men were fed. He was smart, a strong flyer, had good judgment and because of his prior experience with the Thunderbirds, would not be starting from scratch.

Still, it was a tall order. The next day, Neil and Maggie took the F up and began working on show figures, concentrating on entry altitudes, airspeeds, and smooth execution of each maneuver. Over the next several days, the wingies joined in two-ship, then three-ship, and then with the whole Diamond, but we simply didn't have time for the sort of sustained effort required. We couldn't squeeze in training and air shows both, and we were committed to fly live at Wethersfield, Lakenheath, and the other UK bases. Plus, this was not southern Nevada; the weather was being English, making the job a lot tougher.

Charlie Hamm and Hank Canterbury soon joined us, bringing over two more jets hastily painted in Thunderbird colors. Both guys were former Thunderbirds, now instructing at the weapons school. They followed us around Europe for a while, flying the spare aircraft and calling themselves fairy pilots.

Meanwhile, since Mike Miller was not yet back in Class I flying condition, our public affairs officer, Steve Murata, was pressed into temporary service as narrator. Steve was from Hawaii, the only non-pilot officer on the team. He usually stayed at Nellis, working the scheduling and public relations beat. He was a Stanford grad, had a master's degree in journalism and was extra smart. Miller called him the Inscrutable Man, but as a substitute narrator, Steve was first rate, entirely scrutable.

On Battle of Britain Day, we staged into Biggin Hill, the RAF station made famous during the defense of the Isles. The weather was horrid, ceiling OK but with scattered cloud that kept getting in the way and visibility maybe three miles in haze. We could barely make out, let alone line up with, the show line, which, for some reason, was not the old landing strip but a much less distinct trace through what looked like uncultivated farmland. When the Diamond was at his end, Bobby helped Neil as much as he could by giving steering commands back to the line. I would have helped on my end but was maxed out just doing my own job. Due to the visibility, I had big trouble seeing Bob during the run-in for opposing figures. As usual, Bob was flying the line, leaving it to me to find and—we hope—miss him. On the Opposing Inverted, I saw Bob late and had to scramble to salvage the collision effect. As usual, I got my first good look at the ground after popping into the Inverted on Bob's call. I said to myself, "This is awfully low." But before I could ease in my usual too-much-forward stick, I thought, "Well, it's about the same as always." So I just let it fly level, not exactly relaxed—the abdominals would always harden—but quiet, in control. After maybe 30 official air shows I finally did a level Inverted.

Even Mr. Earl thought so. The interminable string of write-ups, "Six, climbing in the Inverted," ended; I never again earned the citation.

It turned out flying level 50-foot Inverteds was about as much fun as you can have with your flying boots on.

W̲e̲ moved to Spain for a few days, taking advantage of the good weather to do high shows, plus sandwich in practice of the shorter Paris sequences. At San Pablo, near Saville, Beckel and I joined the Diamond for the usual six-ship aerobatics. A little slow at the entry for the Wedge Loop, Neil started up anyway in order to center the figure on the crowd. Just past vertical, we all ran out of airspeed.

At zero airspeed there is, of course, no airflow across the flight controls, and it makes no difference what you do, the aircraft is just going to flop around until you pick up some velocity. It's during the transition back to flying speed that you'd better be careful. A little air over the controls starts their return to effectiveness and, if you insist, the airplane can be forced into doing something stupid before it's ready to fly, ushering in some unscheduled excitement. The only good bet is to center the stick and wait for the airplane to start flying—which is what all six of us did, thank goodness.

The problem: I couldn't see the Diamond. Looking across the space they normally occupied, all I saw was Bobby Beckel. We were floating together, as we should, line abreast, but without the Diamond in between us. Upside down in the loop, I knew they were not below me because I could see in that direction, toward the ground. I thought they must be above me and blocked from view by the bottom of my airplane. I just had to leave everything alone and hope none of them drifted into me. Applying some gentle right rudder when I could, I spread it out a bit so as to make space. Finally, one at a time, the Diamond came back into view, and before we bottomed, we'd rebuilt the Wedge, everyone back in place.

During debrief, we ganged up on Neil. He was our new commander and leader, but he had already put us through a couple of deals that got pretty hairy, and since, technically, he was still in training, we could be brutally frank. Besides, everybody was in that second phase, when fear turns to hostility. "Don't you ever do that again." "We don't give a damn about centering the maneuver." "Make absolutely sure you have enough airspeed before you start us up," and so forth, five alpha males taking a short break from their customary role as Radio City Rockettes. Above all, Neil was an adult. He knew he'd screwed up and took his punishment. But we never let him live down the famous San Pablo Zero Airspeed Loop.

In any operational outfit, formation flying is a contract between leader and led. With the team, it was more than that, a collaborative act of creation not unlike M. C. Escher's famous lithograph of a pair of hands drawing a pair of hands.

Here, at San Pablo, a string was broken. Stan Musser, sobered by the experience, never again raised a rude signal to me as we went over the top of a Wedge Loop.

We flew several shows in Germany. At Spangdahlem, we performed under an overcast that started out at 6,000 feet but lowered during the show. Bob and I had a standard escape procedure in case we entered cloud and lost sight of each other in the Loop or Half Cuban. Since Bob flew over the top of me, he let it out in a more pronounced float, and I pulled it in to get around the corner quicker, giving us some vertical clearance at the cross. We ended up using this procedure—not a lot of fun, popping into the suds just as the collision effect was getting interesting.

Next day the weather was beautiful. We flew shows at Wiesbaden in the morning and Ramstein in the afternoon. Something in the Central European psyche responded to the season's first warm temperatures. All Germany donned lederhosen and volksmarched to the air show. We had 400,000 spectators in the morning and half a million in the afternoon, establishing a team one-day attendance record.

After the Ramstein show, we attracted so many autograph

seekers I retreated to the top of my wing to get some lebensraum. A tall German youth was pressed up against the wing's leading edge, about Adam's-apple high, and started to choke. I backed the crowd off and he crumpled under the wing, not to be seen again, at least by me.

———◆———

The Paris Air Show lasted five days. *La Patrouille de France*, the French team, flew a nine-ship act in a small trainer, the Fouga Magister. Their leader initiated a downward Bomb Burst too low so one of the slot men didn't have time to pull out and ended up planted in the grass about 200 meters from show center.

Paris was an exciting place to fly. All the industry was there, making it great fun to visit chalets and see what was going on in the big world of aerospace. We flew our shortened, Le Bourget displays without incident, though the weather had again turned awful. The Diamond made the cover of *Aviation Week*. (And what about the solos?)

As time neared for our departure, I had some special flight planning to do. Following our last Paris appearance on 4 June, we were scheduled to fly the Air Force Academy graduation on the seventh. From Paris to Colorado Springs, we could either fly a long hop on the fifth and another on the sixth, or make one very long hop and take a day off. We opted for the day off.

A decade before, in 1957, three F-100s had flown more than 7,000 miles nonstop from London to Los Angeles, until then the longest flight ever made by single-engine jets. The distance from Paris to Colorado Springs was about the same. We'd need lots of gas, six air refuelings, to get there, but if we made a seventh refueling, we'd arrive with plenty of fuel and could, if we chose, fly around Colorado for a while and set a new record for single-engine jet endurance. Doing so would keep us aloft something over 14 hours.

For refuelable aircraft, the constraint on endurance is usually oil consumption. Jet engines use oil a lot faster than car engines and have no spare tank or other means of adding oil after takeoff.

When we arrived in Colorado, if everybody's oil temperature and pressure looked good, we'd try for the record.

A day ahead of departure, I arranged with airport authorities to have bottled water to take on this long flight. French wine being what it was, we hadn't been drinking much water anyway, and, en route, cockpit air conditioning would further dehydrate us. Regarding nature's other calls, the rest of the guys would have to do their own planning. Early aircraft had relief tubes that dumped overboard. The F-100 came equipped with a small, stoppered bottle that could be drained and rinsed for reuse after landing. I regarded this device as unpleasant and difficult to deploy cleanly and safely. Also, I made it a habit to remember what a fighter pilot needs to do last, just before stepping to the jet.

The morning of our launch, I got to the airport an hour or so before the other guys to do last minute calculations and file a clearance. No water had showed up, but we still had plenty of time. I reminded the French bureaucracy of the request and set about my work.

The other guys arrived. We went over the route, special procedures and radio frequencies we'd use for refueling. No sign of any water.

We couldn't wait. The whole formation—not just the eight of us, but also our first set of tankers—had clearance into French airspace and the transatlantic jet-route structure at a certain time. Any delay would result in cancellation and a one-day slip of the redeployment.

We stepped to the aircraft on time, made normal engine starts and system checks, and taxied, holding short of the runway until our approved departure time. Still no water. By now, I was semi-angry with my French buddies. It was going to be a long time between drinks.

Our tankers were cleared into position, did final engine checks and took off. And, at last, here came one of those little airport-authority Peugeots, a very French-blue light spinning on top. He stopped in order at each airplane. One by one, we raised canopies and reached down to retrieve two bottles of mineral water. Small bottles. Coke-bottle sized. I'd envisioned a substantially larger water ration. Still, it was better than nothing, and I sighed relief as we taxied onto the runway, ran 'em up, and hurried after the tankers.

The flight plan called for us to fly south to Spain, then turn west after crossing the Pyrenees. We took our first fuel after coasting out into the North Atlantic. With my tanks topped off, I slid back to the tanker's right wing and settled in for a long, over-water leg. Reaching down, I grabbed one of the water bottles and twisted off the cap. Immediately, water squirted out the opening. When it was through fizzing, I had maybe three inches of liquid left in the bottom of the bottle, and my flying glove was soaking wet. The dumb bastards (pardon my French) had given us seltzer water! At a cockpit altitude of 8,000 feet, the liberation of gas was spectacular.

We got to Colorado on seven refuelings and two gulps of water. Once there, all of us were in good shape, so Neil set up a meander around the state to add the required flying time. However, air traffic control soon butted in with a message from TAC headquarters that we should land "as soon as possible." So we went burner and speed brakes to get rid of what was now too much fuel and recovered at Peterson Field, having remained aloft 13 hours and 40 minutes. The eight of us had just missed setting a new endurance record for single-engine jet aircraft.

Neil checked in with TAC and learned they'd told ATC we should land "as soon as possible after breaking the record."

———◆———

We staged out of Peterson Field for my first air show at the academy. The road running roughly north-south just east of Falcon Stadium made a good but not great show line, trees and light poles obstructing solo work. A line of low hills just past where we'd like to bottom on the north end added color. But the real problem was altitude. Like visiting football teams, we found our motors produced considerably less thrust in the thin, mile-high air. The jets also handled sluggishly. Here, we entered looping maneuvers near the same altitude at which we went over the top for sea-level shows, the difference in flight control responsiveness quite noticeable.

Doing the pigtails, I corkscrewed up into a livid, ominous-looking cloud stationed right at show center. I'd popped into the suds doing vertical rolls before and it wasn't all that bad. None of the instruments helped much, but if you left everything alone, you'd eventually come back out with the pointy end facing down and could recover visually. Always before, though, I'd rolled up into stratus— not cumulonimbus, the characteristic cloud of thunderstorms.

The United States has the dubious honor of being one of the world's leaders in thunderstorms, with maybe 100,000 occurring within our boundaries every year, so we saw them all the time as we flew around the country. They're the most powerful weather phenomenon on earth, except for hurricanes. "There's a growler," one of us would say of a fully developed mother-of-all-thunderstorms, its anvil building above 50,000 feet. Maggie, now gone from the team, honored these monsters with a special name: Bruno. If possible we gave them a wide berth, but sometimes we had no option. On one letdown into a show site in Indiana, hail badly damaged my paint job, requiring much extra work by the ground crew.

Along a line of mountains like the Front Range on which the Air Force Academy stands, convective air currents pump tremendous energy into cumulus clouds. It was imprudent of me to pirouette up into this particular Bruno, and I couldn't help feeling guilty (as well as apprehensive) as the aircraft was rattled and buffeted, until finally I was spit out the bottom, my sin absolved.

The summer of '67 provided great background music. The Beatles produced *Sgt. Pepper,* its influence unmatched, and others—Cream, Jimi Hendrix, The Doors, The Grateful Dead—created memorable work. The Summer of Love was also a time of strife across the country. The trouble began in Newark, where 23 died, and moved to Detroit, where 41 were killed in the bloodiest uprising in at least 50 years. In October, police beat protesters at the University of Wisconsin–Madison, this action featuring the first use of tear gas on a US college campus. An all-night antiwar rally took place on the Pentagon steps, Norman Mailer one of the notables arrested, the incident furnishing material for *The Armies of the Night.*

In mid-November, *Time* magazine published an interview with General Westmoreland in which he said: "I hope they try something because we are looking for a fight." At the end of the month, Robert McNamara submitted his resignation as secretary of defense. An anti-war Democrat, Sen. Eugene McCarthy announced he would stand against Johnson as a candidate for president. Nearly 600 war protesters were arrested in New York City, including famous baby doctor Benjamin Spock. By year-end, our troop strength in-country had risen to 485,000, with 16,000 combat deaths to date.

———◆———

The sixties was a decade of causes—civil rights, feminism, antiwar protest—and something like unit cohesion developed among civilians. It was a time of solidarity, of movements and groups and tribes.

Before joining the team, I'd bought a $12 acoustic guitar. We took it with us on the road and passed it around at parties. Patterakis was really good, and Mike Miller played cowboy chords. I could strum a little rhythm. After a show at Albuquerque, Jack Dickey dropped me at base ops so I could do the flight planning. He took my luggage to the aircraft, leaving the guitar behind in the rental car. OK, I bought another one, the next BX we came to, the price now up to 30 bucks. When we got back to Nellis, the guys contacted the rental-car outfit and tracked down the old guitar, without telling me. Car trunks in Albuquerque in the middle of August build up a fair amount of heat, so the guitar came back slightly warped. They had the Thunderbird painter lacquer it in team colors—red, white, and blue—and lettered "Marvelous Merrill, the Grants Pass Stunt Pilot" on the back. In a special presentation, they gave it back to me.

Start with the cheapest guitar you can find, warp it, spray it with acrylic, you're sure it's wrecked. Funny thing is, it sounded terrific.

It was a time of groups and tribes, and I'd found mine. I would never have better or closer friends than these men, the seven of us who flew the 1967 show season, including two leaders: Maggie and Neil. Six of the seven ended up general officers. Either it's pretty easy to make general, or this was a good bunch of guys.

Chapter 12

Bomb Burst

Fear and fright are two different things, the emotion of true fear requiring time for culture and preferably a period of helpless activity . . . Fear is the afterbirth of reason and calculation.

Fright is only the percussion cap of fear. It snaps rather than rumbles and its explosion is instantaneous . . . It hits, explodes, and may be gone as quickly, if it does not have time to ignite the keg of fear.

—Ernest K. Gann, *Fate Is the Hunter*

Del Rio could have been the movie set of a West Texas border town. It was rundown and windy, the weather tending to seasonal extreme. The airfield, six miles east of town, was named for 1st. Lt. Jack Thomas Laughlin, a B-17 pilot and Del Rio native killed over Java in the first weeks after Pearl Harbor. The base spread out over a considerable acreage—fairly level ground, desert sage, scrub brush. It was a pilot training base, like the one I'd gone to at Enid, Oklahoma. The team flew in on 20 October 1967 for an air show the next day, honoring a graduating class.

We went through the standard preshow routine. Lead and Five surveyed the show line while the rest of us made the usual round of hospital and school visits or did broadcast and print-media interviews. We picked up rental cars and headed to a motel off base. At a dinner for community leaders, lead cracked the same jokes about each of us and the audience chuckled while we pretended the lines weren't so stale. Next day, proud parents watched as 60 new pilots pinned on wings.

We briefed at noon in the conference room at base operations. As usual, an inspection team of local dignitaries joined us for a photo session before we stepped to the jets. The film *Bandolero!* was in production near the base. Its stars, Jimmy Stewart and Raquel Welch, showed up in the inspection party and caught the crowd's attention. Jimmy Stewart was a Reserve brigadier general, a founder of the Air Force Association, and a big hero to all of us. Raquel Welch was—well, she was Raquel Welch.

Engine start was at 1410. We were wearing white show suits for this one. Lead could choose from among gray, blue, black, or white, my least favorite. We looked like we should be selling ice cream. In addition, I worked hard during the air show and sweat soaked my collar circumference. This wouldn't matter much, except we did a lot of taxiing in trail, often with open canopies. With only six feet between the end of my pitot boom and Bobby Beckel's afterburner eyelids, I took a lot of jet exhaust into the cockpit. Wearing the mask and using 100 percent oxygen kept me comfortable, but the engine soot clung to show suit dampness, leaving a very noticeable ring around the collar when we wore white. At Del Rio, I followed my usual practice, rolling the collar under, once we'd taxied away from the crowd. After the show, as we deplaned, I'd roll it back out, the chimney black still there, but underneath, out of sight.

We taxied short of the runway for a quick check, a couple of our NCOs doing a last minute walk-around inspection. They looked over my aircraft, F-100D, serial number 55-3520—good old Number Six—and cleared it for flight. We took the runway, the Diamond in fingertip, Bobby and I together, 500 feet back.

The Diamond released brakes at precisely 1430. Bobby and I ran up the engines, my stomach tightening against the surge of isolation and exhilaration that came before every air show takeoff. By this time in the season, the team was really clicking. Already we had 91 official air shows under our belt. We'd flown at every kind of site and in all sorts of conditions. We knew what we were doing. It was a super day, the sky a severe clear, the show line a nice long runway with uncluttered approaches. Maybe the wind wasn't perfect: 140 at 12, gusting 17. We'd like about 5 knots, please, just enough to blow smoke off the line but not enough to make the air lumpy or require adjustment in the maneuvers.

Twenty-one minutes into the show, it was going nicely, had a good cadence and rhythm. The script was on automatic, the important information packed into silences between radio calls. We approached the climax of the demonstration, the signature Bomb Burst.

By now I was very experienced at putting on the pigtails; I could judge the timing pretty well and get the rolls truly vertical. I was doing lots of rolls, threatening Beckel's claimed all-time record of 13 (yeah, right!). My crew chief, C. D. James, kept count. If I ever got close to 13, he'd make sure we got credit.

Doing even a few vertical rolls requires establishing a perfectly vertical up line; doing more than a few means you must, in addition, begin the rolls with a ton of airspeed. I grabbed for altitude while Beckel entertained the crowd with his Wing Rock and Roll. Not wanting to be noticed until I popped through the Diamond's smoke, I tiptoed up, staying out of afterburner. The narrator helped by drawing the crowd's attention to the Diamond as it dove into the entry for the Bomb Burst. At what I judged the right moment, I hurried after them, following their track over the ground, keeping their smoke between the crowd and me.

Airspeed built rapidly. The FAA banned supersonic flight during public demonstrations, so I stayed subsonic, but just barely. Approaching the pull, I wanted to see .99 Mach. Then I could light the burner and hold the speed just at the edge of the Mach as I started a 6 ½ g pull into the vertical.

The biggest mistake I could make? Arrive early. With the Diamond about to break in all four directions, if I got there too soon, there'd be nowhere to go. (In a pinch, I'd call the break rather than wait for lead to do it.) If I hit it just right, I'd fly into the apex of the Bomb Burst three to five seconds after the Diamond separated, snap the throttle out of burner so as to make smoke, be perfectly vertical, and be going very fast. As the Diamond pilots tracked away from one another, I'd put on those lazy, lovely pigtails, after which I'd better get the smoke off and figure out how to do a slow speed vertical recovery. Nominally, I should stop rolling at 150 knots indicated in order to have at least a little control authority with which to point the nose, but as my confidence blossomed I'd begun staying in the maneuver and squeezing the last ounce of roll out of the airplane, a practice that made for some interesting low speed recoveries. Oh, well—no guts, no glory.

But this one did not go right. On the afternoon of 21 October 1967, at Del Rio, Texas, I started an aggressive pull into the vertical . . . and the airplane exploded.

———✦———

F-100 pilots got used to loud noises. In the best of circumstances, the afterburner could bang pretty hard when it lit off. And engine compressor stall was fairly common, usually moderate and of short duration but sometimes quite severe. Any F-100 pilot who heard a really loud "BANG!" automatically thought compressor stall and unloaded the jet to get air traveling down the intake as smoothly as possible. So, instinctively, I relaxed stick pressure to reduce the *g* load. By now I was fully into one of those fast-forward exercises where the seasons compress into seconds, leaves changing color while you watch. I seemed to move the stick forward lethargically, even had time to think, "That's no compressor stall." In retrospect, the airplane had already unloaded itself, making my home remedy superfluous, but some ancient pilot lore was at work here: no matter what else happens, *fly the airplane.* Forget all that stuff about lift and drag and thrust and gravity. Just fly the damn airplane until impact, then fly the pieces as deep into the wreckage as possible. Old 55-3520 had quit flying, but I hadn't—just yet.

But it didn't matter much because, immediately, flame filled the cockpit. No decision to make. I had to get out. Grabbing the seat handles, I tugged them up, jettisoning the canopy and exposing ejection triggers under each armrest. Yanking the triggers, I felt the seat catapult into the slipstream. Seat separation occurred automatically and too fast to track, explosive squibs firing to unlock the seat belt and shoulder harness. The seat disappeared. I quickly curled into the semi-fetal posture meant to absorb opening shock, mentally congratulating myself on perfect body position. For one elongated moment, I imagined how proud they'd be at jump school. Then the chute snapped open much too quickly, jolting me back to real time and short-circuiting the transition from stark terror to giddy elation, the evil Siamese twins of parachute jumping.

My helmet was missing. Now, where had it gone? Looking up, I saw a couple of panels torn loose, several shroud lines broken, one large rip in the crown of the parachute's canopy. I would come down a bit quicker than necessary. There wasn't much altitude left anyway. I was going to land in the infield, pretty close to show center, and I needed to figure out the wind so the parachute wouldn't tow me through the sagebrush. Then, too quickly, I hit the ground, bounced, was dragged, struggled with and finally got the chute collapsed. OK. I stood up, maybe in one piece. And a blue van with some of our guys in it drove out to collect me.

It began to sink in. In 14 years and more than 1,400 air shows, the team had been clever enough to do all of its metal bending in training, out of sight. This was our first accident in front of a crowd, and the honor belonged to me. I gathered my gear and climbed into the van just as the Diamond bottomed out, low and right on top of us. At least they didn't have the smoke on.

Somebody wanted to take me immediately to the base hospital, but I demurred. "Let's go over and tell the ground crew I'm OK." So we stopped, I got out of the van, shook hands with C. D., tossed the other crew chiefs an insincere thumbs-up. Jimmy Stewart was still there and came over to say nice things, but Raquel hadn't stayed for the show, so no air kiss. I'd given Mike Miller some ad libbing to do in the middle of his narration and he mentioned maybe we should leave that maneuver, whatever it was, out of the show sequence. That's when I learned I'd pulled the wings off the airplane.

On modern fighters, the wings are positioned well behind the pilot. You can see them in the rear-view mirror or if you look back, but they're otherwise not in normal view. Of course, I was watching the Diamond, ahead and well above me, as I concentrated on getting up to them quickly, but not too quickly. I didn't see the wings come off. All I knew was the airplane blew up.

The F-100 had a large fuel tank just behind the cockpit, forward of the engine and on top the wing center section. When the wings folded, a large quantity of raw fuel from this tank dumped into the engine, which exploded. The shock wave propagated up the air intake and blew the nose off, removing the first six feet of the airplane, all the way back to the bulkhead forming the front of the cockpit pressure vessel. The explosion badly damaged the tail end of the jet also, liberating the drag chute used for braking after landing. As it came fluttering down, some spectators thought my personal parachute had failed.

After it exploded, the engine began pumping flame through the cockpit pressurization lines. Conditioned air entered the cockpit at the pilot's feet and behind his head. My flying boots, ordinarily pretty shiny for an ex-ROTC guy, were charred beyond repair; I never wore them again. Where I'd rolled my collar underneath to protect show suit appearance, my neck got toasted.

It would be hard to say how fast I was going at ejection. I was certainly just barely subsonic when the wings failed, but with the nose blown off, the F-100 is a fairly blunt object and would have slowed quickly. On the other hand, I remained with the aircraft no longer than a second or two after it exploded, not much time to decelerate. When I came out of the jet, windblast caught my helmet, rotated it 90 degrees, and ripped it off my head. It was found on the ground, the visor down, oxygen mask hooked up, chinstrap still fastened. There was also a neck strap at the back of the helmet that helped secure it to the pilot's head. As the windblast rotated my helmet, this strap rubbed the burned part of my neck, causing some bleeding.

The team wore a standard backpack parachute suitable for ejection at either high or low altitude. Opening was automatic, occurring even if the pilot was unconscious after ejection. At altitudes below 14,000 feet, automatic deployment began one second after man-seat separation. This one-second delay let the human body, a draggy design, slow down a little and also separate from the seat, which was even draggier. For flight at very low altitude, the parachute could be made to open without delay. To set up this configuration, the pilot attached a lanyard to the parachute's manual activation device, the D ring. The lanyard was part of the ejection seat, so the parachute was pulled open as the seat fell away. Ordinarily, pilots selected this option only for takeoff and landing, when relatively slow and close to the ground so, if you needed the parachute, you needed it quickly. Otherwise, you unhooked the lanyard. At cruising speed, even at low altitude, the combination of flight path vector and the upward thrust of the seat as it rocketed out of the aircraft would give you some altitude, and it was a better trade to have the one-second deceleration before chute deployment started.

However, the team did so much work at low altitude, we just left the lanyard hooked up for the air show. That's why my chute opened so fast. Too fast, as it turned out. I didn't get enough separation from the seat, which somehow made contact with my parachute canopy after it was deployed, causing the damage I noticed on the way down. Also, the high-speed opening whipped my torso around to align it with the parachute risers, these heavy straps doing further damage to the back of my neck, the body part apparently singled out for retribution.

Walking into the base hospital I caught my image in a full-length mirror. Above it a sign read: "Check your military appearance." Mine looked like I'd been in a gunnysack with a mountain lion. The white show suit was a goner, cockpit fire having given it a base coat of charcoal gray, to which had been added several tablespoons of blood and a final dressing of dirt, grass and sagebrush stain. I could account for the camouflage—from being dragged along the ground—but I hadn't realized my neck was bleeding quite so much. Really good judgment to stop and visit with the ground crew.

The doctors kept me in the hospital overnight. The team came by, Mike Miller smuggling in dry martinis in an emptied milk carton. They were leaving for Nellis the next morning. I told the hospital staff I was leaving too and asked Jack Dickey to pack the stuff I'd left at the motel. I rode the C-130 home with the ground crew. I was sore for a couple of days, but we were about to take a break anyway. The 1967 show season was over.

My aircraft continued on a ballistic trajectory after I punched out, scattering parts along the extended flight path. Most of the engine and main fuselage section impacted about two miles down range from my initial pull-up. I signed a hand-receipt to remove the aircraft from government inventory, its value listed at $696,989. But nobody on the ground was hurt. All the bits and pieces ended up on government property and could be collected for analysis. If there is a good kind of accident, this was it.

The most durable part of the F-100, or so it was thought, was the box at the center of the fuselage where the wings mated. On inspection, my wing center box was found to have fractured because of fatigue cracking, with about 30 more cracks in the vicinity of the one that failed. North American Rockwell, the airplane's manufacturer, tested what remained of my wing center box, breaking it again at a pressure rating that translated to a load of exactly 6.5 *g*'s for my flight conditions when the wings departed. This should not have happened, as the F-100's positive load limit was 7.33.

———◆———

An aircraft's static strength is its ability to take a simple load, without consideration for repetition or cyclic variation. For instance, the F-100 had been designed to encounter a limit load of plus 7.33 and minus 3 g's. Of course, in routine service, the aircraft would experience lesser loads, but these positive and negative limits represented the normally anticipated maximum loads. The aircraft must withstand such use with no ill effects. Specifically, the primary load-bearing structures of the aircraft should undergo no objectionable deformation when subjected to a limit load, returning to their original, unstressed shape with removal of the load.

To provide for the (one hopes) rare instances when the aircraft must endure a load greater than limit to avert disaster, the manufacturer designs in a safety factor, usually an extra 50 percent. The primary structures of the aircraft must also withstand this so-called ultimate load—for the F-100, about plus 11 and minus 4.5 g's—without failure. Such a load will overstress the aircraft, perhaps causing permanent metal deformation, but no actual failure of major load-carrying components should occur. During construction of a new design, static tests, including destructive tests, verify ultimate strength.

However, in service, aircraft accumulate structural damage that, though related to static strength, falls more in the category of wear and tear. If repeatedly flexed over time, metals develop fatigue, usually in the form of minute cracks that can enlarge and propagate into the cross section of aircraft structures. When a crack progresses sufficiently, the remaining cross section can no longer withstand imposed stress, and a sudden, final rupture occurs. In this way, failure can happen at loads much lower than ultimate static strength.

Interestingly, fatigue damage is cumulative. Just as all men will get prostate cancer if they live long enough, so all aircraft structures will fail at some point because of metal fatigue. This is why even the most ruggedly built airframes have a service life. It's also why aircraft are inspected regularly to insure against the stored-up effects of metal fatigue.

In fact, the F-100's load-bearing structures were inspected periodically, except for the wing center box. First, it was hard to get at. But also, it was, in theory, over-engineered. That is, North American's designers projected the spectrum and frequency of loads that would be encountered in service, and primary structures other than the wing center box were engineered to sustain these loads through anticipated service life without fatigue failure. Then the wing center box was made stronger than that. It might fail, but it wouldn't matter because other load-bearing structures would fail first, in the same way that most men die of something else before they get prostate cancer.

But my wing center box had failed, well inside the normal operating limits of the aircraft, from accrued metal fatigue. When the Air Force looked around, other recent F-100 losses looked suspiciously similar. These were cases of aircraft lost on bombing runs in Vietnam. The recovery from a dive bomb pass is a lot like the high speed, high-g pull-up into the Bomb Burst. In the Vietnam cases, the Air Force could not retrieve the pieces and wrote off the aircraft as combat losses. But after looking at my wreckage, specialists examined other F-100s in the fleet and found a lot of fatigue damage. Consequently, the Air Force put a 4 g limit on the aircraft and initiated a program to modify the aircraft by beefing up the wing center box.

Thus, my accident almost certainly saved lives by revealing a serious problem the Air Force could and did correct. But it also grounded the team for the rest of the year. A mod line was set up at North American's Palmdale facility to repair all F-100s, including ours. With luck, we'd get them back by January to start training for the '68 season.

Chapter 13

Solo Leader

A fisherman, who with his pliant rod
Was angling there below, caught sight of them;
And then a Shepard leaning on his staff
And, too, a peasant leaning on his plow
Saw them and were dismayed: they thought these
Must surely be some gods, sky-voyaging.
> —Ovid, retelling the story of *Daedalus*

Normally, the team took time off at Christmas. The departing lead solo flew a few sorties with his old wingman, the new Number Five. The purpose was to introduce single-solo maneuvers done by Five alone: the Eight Point, Inverted to Inverted, and Wing Rock and Roll. Local knowledge, such as how to take timing cues from lead's radio calls, was also passed along, but by now the solo wingie had figured most of this out and the real issue was these single-solo figures. However, our jets were still in the depot having their wing center boxes replaced, so Bobby Beckel was unable to give me any practical training before he headed off to Vietnam.

We did talk at length. According to Bob, the Eight Point and Wing Rock were fairly straightforward. One was just another hesitation roll, an elaboration on the Four Point, not easy, but no new science involved. The other was a slowed-down, dirty roll—dirty in the sense that the gear, flaps, and speed brakes were down. Designed to show the slow-speed handling qualities of the aircraft, this maneuver, too, required some technique but recalled the by now thoroughly familiar Roll on Takeoff.

The Inverted to Inverted was a different matter. It began with a low entry into an Inverted. Approaching show center, upside down, Five rolled rapidly 360 degrees from the Inverted back around to Inverted. Because of the general squirreliness of the F-100, Bobby had scared himself a few times doing this figure at 50 feet. In fact, he said he'd been crossing the maneuvers off his calendar when my accident interrupted, so he didn't have to count down to zero. He recommended I jack up the altitude, which surprised me a bit. Beckel had kept me alive for a year, but I knew from experience how comfortable he was upside down, close to the ground. I took his advice to heart.

Then, Bobby left Nellis, hurrying to Vietnam, not wanting to be the only fighter pilot in the Free World, other than me, to miss the war. With luck he'd be there by Tet, the Vietnamese New Year.

My wingman was Mike Miller, the ex-narrator moving up to Number Six. Rounding out the new lineup, Mack Angel replaced Patterakis at left wing, and Doyle Ruff joined us as the new narrator. Both Mack and Doyle had just returned from combat tours. An outgoing party animal, Mack added a light touch, blending nicely with the type-A overachievers already on the team. Mike immediately dubbed him "Beef Man," a not-so-flattering reference to the fight he seemed destined to have with his waistline. In keeping with his general imperturbability, Mack ignored the slight. A tall, slender Florida State track and field athlete, Doyle also made a first-rate addition to the team. Mike nicknamed him "Slick."

Though he'd flown cross-country with the team and watched air shows for a year, a lot of solo wisdom still needed to be imparted to Mike, so we briefed, and briefed some more, while we waited for our jets to come back from the depot mod line. I stressed especially the principle that held solo flying together: our success, indeed our continued consumption of the planet's meager resources, depended on doing the same thing, the same way, every time, so the other guy knew what to expect. It was a contract.

Mike and I flew our first two-ship on 6 January, me in Dickey's airplane, Number Four, because mine wasn't out of the depot yet. It was the standard solo mission one, a sagebrush burner to the Lake. Cresting the Sheepheads, I kicked Mike out and got ready for my first Inverted to Inverted. I was maybe 1,000 feet above terrain, so no sweat on altitude. I rolled upside down, paused a few counts, then yanked it 360 degrees back to inverted. Somewhere in this roll, the canopy fired.

It was a sort of explosion—"KABOOM!"—right behind the ears, sounding for all the world like the big bang when my wings folded, the last time I flew a red-white-and-blue airplane. Hanging in the seat, nothing between me and the ground but 425 knots of wind, I waited for the next surprise.

Nothing.

Gently, carefully, I rolled it back upright and got my heart restarted. I was at idle power for the maneuver and left it there, so the jet was decelerating, the wind getting easier to live with. Still, it was impossible to talk because of cockpit noise, so I flicked on the smoke switch, our silent rejoin signal, and started a gentle left turn back to Nellis. I didn't want to mess with the seat, like bottoming it to reduce windblast, because I figured it was armed, canopy departure being step one of the ejection sequence. I worked the safety pins back into the seat. Now if something else happened and I needed to punch out, fumbling with the pins would cause delay, but I preferred this to riding a live seat.

Out to my left, I watched as Mike hustled toward me, carrying lots of overtake, wanting to rejoin smartly and show some skill, his first day on the job. He expected me to be doing 425 knots, so he flashed by and out in front like I was flying the Goodyear Blimp. Pulling up to kill off airspeed, he deposited a trail of jet wash that bounced me around in my open cockpit. On the outside of the turn now, Mike slowed, worked his way back and joined on my right wing.

Here is a physical law valid for all carbon-based, molecular life forms: he was *never* to be on the right. He flew my left wing. In six-ship, he flew outside left. If I ever needed to find him, I looked left. Period.

I watched as he joined on the right, by now into that second wave of emotion, angry at myself for being scared.

Mike came up on frequency: "Hey, Ton, your canopy's gone."

I thought how tough it must be, being a genius.

I'd slowed enough I could talk on the radio: "You get your butt over on the other side."

Mike vanished under my airplane and reappeared in the proper location.

I took it back to Nellis for an uneventful landing. No big deal. In the old days, fighter aircraft often landed with the canopy open, though usually not entirely gone.

To get at the wing center box, technicians at the Palmdale depot had removed the ejection seat. After reinforcing the wing, they buttoned up the airplane and managed somehow to get the seat back in so it looked OK but was not properly installed. Under the negative g I used to roll from inverted back to inverted, the seat's armrests displaced upward slightly, just enough to fire the canopy. As an extra-added attraction, in this condition the seat was armed, and putting the ground safety pins back in, as I had for the return to base, made no difference whatever.

We sent the depot a little valentine.

Mike and I flew intensively through January. We spent every minute working on his stuff, teaching him the figures, gradually lowering the altitude, then starting on opposing maneuvers. For the most part, I ignored my own requirement to learn single-solo figures. There just wasn't time. Mike had no shortage of talent or courage, so very quickly we were doing Calypso patterns and the Roll on Takeoff at Nellis. Late in January, the two of us joined the Diamond for six-ship work, then started practicing show sequence at the Springs, and I had no choice but to do the single-solo maneuvers. Eight Points turned out to be a piece o' pie. No problem with the Wing Rock and Roll either. In fact, I could fly this maneuver pretty close to the ground so it looked hairy but was actually quite safe, as long as I unloaded just a little at the right time and didn't let the nose yaw too much. I also found a way to make a slow, lazy entry into inverted for the Calypso. Both the Wing Rock and Calypso entry would be crowd-pleasers.

But Beckel was so right about the Inverted to Inverted. I jacked it up to seventy-five, even a hundred feet, and still it was an armful. I had no problem doing it level; it just seemed slippery in the roll, so I had to do it a little higher than I wanted.

———◆———

Nearing the end of January, North Vietnamese troops launched a major attack at Khe Sanh in the demilitarized zone. Precipitating the single largest battle of the war, this move was in part a massive diversion for what followed. On the evening of 31 January, as Vietnam celebrated the Lunar New Year, Vietcong soldiers attacked in more than 100 cities and towns, including Saigon. With TV cameras rolling, VC commandos occupied the courtyard of the US embassy.

During the chaos of Tet, two events left a deep impression: a handcuffed VC prisoner was shot in the head by South Vietnam's police chief, Gen. Nguyen Ngoc Loan, in front of Associated Press photographer Eddie Adams. The mesmerizing photo appeared on front pages the next morning. The other incident involved the city of Ben Tre, a provincial capital in the Mekong Delta leveled by US bombing. AP correspondent Peter Arnett quoted an unidentified officer as stating, "It became necessary to destroy the town in order to save it." The remark, or some version of it, was quoted often thereafter, becoming a metaphor for the American experience in Vietnam.

The Tet offensive came as a more or less complete surprise, a major failure for the world's most elaborate and expensive intelligence apparatus. Charlie held the cities for only three or four days—the exception being Hue, where he hung on for 25—in the process losing troops at a rate from which he would never fully recover. Nevertheless, Tet was the turning point, a strategic victory for the North. Walter Cronkite, America's most trusted TV news anchor, declared on 27 February that we were "mired in stalemate" and should negotiate our way out. Claiming the Communists had been defeated decisively, General Westmoreland asked for 206,000 more troops.

The American people now stopped believing what their government told them.

We kicked off the show season on 9 March, again at Malmstrom in front of a small crowd, then headed south. We did a show at MacDill, a SAC base near Tampa, in nice weather, but lined up for departure the next day in drizzle and low cloud, the ceiling maybe 300 feet. Because of MacDill's wide pavements, we could get seven aircraft on the runway, lead at the point with three in echelon on each side forming a V. Bob Haney lined up outside Mike Miller, flying outside left, and Jack Dickey took a position outside me, on the right. In good weather, Dickey would make a long move under me and Musser into the slot and Haney would come over from the left side to tuck in behind Jack in Stinger, but today Neil told them to stay in place for a straight-ahead climb until we punched out on top the overcast. We rolled seven, burners cooking, Neil throttled back to give everybody some power to play with. As we rotated for lift-off, a rooster tail of steam and spray bounced off the runway, rising to blend with low cloud. We broke ground and, quickly, started the gear up. At the departure end, I caught sight of bomber crews at the SAC alert facility standing outside, watching us, a rarely seen seven-ship formation takeoff, all noise and steam, then gone, suddenly, like rabbits down a hole, except it was up, into the suds.

———◆———

As Five, I'd picked up a couple of new responsibilities. First, and as an absolute priority, I was going to bring my wingman back after every practice and every show. Mike was a gifted flyer and fearless, maybe even too aggressive, which was OK, as long as I did the thinking for both of us. Given the difficulty of what we were trying to do and the varied circumstances at each show site, my judgment would not always be perfect, but it was what we had going for us.

On cross-countries, I was now Blue lead, so I also had to take care of the maintenance officer and narrator when we split from the Diamond for any reason, most commonly to go to different tankers for air refueling. I liked the increased responsibility.

One nice thing, lead and Five always did a survey flight of the show line, usually in a helicopter, often crewed by Army or National Guard pilots. The chopper guys often seemed intent on helping us question our manhood, but the opportunity to look at obstacles and timing checkpoints was truly the peek worth a thousand finesses.

———◆———

In March Sen. Eugene McCarthy came within 230 votes of beating Lyndon Johnson in the New Hampshire primary. Two days later, Robert Kennedy announced his candidacy.

On 16 March, members of Charlie Company, 1st Battalion, 20th Infantry, Americal Division, slaughtered more than 300 Vietnamese civilians in the hamlet of My Lai. On entering the village and finding no VC, Lt. William Calley and his platoon began killing old men, women, and children, a process interrupted only when a helicopter pilot, Warrant Officer Hugh Thompson, realized what was happening and began evacuating civilians. The initial report by participants claimed 69 VC soldiers killed and made no mention of civilian casualties.

At the end of March, facing defeat in the Wisconsin primary, Johnson withdrew from the presidential race, announced a

New Thunderbird solo pilot, Nellis AFB, January 1967.

Bobby Beckel shows me how to achieve collision effects without actually banging into each other.

My crew chief, C. D. James. C. D. kept me alive for two years, so I figured he could be trusted with the paperwork.

Solo formation takeoff, Nellis, January 1967. Wheels already up and locked, landing gear doors closing. Make a note: When Beckel says he'll get the wheels up quickly, he means quickly. And after we get the gear doors closed, he's going to lower the nose.

With Bobby in Calypso, Palmdale, California, 1967.

Key West, Florida, 1967. We are made honorary "Conchs."
Front row: Stan Musser, Jack Dickey, Chris Patterakis,
Bob Haney. Back row: Tony McPeak, the mayor of Key
West, Maggie Maglione, Bob Beckel, Mike Miller.

Bouncing smoke off the ground at the entry of the Opposing Slow Roll. If I get it right, I'll miss, but feel him go by.

Photo taken by someone in the crowd at RAF Bentwaters, UK, May 1967. For the Opposing Aileron Rolls, I should be a little high on Bobby, but here I'm maybe five or six feet too high. And the photographer was (I hope) 100 feet or so right of show center.

Bobby and I start up into an Opposing Loop.

*Haney and Miller join the Wedge
to form the Outhouse formation.*

*McPeak, Beckel, Eddins, Maglione, Patterakis, Musser,
Dickey. The team prepares for the long return flight from
Paris. We hope to set a record for single engine jet endurance.
Now, where is the water those French guys promised?*

*Neil gives Jimmy Stewart just what he's always wanted:
an autographed picture of the team. Del Rio, Texas, 1967.*

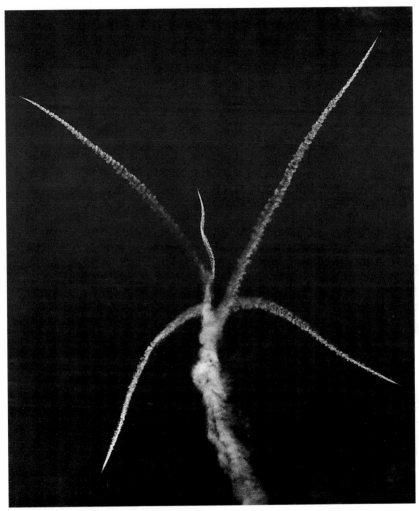

After the Diamond separates for the Bomb Burst, the solo pilot
pulls up through the smoke to do vertical rolls, the "pigtails."
This is what the early part of the maneuver should look like. At
Del Rio, Texas, 21 October 1967, I didn't get very far into the pull.

The wings are gone and what's left of Number Six is on fire, with one of the Diamond aircraft above. Photo taken from video made by a spectator.

Me hanging in the parachute, with my survival kit and life raft dangling below.

My canopy.

When the engine exploded it blew off the first six feet of the intake.

The wreckage of Number Six.

The 1968 Thunderbirds: Neil Eddins, leader; Mack Angel,
left wing; Stan Musser, right wing; Jack Dickey, slot;
Tony McPeak, lead solo; Mike Miller, solo wingman.

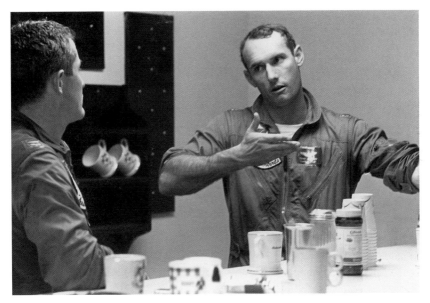

Flying with your hands, something all pilots do. In this case, I'm talking to Mike about inverted flight.

I bring back Number Four, Jack Dickey's jet, without a canopy, January 1968.

*Mike and I walk back to the hangar after a training sortie,
January 1968. We're thinking it's got to improve.*

Mike and I in Calypso, 1968.

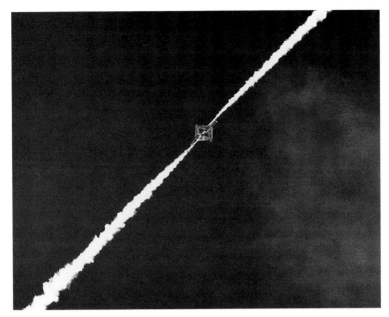

Mike and I pass each other on top an Opposing Loop. Tops were hard. Getting them right made up for a lot of other mistakes.

With Senator Barry Goldwater and General Ira Eaker.

On my wing for an autograph session following an air show.

The team returns to Nellis from a long road trip.

The team near the end of the 1968 season. From left: June Eddins, Connie Angel, Dawn Musser, Lore Dickey, Ellie McPeak, Jacque Miller, Kay Ruff, Cookie Murata. With us, between Doyle Ruff and Steve Murata, Joe Moore, selected to lead the team in 1969–70.

Landing gear and flaps down for the
Wing Rock and Roll, Nellis AFB, 1968.

The 1967 team reunited in Las Vegas, 2003. From left:
Eddins, Patterakis, Musser, Dickey, Beckel, McPeak, Haney,
Miller. I would never have better friends than these men.

partial halt to bombing in the North, and invited Hanoi to begin negotiations.

On 4 April, James Earl Ray shot and killed Martin Luther King Jr., who was standing on a balcony of the Lorraine Motel in Memphis, Tennessee. Rioting broke out in 100 US cities, the flames reaching within six blocks of the White House. The government called out 70,000 troops to restore order.

I was the team's flight examiner and instrument check pilot. As the others came due for annual proficiency checks, I signed them off, doing this during any flight in which I was in a position to judge their competence, even an air show. But for the yearly instrument check, they had to crawl in the back of the two-seater and go under the bag. The check was no real challenge for any of these guys, but at the end of the ride, I got to show them an inverted entry into the landing pattern. It was an eye opener, the first time through one of these, and a nice way to get even for all those antisocial remarks about solo "Dummies."

Usually, nobody flew the F-model in an air show. With eight Ds assigned, we could have one in the hangar at Nellis for maintenance and still have six single-seaters plus a spare available at the show site. The problem came when we lost aircraft, as we had in the '67 midair on the way to Europe. When we ran short of Ds, one of us had to fly the two-seater in the show. The Diamond said not them, since the F's longer fuselage would make the formation look asymmetric. And Five couldn't ask Six to take it since it was a bitch to fly and we protected the solo wingie. Beckel had flown some shows in the two-seater and, for the '68 show season, it was my turn if we lost any jets. On 11 May, in Orlando, Florida, we bent up three airplanes in one mishap.

We briefed a standard high show, Armed Forces Day at McCoy AFB. But when we lined up for takeoff, the control tower reported a sizable thunderstorm seven miles southeast. It looked closer and was moving toward the field, so Neil audibled to a low show, our backup plan when the weather didn't cooperate. Mike and I followed the Diamond, doing our patented Roll on Takeoff and hastened to opposite ends of the show line. The Diamond opened the low sequence with a Flat Pass. Mike and I were on stage next, heading at each other for an Opposing Flat Pass. The rain was by now heavy enough that my canopy looked like I was going through a car wash. I couldn't see Mike, which worried me, even though it was his job to miss me. After we went by each other I called Neil and said maybe we should knock off the opposing work until the storm passed. Neil agreed and stopped the show. He told me to bring Mike and join up with the Diamond. We'd hold clear of the weather, waiting to see if it would get better.

After 15 minutes, Neil gave up and decided to land. The rain had camped out over the field, but we had 12,000 feet of runway and could still see the approach end and touchdown zone clearly. Neil maneuvered to downwind and told us to take spacing. We stretched out on a base leg, me ahead of Mike, the reverse of our normal Calypso landing order. Neil and Mack Angel landed OK, but Stan was blinded by heavy rain immediately on touchdown. He couldn't see ahead of himself, overtook Mack about 4,000 feet down the runway and swerved left too late to avoid hitting him. Stan's right main landing gear rode up and over Mack's left wing, removing about three feet of it and shearing off in the process. There was some radio chatter between Stan, Mack, and Neil as Stan continued, sliding down the wet runway on nose wheel, left main gear and right wing tip. He passed in front of both Mack and Neil (who had nearly stopped) before departing the right side of the runway into the grass infield, where his nose gear collapsed. Behind them, Jack Dickey, unable to see much and hearing the commotion on the radio, jumped on the brakes and blew both main tires, shedding rubber and metal as he ground down the brake stacks. Jack transmitted a warning to me that he'd stopped short, in the middle of the runway.

From my point of view, half a mile on final, rain hung like a curtain over the approach end of the runway. I could see the first 200 feet or so of the overrun, with its distinctive markings, but couldn't make out the first brick of the actual landing surface.

I told Mike, "OK, let's go somewhere else."

We motored over to Herndon, Orlando's general aviation airport, which had a fairly short (for the F-100) runway that terminated in a lake, so the drag chute needed to work. Mike and I headed for the bar and were rapidly getting illegal for flight when we got a phone call from Neil. The airplane parts had been cleared off the runway at McCoy, and he wanted us back over there.

F-100 pilots learned how to improvise repacking the drag chute, but this was the only time I ever actually had to do it. Anyway, we somehow got our birds ready and made the short hop over to McCoy, now basking in Florida sunshine.

So we were short three Ds. One (Jack's) could be fixed pretty quickly. One (Mack's) could be fixed someday. One (Stan's) would never fly again.

Next morning, four of us departed McCoy for Nassau, the Bahamas. Stan flew my jet. Mike, in Number Six, filled in at left wing. I got issued the F-100F. We counted the Bahamas as overseas, so I had the flight surgeon in the backseat. Once we hit the island, Neil kicked Mike and me out, the Diamond became a two-ship, and we did arrival maneuvers. The doc, who didn't realize how much harder solo work was in the two-seater, thought this was great fun.

For 1968, I would end up setting an unwelcome record: most air shows flown in the family model.

We flew five shows in Toronto at the Canadian National Exposition. The Blues had lost a solo pilot there a couple of years back, the accident making a big impression on the Canadians. Air show officials were emphatic: no maneuvers below 500 feet. If they saw anything below 500, we could pack up and leave.

Neil took them seriously, and I said, "OK, Mike and I will jack it up." We were flying out over the lake anyway, making it a little harder to judge altitude. So I got to do the Inverted to Inverted at 500 feet, five days in a row.

OK, maybe 200. Anyway, I finally had some concentrated practice with an altitude cushion and could work out how to do it. The rest of the year, I was all right with the maneuver, except for a show at Little Rock, where, again, I was in the two-seater. That big, long nose wiggled too much, and I got low enough to reseal the runway.

On 20 May 1968, I pinned on the rank of major, becoming a field-grade officer, another on-time promotion, but this one a biggie. My early track record might have ruled out this advancement, so I felt lucky not to have been passed over. Already many of my peers had pushed in front of me. I had no complaint; these are mostly good guys, like Stan Musser. But if I was ever to make headway in the Air Force, I'd better get moving.

In Los Angeles, a 24-year-old Palestinian named Sirhan Sirhan shot Robert Kennedy moments after he claimed victory in the California primary. Kennedy died 6 June 1968.

On 1 July, Gen. Creighton Abrams replaced Westmoreland as US commander in Vietnam.

In the summer I got to participate in a test program. Too many pilots were spinning aircraft or encountering other out-of-control conditions and not recovering properly. We didn't spin fighters on purpose, so the last spin experience most of us got was in the T-28 during primary flying school. A potential solution was to station a handful of T-33s at each fighter base and let everybody get spin training once a quarter.

Unhappily, each jet has a little different spin recovery method, and this was what pilots needed to rehearse. Practicing the T-bird's prescribed procedure would be negative training. The issue was whether any fighter's recovery technique would work well enough to be safe for use with the T-33. An instructor pilot was flying a T-bird around TAC bases to see what happened when line pilots spun it, then used the recovery technique prescribed for their own airplane. I was the F-100 guy selected, since somebody figured I'd had a few interesting low-speed recoveries in the jet. I hopped in the front of the jet, took it up and spun it a dozen times, recovering nice as pie each time using the F-100's standard recovery technique.

Nothing ever came of this safety initiative, maybe because of cost, but it was a great idea.

In midsummer we staged a show from NAS Love Field, near Dallas. The show site was an open field some miles southwest of the Navy station. A string of power lines ran at 90 degrees to the show line on one end. Neil and I noted this during the survey flight. It looked a little close, but maybe we could do normal solo figures.

Just into the show, recovering from the Opposing Inverted, I managed to graze the power lines with my belly. I felt the hit and knew my tail hook had been yanked loose from its stowed position because I got a warning light in the cockpit. The F-100's tail hook wouldn't retract in flight, so it was going to stay down.

Mike joined up for the Four Point and, as he was coming aboard, radioed: "Ton, your tail hook is down."

I rogered, asking, "See any other damage?"

Neil snapped, "What's going on?" the decibel level high because the solos were causing trouble again.

Mike said I looked OK otherwise, so I told Neil we could continue, which we did.

Love Field had arresting gear deployed at several spots across the active runway. I'd get an automatic barrier engagement when I landed, which was a no-brainer. I'd just recover last so as not to close the runway for the other guys.

After landing, the crew chiefs got me out of the wire and secured the tail hook. I taxied back and shut down. It turned out my horizontal stabilizer had a good bit of damage, and (surprise!) we found matching damage to Mike's aircraft. He'd hit the power lines on the Opposing Slow Roll. Mike said he'd tried to tell me about it but the transmission got buried in Diamond's radio calls.

Angry, Neil said to me, "OK, smart aleck, you call Nellis and tell them what you two guys did."

I got on the phone and mentioned casually to the command post duty officer I'd hit some power lines. Luckily, it was a weekend and he was not exceptionally alert. "No," he declared, "You mean phone lines. Power lines are thick cables that would tear up your jet."

"OK, phone lines," I said.

But some folks in the west end of Dallas lost electricity for a while.

———◆———

We often flew on the same bill with civilian stunt pilots. Among the best was Dick Schram, who did an act called the Flying Professor. He performed in a stock, usually borrowed, Piper Cub. He appeared in formal attire, very professorial looking but maybe seeming a little inebriated, holding a large book titled "How To Fly." He would stagger to the Cub, manage to get it started and off the ground, then proceed to fly the most hair-raising, grass-clipping aerobatics imaginable. He was on his back at the top of a loop at lower altitude than anybody I'd ever seen. More than a talented pilot, he was a great guy. But we lost him in 1969 at Reading, Pennsylvania, when he did not recover from a hammerhead stall. He was always proud of his son, who later served a tour as a support officer with the Blue Angels.

Another we often flew with was Bill Fornoff. Bill had a postwar Navy fighter, the F8F Bearcat, and put on a great show. But he always seemed maxed out, on the edge of his personal envelope, no slack left. Too often he came up after a show to say something like, "Did you see what happened to me when I did that (whatever) maneuver? Boy! I just managed to get it back under control." I wasn't convinced Bill was going to make it, and he didn't. Even for air shows—maybe especially for air shows—you have to fly within yourself, hold something in reserve.

Harold Krier was *the* aerobatic show pilot of the 1960s, setting the style for many others. Silky smooth, his aerobatics were big and on line. No frantic tumbling for him. But he, too, was lost in 1971, when his chute did not deploy during spin tests of a new aerobatic special.

Art Scholl, another Flying Professor, flew a Super Chipmunk. The National Aerobatic Champion in 1974, he'll be remembered for his precise, aggressive flying style. Art took over from Paul Mantz as Hollywood's premier movie stunt pilot and subsequently lost his life during the filming of *Top Gun*.

Bob Hoover was maybe the best of the bunch, a splendid performer with well-tested judgment. Early in the 1968 season, he saw me do the Wing Rock and Roll and advised me to raise the altitude and moderate the amount of bank and yaw. This was typical Hoover, always urging restraint.

Early fall is the best time to fly shows in Alaska. The days are still long, and if you time it right, the salmon are running. We had shows scheduled at Anchorage and Fairbanks and staged to some of the remote radar sites. Neil loved to fish, so we landed at King Salmon Air Station and spent a couple of days at a camp run by the Air Force. The kings were already gone, but the river was thick with silvers and none of us had any trouble catching our limit in a few minutes each morning. We spent the rest of the day inside playing bridge or poker on account of small flies (the locals called them white socks) that made it impossible to stay outdoors for long. Eddins, our maximum leader, was quite good at bridge, his bidding a little raw but basic card sense making up for it in the play of the hand. Not so in poker, as he had no talent for dissimulation. Like a Labrador retriever, he jumped as far in as he could as soon as the float splashed, the rest of us just tossing in our hands.

We flew a show at King Salmon for a crowd count of 65, which must have included sled dogs. Afterward, the crew chiefs had to wipe a heavy layer of insect blood off every leading edge.

We ended up loading two tons of salmon into the C-130 that followed us around as a support aircraft, fish that were going to taste pretty good back at Nellis, if the C-130 crew kept them iced down. Heading back from Alaska, we were going to stop first at Reno for the air races, so our salmon would be on the ground there for a day or so.

Mike Miller and I made plans. The C-130 took off for Reno ahead of us, but we would catch and pass above it along the Pacific Coast of Canada. Neil got them to come up on our discrete frequency. I chose a small, round island unnamed on navigation charts, and pointed it out to the C-130 crew. Mike simulated a trumpet flourish and we named the island after our C-130 guys, giving it their call sign.

The fish arrived at Nellis in good shape.

In November, Richard Nixon, who claimed to have a plan to end our Vietnam involvement, defeated Hubert Humphrey in a close election. The ticket of George Wallace and retired Air Force general Curtis LeMay got 46 electoral votes.

We flew our last show of the season and came home on 27 November 1968. I was in the family model, as usual, but with Jack Thurman, the newly selected solo wingman, in the backseat. We did arrival maneuvers at Nellis, and I made a nice, slow entry into inverted for my last Calypso pattern—no lower than normal, but maybe an unsettling sight for Jack. I was at the very end of the learning curve for inverted flight, and he was looking up it for the first time.

Later, I came to think it a mistake to let Thurman ride through this Calypso traffic pattern. To make things worse, Mike overcorrected to stay in position and bumped my wing with his fuselage, giving us a noticeable nudge while we were upside down. After pitching up to downwind, I could see my wing tip had been bent into a little winglet. Thurman must have wondered at that point what he'd gotten himself into.

This was the last trip home for Eddins, Dickey, and me. Stan would stay for a third year and fly slot. Maj. Gen. Zach Taylor, commander at Nellis and a nice man, met us with a red carpet and champagne. He said he was happy, not having to watch me do any more Wing Rocks.

My last flights as a Thunderbird took place two days later, on 29 November. I flew both sorties with Mike Miller in the F, giving helpful hints on lead solo figures and making my final passes up the runway, upside down.

Then the weapons school scheduled a couple of sorties to the range so I could get recurrent in bombing and gunnery and take a needed annual instrument check. I'd report to Vietnam with all the squares filled.

Logbook: Thunderbirds

1967–68	First Pilot	IP	Total	Official Air Shows
F-100D	686.5	111.3	797.8*	199

Qualifications:

Demonstration Pilot

* Midway through calendar year 1967, the Air Force switched to a digital presentation for flight logs.

Chapter 14

Not Much of a War (But All We Got)

. . . He'd said, What about Nam? They had all been there
and each of them had thought about it some more and
said no, Nam was bad, but it wasn't bad duty, it was part
of it. Part of what? Part of being in the Marines.
— Elmore Leonard, *The Hunted*

Crossing the Pacific, we refueled at Hickam, in Honolulu, and again at Clark, in the Philippines, where I disembarked on Tuesday, 10 December 1968. The plane was filled mostly with GIs who pressed on into the fight. A few fearless fighter jocks had to attend Jungle Survival School.

A new class started jungle school every Monday. I was anxious to join this week's class rather than wait around for the next one. I'd already spent time resettling Ellie and boys into civilian quarters[33] and detoured four days to Florida for refresher training on over-water bailout (which turned out to be pretty good instruction, including my first shot at parasailing). I made straight for jungle school, barged in on the officer in charge, a sleepy lieutenant

---

33 That's right, the government removed families from base housing when sending sponsors to Vietnam. As of December 1969, I'd been in the Air Force 12 years and had unpacked furniture into 16 addresses.

colonel. Making the most of a natural modesty, I told him withholding me from the fight would weaken the war effort, perhaps fatally. He was underwhelmed. This little unpleasantness in Vietnam had gone on for some time and seemed likely to last a bit longer. I'd get my chance. Plus, I'd already missed the first day of academics. I mentioned how I was an honor graduate of every variety of survival school and could recite the academics from memory. No sale.

So I hung around Clark, using some of the time at the firing range. I tried out the M-16 rifle, still fairly new but already standard issue for infantry. Made of aluminum alloy and plastic, it fired 700 high-velocity bullets a minute, giving it great stopping power. I thought its all-around usability would make the M-16 a classic.

By contrast, aircrews still carried the .38-caliber revolver for personal defense. This clunker was inaccurate at anything beyond about 25 feet, for me at least. Its worst feature: having to reload after six rounds, an act that, if you needed to do it quickly, required either specialized equipment or superhuman dexterity, reinforced by lots of practice. It was not easy to visualize how it could be done at all in the warmth of a close-quarters dialogue with potential captors. (A cleaned-up version of the standard aircrew assessment: file off the sights so it won't hurt so bad when they stuck it where the sun never shines.) Our counterintelligence guys had a cut-down version of the timeless Colt .45, which would have been a much better sidearm for aircrews, but I couldn't figure out how to pry one loose from the system.[34]

Jungle school turned out to be enjoyable, plus I learned quite a bit in the academics. Negrito guides—small, nearly pygmy-sized mountain people indigenous to the Philippines—provided much

---

34 Years later, the services would standardize on the Beretta 9 mm, a fine personal weapon carrying a 14-round clip, plus one in the chamber, if you wore it that way, and (for me, at least) as accurate as the much loved Colt .45. One of the many small pleasures of being promoted to brigadier general was that the Air Force issued you a personal Beretta, which you could subsequently buy and take into retirement.

of the field instruction. One of the two winning strategies for jungle survival: parachute into a banana grove. Following this simple advice pays a multiple dividend: concealment, housing, and nourishment. It also would help to find a friendly Negrito, it being amazing what they could do with a machete and a banana tree.

The last part of jungle survival was the escape-and-evasion problem. At sundown, we got a head start, then they turned loose the Negritos. Each of us was given three chits the Negritos could trade for bags of rice. We had to give up a chit to each Negrito who made contact. If we ran out of chits, we were captured, becoming POWs for the night. Since Negritos were great trackers and liked rice, most of the class ended up in jail.

The exercise area was an enormous stretch of jungle and mountain. I set off alone, going as fast as I could in a straight line to what I figured was the most isolated edge of the area, climbed up to a high, limestone ledge that had good cover, and went to sleep, notwithstanding moderate to heavy rainfall. I came in next morning, damp but with all my chits.

That's the other strategy: don't get caught.

Now the problem was getting to Vietnam. Aircrews completing jungle school were scheduled for the next inbound passenger transport, coming through in a couple of days. Waiting for that to happen would get me to Tan Son Nhut, the main administrative base near Saigon, following which I'd need to get a hop to my base of assignment, Phu Cat. I went down to base ops looking for a better deal. By pure luck, a C-141 loaded with 20 mm ammo was filed for Phu Cat, leaving immediately. They had lots of room, but couldn't carry passengers with hazardous cargo aboard. So I got myself manifested as an ammunition courier and arrived at Phu Cat on Friday evening, 20 December 1968, in time to be included in the year-end troop-strength count, which would show a record-high 540,000 of us in-country. So far, we'd lost 30,000 killed, the rate for 1968 being about 1,000 a month.

By late 1968, we were flying F-100s at four in-country bases: Bien Hoa, on the outskirts of Saigon; and Tuy Hoa, Phan Rang, and Phu Cat—these three strung out along the coast, with Phu Cat the farthest north.[35] As the Army divided up the real estate, Phu Cat was part of II Corps.

US engineers built the air base at Phu Cat in 1966, plopping it down on top a 3,000-foot dirt strip the French had scratched out. It occupied just barely high ground, a pushed-up flat spot sitting in rice-growing lowland, with mountains on three sides. The 37th Tactical Fighter Wing stood up there in March 1967. Just over a year and a half later, as I arrived, the wing had three regular fighter squadrons assigned, the 355th, 416th, and 612th, and Iowa's Air National Guard squadron, the 174th. About half the 355th's pilots and maybe 75 percent of its enlisted troops were also Guard, mostly from New Jersey and Washington, DC. The war was already advanced in years, and the active Air Force was beginning to show signs of wear. We needed help from the Guard guys to sustain the effort.

In addition to its fighter squadrons, Phu Cat had rescue choppers (HH-43s), AC-47 gunships, C-7 light cargo lifters, EC-47 electronic warfare aircraft, C-123 Ranch Hand spray aircraft, and both RF-101 and RF-4 reconnaissance (recce) birds. A squadron-sized unit of high-speed forward air controllers, officially called Operation Commando Sabre, was known by its call sign, Misty.

Base facilities were surprisingly good. Naturally, we had a chapel, library, post office, Officers Club, and barbershop (haircuts, 35 cents). But Phu Cat also boasted a swimming pool, a Korean laundry, a well-stocked BX, evening classes offered by the University of Maryland Extension Division, even a nine-hole golf course fashioned from former rice paddies. Aircrews lived in two-man portables, demobilized trailers set on concrete pads. These featured

---

35 Two additional in-country fighter wings, one at Cam Ranh Bay, the other at Da Nang, operated F-4s.

a shared bathroom separating single bedrooms at either end and swamp coolers designed to work until needed. My trailer mate was a recent pilot-training graduate named Gib Ahl. We partnered in paying "mamasan" a few dollars a month to keep the place cleaned up. Like the VC they probably were, mamasans wore black cotton "pajamas" and conical straw hats. They usually hunkered down in a squat, an uncomfortable-looking position they could hold for hours.

Each squadron clustered its aircrew trailers around a central patio, enclosed by self-help—that is, with volunteer labor and liberated materials—to create a hooch. The design features and workmanship in these hooches reaffirmed my conviction that it was impossible even to guess at the talent residing in a fighter squadron. A center of social activity, squadron hooches would have put the Officers Club out of business, except there was almost nothing to do, off-duty. After you visited the BX, barbershop, and laundry, you still had a year to go.

One reason for the lack of activity: nobody went off base. For some reason, we didn't feel welcome out there. Before US and Korean ground forces cleared the area in 1966 it was a VC training center. Route 19, the main road carrying supplies from the port at Qui Nhon into the Central Highlands, ran along the base's southern edge. A few miles west, at An Khe and Mang Yang, Highway 19 cut through mountain passes known as Ambush Alley. In 1954 the French lost three crack battalions there in a fight with the 803rd Vietminh Regiment. (Showing a flair for such things, the French buried their dead standing up and facing west, toward Paris.)

It was our good fortune to be colocated with the ROK Tiger Division. The Koreans gave us reasonably good security, being well known for not taking any snot off anybody. Nevertheless, we merited the occasional Vietcong assault. One particularly memorable foray occurred the night of 23 February 1969, when VC fighters attacked more than 100 targets across the country, including some in Saigon. Sappers penetrated Phu Cat's perimeter defenses.

Our security force captured a couple, along with a quantity of B-40 rockets, some hand grenades, and other explosives. We all kept a flak jacket and steel hat under our cots; this incident made me appreciate these, as well as the sand-filled blast walls bunkering my trailer. Still, the ROK presence made us rather safe at Phu Cat. We took nothing like the pounding they were getting at Bien Hoa or Da Nang.

We also had the US Army on station, in the form of a battery belonging to the 41st Artillery Group. From time to time, they fired in support of distant ground operations, but they seemed to shoot most of their rounds into a nearby hill we called Target Mountain, calibrating their guns, I suppose. Local knowledge: don't worry about an earth-shattering "BOOM! SWUSHHH." That's the good noise. It's when you hear "SWUSHHH, BOOMMM!" you'd better duck.

The wing had world-class leadership. The commander was Col. Leroy Manor, who would attain the rank of lieutenant general and achieve some fame as planner of the Son Tay Raid. The vice commander, Col. Richard Henry, was also destined for three stars and major responsibilities in the space business. The director of operations was Col. Wilbur "Bill" Creech, later the enormously influential four-star commander of Tactical Air Command. I had an alumni connection to Creech, who was an early-vintage Thunderbird wingman. Creech's assistant was Col. Evan Rosencrans, a great guy, also later a three-star. Flying an overmatched P-80, Rosencrans had somehow managed to get a MiG kill in Korea.

My orders assigned me to the 612th Fighter Squadron as a line pilot. I spent the first few days on mandatory briefings and indoctrination, a process compressed for me. By this point in the war, most of the experienced fighter jocks had already done time in Southeast Asia. A few got caught in schools or controlled assignments, like my two-year Thunderbird tour, and showed up late, but by and large, the Air Force was emptying the cupboard, cleaning out Air Training Command, flushing older officers out of staff jobs, even retreading a few bomber or transport guys who would return to their professional mainstreams with bragging rights. The pattern held for many 612th aircrews, so even though the squadron was fully manned, it was rather short on experience. They knew I could help, as soon as they got me through the new-guy treatment, and cut corners where they could. I flew my first combat sortie on Boxing Day, then was scheduled every day, finishing December with six combat sorties and 8.4 combat hours.

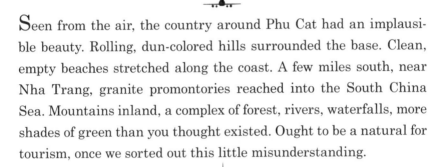

Seen from the air, the country around Phu Cat had an implausible beauty. Rolling, dun-colored hills surrounded the base. Clean, empty beaches stretched along the coast. A few miles south, near Nha Trang, granite promontories reached into the South China Sea. Mountains inland, a complex of forest, rivers, waterfalls, more shades of green than you thought existed. Ought to be a natural for tourism, once we sorted out this little misunderstanding.

Bob Hope visited the base on 28 December. The noted pro football player Rosey Grier was part of Hope's troupe, but the real draw was Ann-Margret and a chorus line called the Gold Diggers. Women did come by Phu Cat on occasion. Red Cross girls, "Donut Dollies" stationed at Qui Nhon, visited weekly but did not tarry. From time to time, a touring girl rock 'n' roll band from Korea entertained. Otherwise, not much, so the sight of Ann-Margret and her Gold Diggers was uncommonly welcome.

Bob Hope did two shows a day all over the theater during the Christmas season. Like generations of GIs, we gave him a stormy reception.

Two kinds of tasking were given to in-country fighter squadrons. The first was called "preplanned" because higher headquarters laid on some number of these sorties the day before, allowing aircrews to do mission planning. Most preplans tasked two-ship flights to take off, proceed to a location and check in at a stated time with a forward air controller.

The in-country FAC was an Air Force pilot assigned to an Army battalion. Living with the battalion, he knew their people and capabilities and, most important, what they were trying to get done on any particular day. Then, flying slow, propeller-driven aircraft—mostly O-1 Birddogs—he was aloft over his allotted real estate, getting to know it by heart. Airborne, he had a lot to do. He kept track of Charlie, often dodging ground fire and shooting back with a sidearm or M-16 stuck out the door. In addition to keeping his little bug smasher right-side up, he had three radios going all the time: FM with forward ground elements, VHF with the battalion tactical operations center, and UHF with arriving and departing fighter aircraft.

On initial radio contact, the FAC found out how much playtime we had and served up a standard briefing: target description, desired munitions effects, attack vector, location and distance to nearest friendly troops, and so forth. When we were in visual contact, he rolled in and fired a 2.75-inch folding-fin rocket with a white phosphorus (WP, or "Willie Pete") charge that produced a puff of smoke on impact. If the mark was on target, the FAC said, "Hit my smoke."

Often, there was a fair amount of bluster here. When there was no real target, you might as well hit his smoke as anything else. It always reduced my skepticism if the FAC said something like, "OK, from my smoke, look 50 meters north where the road passes the edge of the tree line. The target is just off the west side of the road in those trees." In any case, the game was, do what he said. He watched us through every roll-in and cleared us to release on every pass. No clearance from him, no drop.

The usual format was to release bombs one or two at a time,

climbing back to safe altitude after each pass. This gave you an opportunity to assess your work, see what the wind was doing, and if needed select offset aim points. If the FAC liked your first result, he might move you to a new target. If he thought you could do better, he'd keep you on the target and issue adjustments. An altogether less satisfactory technique was to clean everything off the wing on the first go, something called "one pass, haul ass." If you didn't score well the first time, it was all over. The only good excuse for doing this was you had to get home for some reason. (The Navy often used this tactic because they wanted to get back to the boat with enough gas to miss the wire a couple of times and still divert to Da Nang.) Pilot concern about ground fire was not so good a reason. The in-country gun threat was not worrisome enough to rule out multiple passes on a target.

Besides preplans, there was a second category of mission called "immediates." Action might develop quickly, as when the VC or North Vietnamese Army (NVA) attacked, and for fleeting targets there wasn't time to preplan. Flights en route to preplanned targets could be diverted to immediates. Alternatively, each squadron kept a few jets on 15-minute alert, aircraft that could be scrambled for immediate tasking. In periods of intense activity, such as during the Tet Offensive, we might have lots of what the Air Force called "lucrative" targets, and the number of aircraft on alert was increased. But usually you scrambled off the alert pad only to find there wasn't much happening when you got to the scene. Even so, if you were lucky, immediates could be interesting in that there was at least the possibility somebody needed help. The best such case was called "troops in contact," meaning Big Green had cornered some guys in black pajamas. The ensuing sortie was essentially the same as a preplan; that is, you checked in with a FAC and did what you were told.

When finished, the FAC scored your results, providing battle damage assessment, or BDA.

As for weaponry, in the dive-bomb mode, we launched with four 500-, 750-, or 1,000-pound low-drag bombs, called slicks. These fit the World War II image of a free-fall munition: a streamlined body, a fuse in the nose and some stabilizing fins in back. The fuse had a little propeller on the front that had to turn through a few RPMs before it would arm, and some safing wire that kept the propeller from turning until the wire was withdrawn as the bomb fell away from the aircraft. Slicks were usually set to detonate on contact, but sometimes were delay-fused so the bomb penetrated before going off—handy for getting through jungle canopy or down into bunkers—or set up with fuse extenders ("daisy cutters") so the bomb exploded a few feet above ground level, greatly enhancing blast and fragmentation effects. Occasionally, we used daisy cutters to blow away foliage and prepare a landing zone for helicopters.

Instead of dive-bombing, maybe half the time we attacked from low altitude, either level or in a shallow dive. For such attacks we used high-drag bombs (snakeye), napalm, or a high-drag/napalm mix (snake and nape). High drags were simply slick bombs rigged with a retarding device—big, alligator-mouth fins that opened to decelerate the munition once it came off the wing. Napalm was basically gasoline turned into jelly by mixing in some aluminum thickener, carried in a canister that tumbled and slowed down quickly after release, resulting in the same sort of safe separation accorded by high drags.

We always launched with hot guns, but strafing was a sort of dessert. We would offer the FAC the option and, if he didn't want it, we'd contact a controlling agency on the way home and check for targets of opportunity.

Strafing, or using high drags and napalm, got us pretty close to the target, making for much greater exposure to ground fire. The trade-off was very good accuracy, meaning this was what we did when working really close to friendly troops.

To borrow from Tolstoy, all good bombs are alike, but every bad bomb is bad in its own way. The worst and most devastating mistake is to kill friendlies. We went to very great lengths to avoid fratricide. This was the main reason we had Air Force people with every Army combat battalion and did not bomb unless the FAC had real-time radio contact with the troops. Nothing I saw justified increasing the risk the grunts were taking already. There had been a few in extremis cases of our guys calling fire down on top of themselves. Otherwise, their safety was an absolutely overriding consideration.

Another bad mistake, dropping a dud bomb, was mighty easy to do. All combat aircraft have mechanisms for deliberate safe release or jettison of external stores. Prior to drop, you needed to check and double-check that the switches were set for *live* release. Moreover, munitions typically have built-in safety features that require some time-of-fall after release to allow for safe separation. Bombs dropped too late, so they didn't have time to arm before impact, or mistakenly dropped safe because of a switch-setting screw-up, or even those jettisoned during an in-flight emergency were, for sure, handed over to the other guy as high-explosive raw material, saving him a miserable trip down the Ho Chi Minh Trail.

And if you worked at it, you could defeat even the cleverest munition safety features and get caught in the fragmentation pattern of your own bombs. This kind of fragging should be easy to avoid, but it was always tempting to get closer to the target, to refine the aim point just a little more. Also, pilots can experience a sort of target fixation, which is unhealthy. For whatever reason, a late release might leave you with too little time to pull away.

Fragging yourself was embarrassing and couldn't be covered up. At the end of every sortie, aircrews did a careful walk-around with the crew chief. Any small holes in the airplane had better be round, like bullet holes, not jagged, like bomb fragments.

Gun defenses of primary interest to the pilot fell into two classes: machine guns, generally .50 caliber or smaller, and antiaircraft artillery (triple-A), usually larger than 20 mm.[36] The triple-A round is explosive and generally incorporates an automatic self-destruct feature meant to protect the gunner by blowing up rounds that miss so they come back to earth in small pieces. Small arms and machine guns fire solid metal slugs that will not self-destruct.

As far as I could tell, there wasn't any triple-A in-country. Here, the threat was limited to small arms and machine guns. These would be effective up to maybe 3,000 feet max, so above this height you might as well be home in bed. When we did come down for low-altitude attack, the gunners had to figure out how to hit us. Like skeet shooters, they needed to predict where we'd be in a few moments—the bullet's time-of-flight—and fire at that point, a procedure taking some skill. One of our great advantages was that, unlike clay targets, we could adjust our speed and direction and therefore the gunner had constantly to update his guess about where we'd soon be, a process called target tracking. Tracking is not at all easy to do, so ground gunners sometimes resorted to another tactic: pick out a likely impact point and fire as many projectiles as possible at that point, hoping to score hits as the aircraft flew through the barrage. The technique used in South Vietnam was for the most experienced or skillful soldier to chose the point to be barraged, then the other troops mimicked him, firing on full automatic at his signal. Obviously, barrage fire is quite inefficient and wasteful of ammunition—really a desperation measure—and should be seen as evidence that something much better than small arms or machine guns is needed to defend against competent, high-speed attack.

Certainly, I was convinced I had an overwhelming advantage in the in-country contest with earthmen. I spent almost no time

---

36 Both "caliber" and "millimeter" refer to bore diameter—that is, the width of the projectile and corresponding opening of the barrel. The British/US usage is to measure this in inches, with the result written as a decimal fraction; i.e., .38 caliber. Thus, a .50 caliber machine gun has a projectile width of half an inch.

straight and level lining up a target, instead flying a constantly turning flight path (a curvilinear approach) until just prior to weapon release, then rolling out momentarily, punching off the munition, pulling hard (5 to 6 *g*'s) until my nose broke the horizon, turning aggressively in either direction, and continuing the pull-up to safe altitude. My unpredictability meant it was going to take a pretty good gunner to get me, and even then he'd need some luck— what we called a golden BB.

Although we did not have in hand the technology to be effective at night, Charlie waited for sundown, and it was important he not get a free ride. For one kind of night tasking, the intelligence guild down at Military Assistance Command-Vietnam's Saigon head- quarters simply selected geographic coordinates where there might be activity. We launched and made radio contact with a controller at a ground radar site who vectored us for a medium-altitude, level run at the coordinates. We dropped our bombs simultaneously on a countdown from the controller. The radar system supporting this type of attack was called Sky Spot. Our name: Sky Puke. It was very unlikely we did any worthwhile damage.

We sometimes made visual attacks at night. AC-47 gunships supported us, using high-illumination parachute flares. At inter- vals, they'd dump a flare, lighting up a small piece of acreage. A FAC then marked the target, or sometimes the gunship would mark by strafing, a spectacular show when its side-firing Gatling gun blazed away in the dark. Typically, night visual attacks were made with high drags or napalm, using shallow dive angles. We worked in and out of the milky, inverted bowl of flare light. It was a weird sensation, the sudden transition from visual conditions under the flare, up into the dark, on instruments, then back again into bright light, a stark, descending terminator separating the two phases. Easy to get disoriented. The flares sometimes burned out before hitting the ground and hung there, waiting to be run into. Often the ceiling and viz were right at the margins of workability, adding excitement. Maybe the worst part was you could see the ground fire coming back at you, fire you didn't even suspect in the daytime. Not a lot of fun, but the sorties I flew were down south, where the Mekong had produced one of the world's great deltas, opening into the South China Sea and creating fertile land at the rate of about 100 meters a year. It was hard to know whether we were advancing or retarding the growth rate with our swimming-pool construction.

But at least down in the delta you wouldn't be banging into any hills.

—✈—

Occasionally, we got tasked to seed antipersonnel mines along suspected infiltration routes. The payload consisted of many tin-can-sized bomblets, each with attached trip wires that spun out some distance on ground impact. In theory, anybody coming down the trail would have to be careful, especially at night.

Mine laying was not a sought-after mission. The mines came in tube-filled dispensers, streamlined canisters carried under the wing. At the target, we fired a small explosive charge that blew a plug off the front of the canister so wind pressure could enter and force the mines down the tubes and out the back. It took about 15 seconds to empty the tubes. During this interval, we were committed to straight-and-level flight; any maneuvering would cause the mines to strike the airplane. In addition, there was a speed limit above which, even straight and level, the mines would impact aircraft tail surfaces. So here we sat, at low altitude, straight and level, slower than we'd like, along a suspected infiltration route, just where you were most likely to get whacked.

Our enthusiasm for this mission was not increased by reports that Charlie just collected the bomblets and used them to make booby traps.

—✈—

One kind of preplanned mission I did like: escort duty. In the Central Highlands, Pleiku and Kontum were kept supplied by convoys that ran up Route 19, from Qui Nhon through the pass at An Khe,

Indian country almost all the way. When tasked, we ran a continuous weave over the convoys, ready to jump anybody who stuck his head up. We also flew escort for AC-47 and AC-123 gunships, good at working over jungle areas with their side-firing cannon but unable to defend themselves well.

And we flew top cover for the C-123s used in Ranch Hand missions. These guys, call sign Cowboy, sprayed herbicide to remove foliage and open up infiltration routes to observation. Commercial agricultural chemicals were used, shipped to Vietnam in color-coded drums, the origin of the names Agent White, Agent Blue, Agent Orange, and so forth. Flying old, slow aircraft, Cowboy was committed to low-altitude, straight-and-level flight, usually in three- or four-ship echelon. They were grapes, ripe for the picking.[37] The VC and NVA responded ferociously with small arms and machine guns—very hard for us, weaving overhead, to see, and impossible to hear. Usually, our first indication of trouble was a radio call from one of the Cowboys saying he was taking ground fire. The trick for him was to keep his voice as matter-of-fact as possible; for us, it was to see something through the foliage along his flight path. We usually had a slow FAC with us, but even he would have a job spotting the source of ground fire. In any case, we wanted to get our nose on the bad guys quickly, without waiting for the FAC to put down a mark. Cowboy sometimes helped by kicking a smoke grenade out the door the moment he started taking fire. We looked for something along the ground track behind that smoke. We carried pods of 2.75-inch folding-fin rockets, effective when you don't know exactly where the target is and need to scatter ordnance over a wide area.

I was enthusiastic about escort missions of all types because these people genuinely needed the support. More than once,

---

37 One notable survivor, a C-123 called Patches, is in the Air Force Museum at Wright-Patterson AFB, Ohio, carrying the honorable scar tissue of some 1,000 bullet holes.

someone sidled up to me at the bar and said, "When you guys weren't overhead, we got our butts kicked."

A key consideration when working with Agent Orange: keep your oxygen regulator set at 100 percent.

It was soon clear the Army was running the in-country war, including the air part. Down in Saigon, our senior headquarters, Seventh Air Force, performed mostly administrative functions— not a criticism, just a statement of fact, often forgotten in the subsequent debate about airpower's effectiveness. Wars should be fought jointly, and the Military Assistance Command-Vietnam was in theory a joint command in overall charge of the effort. Repeatedly and unsuccessfully, the Air Force argued for representation on MACV's senior staff, including making a determined effort to have an airman assigned as second in command. Gen. William Westmoreland, in charge of MACV for much of the critical period of the war, wouldn't have it. Army officers filled the deputy job and all the important staff positions, making MACV a thinly disguised Army headquarters.[38] The situation did not improve under Gen. Creighton Abrams, though by common agreement he was a more talented commander. Nobody in authority at MACV seemed to have any idea about what to do with airpower.

The result was just the sort of Air Force the Army had always dreamed of. It amounted to giving supported Army battalions a guaranteed number of sorties per day, whether or not they had anything in front of them worth blowing up. We pushed close air support, rather than waiting for it to be pulled. The Army liked it and because Vietnam lasted a while, got used to it.

After the turn of the year, I learned that my Thunderbird replacement, Jack Thurman, had been killed in training. On 9 January,

---

38 The Seventh Air Force commander did carry the honorific title of MACV deputy commander for air.

he and Mike Miller, now the lead solo, somehow collided while practicing the Four Point. Mike got his damaged jet back to Nellis, but the team had a two-and-out policy. Have one accident, like mine at Del Rio, OK, as long as it's the airplane's fault, not yours. Have a second accident, it doesn't make any difference whether it's your mistake or just bad luck. Counting his midair on the way to Paris, this was Mike's second accident. So he left the team, replaced by a superstar weapons school IP named Mike Kerby, and the Thunderbirds began a period of five-ship, single-solo shows that lasted seven years.

Winter is the time to fly in Vietnam. Temperatures are mild, nights cool, the flying weather as good as it will get. I logged 25 sorties in January, all of them as a flight lead. On 23 January, I logged my first combat hours as an IP. At that point, a month in, I was checking out the new guys. I closed January with 31 combat sorties and 55.6 combat hours.

Bill Creech asked me to come by for a chat, the end of January. He had a problem with Misty, the fast-FAC outfit. Base security personnel used flares to signal for help when a patrol got jumped. Ordinarily, Misty pilots behaved well at the Officers Club, but occasionally some evil person would push one of them to the floor and force adult beverages down his throat. Once loosened up in this way, Misty pilots thought it hilariously entertaining to pop a flare out the window and watch the response. This got old quickly with the forces of law and order. Creech had previously called in Clyde Seiler, the Misty commander, and told him to knock it off. Seiler may or may not have taken this counseling seriously. He was from the Colorado Air National Guard, federalized and spending a year abroad. In any event, Creech was not a man to be fooled with. When his resolve was tested by an immediate repeat performance, he relieved Seiler of command and put the Officers Club off limits to all Misty officers.

Seiler left Misty in mid-January and returned to his squadron at Phan Rang. Dick Hepworth, the next senior officer in Misty, had joined the outfit only recently and so was not yet fully accountable for its off-duty behavior. Hepworth moved up to commander, and Creech offered me the job of ops officer, the number two. He explained that ordinarily I would not qualify for Misty, since I had not yet accumulated the required 100 combat missions, but he hoped I could help control the wildness of some of the guys.

Chapter 15

Misty

*If the . . . major highway to Washington were bombed
out, the disruption of United States supplies and services
would be enormous and the military consequences in
wartime would be grave.*

*Here it is hardly felt. Traffic and supplies simply
flow around and past the point of interruption and the
damage . . . is quickly made good.*
— Harrison E. Salisbury, *The New York Times*

North Vietnam was shaped like a funnel, bounded on the east
by the South China Sea and on the west by the Annamite Mountains. A heavily fortified demilitarized zone corked the bottom of
the funnel, so supplies moving through North Vietnam's southern
panhandle had to sidestep across the mountains into Laos. Here,
with unbelievable effort and at great risk, the North took over a
piece of real estate the size of Massachusetts and on it built and
maintained an extraordinary infrastructure that in many ways
mirrored the one constructed by Americans in-country, complete
with hundreds of miles of highway, communications centers, ammo
dumps, stockpiles of food and fuel, truck parks, troop bivouacs—
altogether, enough to sustain a field army, and all of it out of sight,
except for the trace of the road itself.

In the panhandle and along the Laotian bypass, we attacked traffic, roads, bridges, and suspected marshaling points. The weight of effort could get quite heavy, especially when bad weather or the various bombing "pauses" diverted sorties to road interdiction. At the outset, forward air controllers flying slower, propeller-driven O-1s or O-2s directed the attacks, just as they did in-country, but sturdier air defenses gradually spread south, and the panhandle, in particular, quickly got too dangerous for slow FACs.

In June 1967, Misty—the official name was Operation Commando Sabre—stood up at Phu Cat. The idea was to use two-seat F-100Fs as fast FACs to do the mission of visual reconnaissance and strike control in the higher-threat, out-country environment. Misty recruited a small group of pilots, volunteers drawn from all four in-country F-100 bases. The mission was going to be difficult and dangerous and everybody knew it, but volunteering for Misty meant a reprieve from tree killing, at least for a while, and it was about the only way an F-100 pilot could get involved in the out-country war, otherwise flown by F-105s and F-4s. Misty became a haven for the hardcore. A Korean War veteran and seasoned fighter pilot, Maj. George "Bud" Day, was Misty's first commander. His ops officer was Maj. Bill Douglas, a warrior type I'd known and admired when he was assigned to the 48th Wing at Lakenheath. Day, Douglas, and others of the initial Misty cadre worked out employment tactics, based on their own fighter expertise and the hard experience of slow FACs.

Many distinguished fighter pilots followed Bud Day and Bill Douglas into Misty. Don Shepperd (Misty 34) later left active service and signed on with the Air National Guard, rising to become its chief as a two-star. Dick Rutan (Misty 40) somehow managed to log 104.5 Misty missions. The half mission came in August 1968, when he was shot down and subsequently recovered. Rutan and Jeana Yeager would one day circumnavigate the globe on a single tank of gas in *Voyager,* designed by Dick's brother, Bert. Roy Bridges (Misty 60) became a test pilot, astronaut, space shuttle commander, general officer, and commander of the Air Force Flight Test Center at Edwards AFB. Ron Fogleman (Misty 86) served as the Air Force's 15th chief of staff. Lacy Veach (Misty 93) survived getting shot down on April Fools' Day, 1969, to become a Thunderbird solo pilot and astronaut. Jack Dickey (Misty 105) joined the outfit in mid-April, replacing me as ops officer when I moved up to commander. Hank Buttelman (Misty 142), the last Misty commander, had seven kills in Korea. By the time the squadron stacked arms in the spring of 1970, a total of 157 fairly good fighter pilots had earned the right to call themselves Mistys. I was Misty 94.

Bud Day managed just 21 hops before getting shot down in North Vietnam's panhandle. Captured, he spent the next five and a half years in jail. His escape attempts and steadfastness while in enemy hands won him the Medal of Honor. Day tells the story in a book titled *Return with Honor.*

Honor is a gift we make to ourselves, and Misty was nothing if not generous. In all, 35 of the 157 Mistys were shot down during their stay with the squadron, two of them twice. Seven were killed, three captured. Fully a third of all Misty sorties into the panhandle ended up in rescue efforts, often one Misty capping another, downed by ground fire. For some reason, the loss rate did not much abate when, in October 1968, President Johnson stopped all bombing in the North, a "pause" that lasted four years. As I joined the outfit, at the beginning of February 1969, Misty was flying seven sorties a day, all of them into southern Laos, site of the scenic Ho Chi Minh Trail.

The trail started at Mu Gia and Ban Karai, the two mountain passes that connect southern North Vietnam to central Laos. Major roads running up into these passes from the Vietnamese side split immediately upon exit into Laos, forming the beginnings of a network that cut at first through spectacular karst, cliffs built up from limestone deposits in which erosion had produced fissures, underground rivers, sinkholes, caves—all just perfect for hiding supplies

and guns. Then, in more open country, the trail continued south
to intersect Route 9, the old French road running west across the
waist of Laos from Savannakhet on the Mekong, through the important district center of Tchepone. Route 9 kept going east into South
Vietnam, passing Khe Sanh just south of the demilitarized zone,
and pressing on to Dong Ha on the coastal plain. (An evil-looking
offshoot branched into the A Shau Valley and on to Hue and Da
Nang, farther down the coast.) But most of the road traffic headed
south out of Tchepone, entering very rugged country—mountain-
ous, forested, cut up by rapid water. At intervals, offshoots swerved
into Vietnam, bumping into Special Forces outposts established in
blocking positions. Approaching the tri-border area, the trail joined
the old Route 110, the Sihanouk Trail, coming up from Cambodia and running west toward Kontum and Pleiku. A well-traveled
tributary continued south, penetrating northeastern Cambodia,
from which it threatened the strategic town of Ban Me Thuot. Still
farther south, near places known to Americans as the Fish Hook
and Parrot's Beak, tentacles menaced Saigon and the delta.

Interestingly, the North Vietnamese didn't call it the Ho Chi
Minh Trail. The Truong Son Mountains form the Central Highlands, running nearly the full length of Vietnam along its border
with Laos and Cambodia. For the North, the trail was either the
Truong Son Strategic Supply Route, or Highway 559, in honor of
the 559th Transportation Group, NVA road-building pioneers.[39]

—▲—

When North Vietnam defeated the French, it closed the deal at
Dien Bien Phu. Rebel Vietminh forces ran heavy guns, ammunition, and much other support out to that desolate spot over roads
that started as single-file jungle trails and were gradually widened,
smoothed and made worthy for truck traffic. In large measure, Dien

---

39 The numerals 559 memorialize the month (May) and year (1959)
the government of North Vietnam reached a formal decision to provide
active support to the insurrection in the South.

Bien Phu was a contest in which the French tried to shut down this supply line and the Vietnamese tried to keep it open. The outright winner, Gen. Vo Nguyen Giap, was still around as of 1969 and seemed not to have forgotten anything. On the other hand, Lyndon Johnson's national security adviser, McGeorge Bundy, questioned whether France's 1954 experience was "at all a useful analogy" for helping decide US policy. Defense Secretary Robert McNamara agreed with Bundy.

—··▲··—

To a close approximation, the tactical fighter mission in a theater of operations consists of three activities: air superiority, interdiction, and close air support. The classification of combat roles is also a list of priorities. We must take care of air superiority first because we need unimpeded access to airspace in order to do the other work. Beating the opposing air force is therefore job number one, though it's important to understand that MiG killing is not all there is to it. Hostile ground fire also reduces our freedom to use airspace. Thus, defense suppression—knocking out antiaircraft artillery, surface-to-air missiles, and the command and control systems that make integrated air defenses possible—is an essential part of the air-superiority task.

Interdiction comes second. Interrupting the other side's flow of personnel and matériel support is by a wide margin the most efficient way to wear down opposing surface forces. Along a line of communications, people and goods are bunched up—in supply ships, on troop trains, in road convoys—and can be dispatched in quantity at some distance from the front, never to become a factor in the ground fight.

As its name implies, close air support (CAS) is not done at a distance, but near enough to friendly troops that we must take safety precautions. Typically, an Air Force forward air controller is assigned to and serves with our ground units, making sure that CAS is done only in a way and at such times and places as the Army wants.

In truth, CAS is by far the least efficient way to employ airpower. Nonetheless, the Air Force can get enthusiastic about it, especially if our green guys are in trouble. In a troops-in-contact emergency, nothing feels better than doing close air support, and every airman will show up, even if all we can do is fly over and make noise. But, if we are effective at air superiority and interdiction, these efforts in themselves will likely tip the scales, and the Army will need a lot less close air support.

The Army's take on all this: the Air Force gives pride of place to air superiority because what fighter pilots want to do is chase MiGs, make ace and sleep between clean sheets. I plead guilty, though the charge would be more telling if the Army hadn't over the decades spent such large sums on ground-based air defenses. Clearly it does not savor the prospect of coming under air attack. But in the years since it became a separate service, the Air Force has fought the air superiority battle deep in enemy territory—over the Yalu, over Hanoi, over Baghdad—with the result that none of our soldiers has seen a hostile aircraft in more than half a century. As this is written, literally nobody serving in the Army has ever been attacked by enemy aircraft.

As for interdiction, the Army almost universally abhors it as a waste of sorties that should be given over to close air support. First, the ground commander has little or no say in interdiction targeting because the attacks occur well away from the front line and the safety of friendly troops is not an issue. Interdiction is an Air Force show. Then, too, the Army cites the record: interdiction has seldom—no, make that never—worked. In World War II, the Air Corps pulverized the Italian road and rail network behind the Siegfried Line, and the Germans withdrew only after fierce ground attack. In Korea, Operation Strangle proved similarly unsuccessful in rolling back North Korean and Chinese forces. Only the isolation of the Normandy beaches for D-day might be claimed a success for air interdiction, and special factors were at work in that case.

Close air support is what the Army controls, what it can see, and what it wants. Indeed, more than a few GIs are alive today because of a little judicious CAS. Therefore, the Army has been keen to see the Air Force equip itself with aircraft like the A-10, of such limited capability it can be used *only* for close air support.

The quarrel between the Army and Air Force goes to basic doctrine, the faith-based thinking done in each service. Airmen believe that in the American style of war, airpower is always necessary and will sometimes be sufficient, that it can and should be employed more or less autonomously to produce desired effects or even decide the outcome. Soldiers believe that airpower is important, even invaluable in a supporting role, but, always and ever, it is the engagement on the ground that counts. For the Army, the idea that airpower can never be decisive on its own has the authority of belief in a 4004 BC seven-day creation event, followed by a flood.

Here in southern Laos, the opposing views would once again be put to the test.

$$-..\!\!\blacklozenge\!..-$$

Initially, Misty pilots flew a four-month, or 60-mission, tour, after which they returned to their home bases and resumed regular aircrew duties. Because air defenses were not so tough in Laos, the mission limit had been raised to 100, a number that could in principle be reached in four months, though logging 25 Misty sorties a month required some enthusiasm.

A new Misty got his first five sorties in the backseat, balancing this out later with five in the front as he neared end of tour. Other than that, we took turns, front and back. The front-seater flew the aircraft. The back-seater served as a second set of eyes, helping find targets and spot ground defenses. When we found something, we called in fighters. The back-seater worked the radios, briefing on tactics and such basics as target elevation, wind, and known defenses, and suggesting vectors to the nearest friendly airfield and best bailout areas. He also carried a handheld camera for photo recce and to record bombing results. The front-seater fired rockets or sometimes strafed to mark targets.

Visual reconnaissance was the heart of the job, and it was an acquired skill, one reason we flew our first five missions in the backseat. Before every launch we studied the area in painstaking detail, using large-scale maps that plotted all known artifacts, especially the sightings of previous Misty flights. Over time a lot of junk had been deposited on the trail, some of it camouflaged to look like live equipment so as to invite attack. Our job was to find the real trucks and figure out where the guns were.

Most of us started off thinking it ought to be dead easy to spot movers, but these guys didn't want to be seen and anyway traveled mostly at night. Support facilities were also hard to find. We looked for likely truck parks, any sign of human activity, budding infrastructure, some gardening. By practicing a lot and using our imaginations, we could sometimes see something out of place—maybe a different tone of green or, back away from the road and high in the foliage, some light dust that wasn't there yesterday, a few straight lines instead of nature's complex curves. These we noted and photographed.

It was also important to look for signs of traffic and estimate its volume. In Laos, spring of 1969, a thick coating of dust hung in the trees on both sides of the trail, and every morning the road was wet for 100 meters in each direction from the exit of any ford.

Misty put up seven sorties a day, every day of the week, maintaining a continuous presence over the trail from before first light until we could no longer see in gathering darkness. Intelligence, weather, and other briefings started two and a half hours before takeoff, so the pre-dawn launches made for some early get-ups.

Inbound at medium altitude, we contacted Hillsboro, the airborne command center that managed the flow of aircraft into Laos. Everybody with ordnance checked in with them, and when targets of opportunity popped up, Hillsboro could redirect fighters from their prebriefed assignments. They expected us and knew we'd work the trail at low altitude from the tri-border region to Mu Gia Pass.

At length, we let down into the working area. Speed would build quickly, our F-100Fs relatively clean. Under the wings, we carried only a set of 335-gallon fuel tanks and two pods of marking rockets, each holding seven 2.75-inch Willie Petes.

At low altitude in the threat area, our tactics were (a) don't slow down and (b) jink. In the panhandle, Misty had tried to stay above 400 knots—*speed is life*—and at four to five thousand feet above terrain—*altitude is life insurance*—unless they had to go lower, either for a close look or to get under weather. In Laos, the trucks and other quarry hid under trees; you had to give away the altitude cushion to find anything. We offset the increased exposure by pushing the speed up to 500 knots. My rule: whenever the clock showed less than 500, right into afterburner and build it back up. I gave this no thought; it was automatic. With our external configuration, the Hun would just about sustain 500 knots in military power, but if I had to do any maneuvering or climb for any reason, I was in and out of burner constantly.

The other important Misty technique was flying a continuous random weave, or "jink," calculated to spoil a gunner's tracking solution by repeated, unpredictable change of the flight vector. I kept the airplane in a constant *g* and a half to 2 *g* turn. But jinking yourself out into empty jungle, while doing wonders for exposure, didn't get the job done. The trick was to jink and stay over the trail.

On the deck, we began looking for trucks. Drivers tried to pull in before first light, but maybe a vehicle had broken down and couldn't get off the road. Their standard truck, a six-wheel Russian-built ZIL 157, would take five tons of cargo up to 40 miles an hour. These were good trucks—the driver could even adjust tire pressure on the move to accommodate varying road conditions— rugged and reliable but pounded hard by the trail. If one broke down and couldn't get off the road, they'd quickly camouflage it and try to set up guns nearby. The camouflage wouldn't fool us because it would be a brush pile in the middle of the road that wasn't there yesterday, and, with luck, we'd get there before the guns did. Our play: the back-seater called Hillsboro and started some iron heading our way. We'd go into a holding pattern, keeping an eye on the brush pile. The F-100F carried a mix of high explosive and armor-piercing bullets, 220 rounds loaded in its two 20 mm cannons. If the brush pile tried to get up and move before help arrived, we'd roll in and strafe.

Once the fighters showed up, they'd have a hard time seeing the truck. The eye had to be trained for this business. So we'd mark it with Willie Pete and tell them, "Trust us, it's a truck." If we ran out of rockets, we could mark by strafing. The rest was like shooting fish in a barrel, except we used high explosives.

If we were lucky, it would be brush piles, plural, since other trucks could get trapped in a column behind the cripple. If we caught multiples, maybe we strafed the back brush pile anyway, just to make sure they hung around. I was favored by such luck only once when, at dawn one day, I came across 13 trucks stopped on the side of a cliff—no way to U-turn out of there—a beautiful sight and one of my best mornings in Southeast Asia.

Very occasionally we spotted a single truck still moving, most likely a particularly aggressive driver who wanted to get that last kilometer in before calling it a day. This guy we strafed right away to get him stopped. Too bad, really. Less dedicated, he'd be safe asleep.

But usually there was no excitement, just empty dirt road. Then we started looking for what was different, what was there today that hadn't been there before, or maybe what should be there but wasn't.[40]

After about an hour on the road, we'd be low on gas and have to go to the tanker. Concurrently, the next Misty sortie would be descending into the area. Staggered launches kept at least one

---

40　Before this ended, I'd log 98 missions and 360-plus flying hours with Misty, almost all of it at low altitude over the trail, and never dodge a single bird. Where were the birds?

Misty, and usually two, on the trail from dawn to dusk. We tried never to spend more than 30 minutes in the threat envelope without another Misty around somewhere for mutual support. We did plenty of talking back and forth and if either of us found something, we both worked it, covering for each other during absences for air refueling.

We cycled twice to the tanker, making a total of three trips into the operating area. KC-135s orbited at 20,000 feet, "anchored" in color-coded tracks—yellow, brown, cherry, peach—at various points in South Vietnam, Laos, and Thailand. Misty used all of them, most commonly a track over the Central Highlands. The tankers monitored our working frequencies, especially the search and rescue freq, and would turn and fly toward the action when they knew Misty was headed their way on fumes.

Weather could render any of the refueling anchors nearly unusable, especially in the afternoon. Vietnam is in the East Asian monsoon zone. From October to March, a winter monsoon blows in from the northeast, drawing warm air off the South China Sea and feeding water and energy into towering thunderheads over the cordillera. The tanker guys did their best, hunting for calm air, but some of my refuelings took place in biblical rain and turbulence that scared me a lot more than ground fire. The front-seater took the first refueling, and he'd better not miss his initial hookup attempt. Second trip to the tanker, the back-seater got his chance, with something from the Budweiser food group at stake.

With two air refuelings, the average Misty sortie ran nearly five hours, most of the time spent at very low altitude in a continuous, high-speed jink. The backseat was tougher than the front because it was hard to get set, not knowing exactly where the guy up front was going with the airplane and being pretty well loaded down with maps, binoculars, and camera gear.

Finally, we would check out with Hillsboro, return to base, land, de-arm, taxi back and shut down. We debriefed in the maintenance shack for half an hour before catching a crew van back to the squadron for a painfully meticulous intel debrief of all we'd seen and done.

Start to finish, it was easy to throw 10 hours at a Misty mission. All of us were of the "some is good, more is better" school of flying, but doing this day in, day out, it was possible to build up a sore butt.

Back and forth, over and across, up and down the trail. Gradually you memorized it, acquired command of its twists and turns, knew what it would do next, could anticipate what you must do to stay on it—a job requirement, not just nice to have. Slash-and-burn agriculture made for seemingly permanent haze over Laos. Three miles was good viz, and at 500 knots you'd spend a lot of time groping for the road if you hadn't stored in memory every branch, detour, and piece of junk.

At scattered intervals, small grass huts stood some distance from the trail, usually a little cultivation at the side. A bucolic scene. We had blanket authority to attack anything that moved within 200 meters of the road, but the rules of engagement also said leave these huts alone unless we took fire from them.

Except, there were no friendly faces down there.

Chapter 16

Speed Is Life

And travellers, now, within that valley,
Through the red-litten windows see
Vast forms that move fantastically
To a discordant melody;
While, like a ghastly rapid river,
Through the pale door
A hideous throng rush out forever,
And laugh—but smile no more.
—Edgar Allan Poe, "The Haunted Palace"

I let down into sunny southern Laos one morning, the midmorning go, not o-dark-thirty, not descending into a black hole. I wanted to be on the deck at a river feature we called the Dog's Head, a convenient starting point for a run up the trail. North from the Dog's Head, I used standard tactics: a random weave along the road, making my flight path unpredictable, using full throttle and a touch of burner whenever airspeed dropped below 500. Shortly, the trail began a gentle climb up to a plateau called Chavane. Years ago the French had built an airstrip here so they could fly in rich people to kill tigers, a manly activity suspended for the duration. The road forked at Chavane, one branch running east into South Vietnam toward the Special Forces camp at Kham Duc, the other continuing south through the Dog's Head to Route 110.

Cresting the hills just short of Chavane, I spotted three aircraft coming at me in loose spread, leaving characteristic smoke trails that told me these were F-4s. This struck me as odd. There shouldn't be anybody down at low altitude in this part of Laos. I knew some of the guys out of Da Nang were testing the Phantom with spray defoliants, a much-detested mission because, like laying antipersonnel mines, it mandated low and slow flying to ensure good dispersal. But if these guys were doing that, they should be farther north. More likely, they'd finished a sortie, expended their ordnance and were sightseeing. They needed to climb and go home at medium altitude, above the gun threat. Anyway, I watched as they turned east at Chavane, heading back in-country.

As they made the turn, ground fire hit one of them. By now I was right on top of them. I watched as the two seats came out of the jet, one continuing the normal parachute-opening sequence. I circled, eyes padlocked on the other seat. It separated from the pilot much too slowly, then the chute streamered instead of opening, its human cargo taking too long to hit the ground, maybe because I was concentrating hard, trying to pry the parachute open by brain wave. But it wouldn't open, so I switched back to the good chute, tracking its progress into dense jungle north of the old airstrip. The canopy hung up in the trees like laundry, giving me a fix on location.

—⊿··—

Here in Laos, news of a downed airman traveled like blood in water, Misty usually located where the wet stuff was reddest. I capped the position and called Hillsboro to get rescue fired up. Rescue was well organized throughout the theater, but in-country pickups tended to be improvised, the helicopter swarm rallying from all quadrants. The out-country effort was more structured. A rescue coordinator—a C-130, call sign King—always stayed airborne. This version of the C-130 was also an aerial tanker and could refuel the rescue choppers—HH-53s, call sign Jolly Green. King and the Jollys worked with A-1s, heavily armed prop jobs that scrambled off alert pads at Udorn (call sign Sandy) or Pleiku (call sign Spad).

These A-1 guys were, at a minimum, courageous beyond belief. They flew into the toughest flak, took over on-scene command, and suppressed ground fire while Jolly Green came in for the pickup. If anything, the chopper crews had even bigger cojones.

King was used to working with Misty. Nearly a quarter of the first 93 Mistys got themselves shot down. We helped recover most of our guys, giving us unwanted expertise. Alone among nonrescue professionals, Misty had official certification for on-scene command of rescue attempts. In a hot area—almost always the case—we created local air superiority. That is, we directed fighter attacks to knock out the guns. Sandy or Spad would wait to be cleared in by us. Even so, they often flew into a steel wall, and we had to do some additional gun suppression. But if everything worked as it should, Sandy took over, checked out the area and cleared in the Jolly Green, then orbited overhead to cover him. Jolly had to come to a hover over the downed aircrew, most likely sending down a PJ, a highly trained pararescueman who helped get the downed flyer onto the hoist. The PJ did high-risk work, but I never heard of one being left behind. If Jolly came out at all, he'd bring his PJ with him, but he might have to stay in a hover for what would seem an eternity.

—··✈··—

Back at Chavane, I started hearing radio calls on guard channel. We had to be careful because so many aircrew survival radios had fallen into the wrong hands. Pilots established individual code words so they could authenticate themselves when they were trying to get rescued, but my guy was only partly coherent. He couldn't tell me his call sign or even his name, though he remembered he was flying out of Cam Ranh. He couldn't see his parachute, so couldn't tell me where he was *from* it. He sounded hurt, maybe in shock.

Relieved by another Misty, I went to the tanker for gas. Returning, I took over just as Jolly Green and some Spads approached from the south. The chopper made three attempts to hover in the vicinity of the parachute, getting shot up each time. Spad worked the jungle over, trying to keep the gunners' heads down. The downed pilot stopped talking, then the parachute canopy disappeared, yanked down from the trees. Jolly took one last look, getting his copilot wounded, and went home.[41]

No friendly faces down there. At least if you got whacked in the North, you stood a good chance of being taken prisoner. The North Vietnamese and their allies, the Pathet Lao, controlled all of eastern Laos, from China to Cambodia. Nearly 600 American aircrew men would go down here. Only nine ended up in North Vietnamese POW camps and were repatriated. It was not that they took no prisoners—at least two of our guys escaped captivity in Laos—but nobody was ever released from here. Thirty-plus years later, 421 US servicemen shot down in Laos remain unaccounted for—258 of them Air Force.

For the pilot of a modern jet fighter, guns should not be a threat. This would not be true if bullets were photons, traveling at the speed of light—which is why developments such as laser or "ray" guns are so interesting. With these futuristic weapons, the projectile is fast enough that for all practical purposes the target is stationary and you can just point at it. But with conventional ammunition, bullet time-of-flight is significant, and a gunner can't expect to hit a moving target he aims right at. He has to calculate the future position of the target and fire at a predicted intercept point in space. Working out how much lead to use can be quite a test. Modern air defenses employ radar or optical devices to determine target speed, range, and direction of travel and feed

---

41 Nearly 40 years later, in 2006, friends and family of the two F-4 crewmen made contact and gave me information on this 8 May 1969 incident: the front-seater, Maj. Bill Brashear; the back-seater, 1st Lt. Jerry Mundt; their call sign, Boxer 23. They were at low altitude because the mission was to seed the trail with antipersonnel mines. Their names are among the more than 58,000 inscribed on the Vietnam Veterans Memorial Wall.

this information to electronic computers that rapidly calculate the lead requirement—initially a "point" solution, good, literally, for only an instant. What the gunner needs is a "tracking" solution, one that takes account of target motion over time, a continuously updated prediction about future position that adjusts the aim point accordingly.

Plenty of variables not controlled by the gunner—range to the target, its speed and direction, its acceleration (the rate at which target speed and direction are changing), ammunition quality and ballistics, wind—complicate the calculation. Even against large, relatively slow World War II bombers, gunners faced long odds because high-altitude bomb runs increased the bullet's time-of-flight and required considerable lead for target motion. Antiaircraft artillery had good success in World War II mainly because the bombers were tied together in cumbersome formations and committed to long stretches of straight-and-level flight. These tactics allowed radar-aimed guns to make relatively accurate predictions about the target's future location. Against a small, fast, highly maneuverable fighter aircraft, the gunner's task is to "hit a bullet with a bullet." Moreover, fighter pilots are not locked into a single, stereotyped style of attack. They use a variety of tactics, approach the target from any direction, and can maneuver the aircraft, changing speed, heading, and g load virtually throughout the attack. In essence, the gunner must hit a smart bullet with a dumb bullet.

On the trail, there were few radar-laid guns. Typically, the gunner had to rely on iron sights and his own judgment to figure out a tracking solution—hard, but not impossible, and experience helped. But then he had to manipulate the gun and get it aimed in harmony with his lead estimation. Machine gunners usually stood in a trench or pit to bring the weapon up to eye level. With triple-A, larger than machine guns, the gunner occupied a seat on the gun pedestal. Gun manufacturers tried to reduce the workload with mechanical aids that made the barrel traverse in elevation (generally, the gunner cranked a hand wheel) and azimuth (sometimes he used foot pedals, but with smaller-caliber triple-A had to shuffle his feet to swing the seat around the gun mount). Still, manhandling either a machine gun or a triple-A piece could be hard work, especially to get the gun moving fast enough to follow low-altitude, high-speed targets.

If the gunner could figure out a tracking solution and if he could get his gun aimed, then he could score hits—if we cooperated by holding steady conditions of flight. So we followed the standard practice of jinking, changing something—heading, speed, altitude—at intervals shorter than the bullet's time-of-flight. If we made ourselves unpredictable, he'd hit us only if he was lucky. And if he was lucky, he wouldn't be a gunner.

Why then, did gunfire account for more than 80 percent of our losses in Southeast Asia? Well, many of the aircraft lost to guns were slow movers, especially helicopters, or fan jobs like those used by slow FACs, much easier targets. But guns also bagged lots of modern fighters, not all of them flown by careless or inept pilots.

In the North, guns were effective against fast movers largely because of the influence surface-to-air missiles (SAMs) have had on our thinking and tactics. SAMs guide to the target, adjusting the predicted impact point after launch, so they overcome the difficulties associated with projectile time-of-flight. In short, the SAM shooter has himself a smart bullet. Therefore, we considered the SAM our biggest threat and tried to defeat it first. The compromises required to handle SAMs made us more vulnerable to guns and interceptors. In the North, it was the presence of SAMs, netted in an integrated air defense, that created a system far more imposing than its individual parts.

But here in Laos, there were no SAMs (yet), or MiGs either. For now, it was a pure guns deal, and pure guns you should beat every time, unless you got careless, or unless somebody issued the other guy a silver bullet—which could happen if it wasn't your day.

As Misty's ops officer, one of my duties was to prepare the weekly operations summary. The OPSSUM went to Seventh Air Force HQ, in Saigon, becoming part of the official record of the war. Seventh added up all the OPSSUMs and forwarded a consolidated report to Washington, providing incontrovertible evidence we were winning.

For my first one, I wrote up a few pages and sent the draft down for review by Bill Creech. I got it back totally nuked—sentences crossed out, grammar changed, spelling fixed, whole new paragraphs penciled into the margins, nothing left of my original except the date/time group. The bad part: when I had the message retyped, it was better. I'd run into an officer who could write.

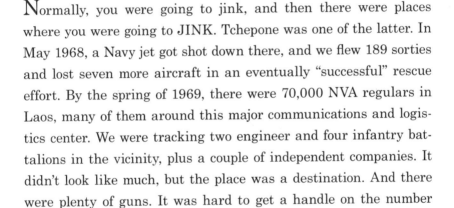

Normally, you were going to jink, and then there were places where you were going to JINK. Tchepone was one of the latter. In May 1968, a Navy jet got shot down there, and we flew 189 sorties and lost seven more aircraft in an eventually "successful" rescue effort. By the spring of 1969, there were 70,000 NVA regulars in Laos, many of them around this major communications and logistics center. We were tracking two engineer and four infantry battalions in the vicinity, plus a couple of independent companies. It didn't look like much, but the place was a destination. And there were plenty of guns. It was hard to get a handle on the number because the figure was growing so fast, but we must have identified a hundred gun positions around the town, any of which could be occupied on any given day.

I saw a lot of Tchepone and never took to liking it. Up around Mu Gia, the NVA had for some time been using radar-controlled 37 and 57 mm triple-A, and now larger-caliber 85 and 100 mm guns were moving into the pass, bumping radar-controlled medium guns south to Tchepone. Not good.

Ron Fogleman (we often used the more politically correct "Fogleperson") and I flew a Misty sortie on 4 March. I suppose the NVA might have wasted a little ammo had it been able to guess

that two future Air Force chiefs of staff were up there in the same
jet. Fogleman and I would have found the prospect quite believable,
but somehow our confidence did not communicate to the gunners,
who treated us with no special urgency.

Fogleman's first assignment out of flying school kept him in Air
Training Command as an IP, so this combat tour was his initial
fighter experience. From a technique standpoint, he was still a little short on finesse, and I won the refueling bets that day. But one
thing about Fogleman: he was a straight-out warrior. Everybody
in Misty went looking for trouble. Fogleman found it. He sincerely
believed he was supposed to beat the crap out of the other guy. It
was the other guy who got wounded, who was taken prisoner, who
died.

He was productive beyond belief.

The climate in Laos is monsoonal, but, for Misty, it was more like
three distinct seasons. In summer and early fall, southwesterly
winds off the Gulf of Thailand produced a pattern of low cloud and
rain that pushed the Mekong and its tributaries out of their banks.
We continued to watch for traffic, but flooding made the trail pretty
much impassible, so mostly we kept track of the guns and infrastructure development. From about October to the middle of May,
the wind shifted to northeast, bringing in moisture from the South
China Sea that was precipitated by the cordillera and dumped
mostly on Vietnam. (So when the weather was bad in Vietnam, it
was good in Laos, and vice versa.)

The northeast monsoon itself had two fairly distinct components.
A cool dry season lasted into January and gave us the best weather
for air operations, though even then visibility was not great because
of smoke and haze. Flying conditions gradually worsened during
the hot dry season, from February into May. Toward the end of this
period we were in for very high humidity, terrible visibility, and
occasional heavy thunderstorms.

My time to visit was during this hot dry phase of the northeast monsoon, and Laos looked somehow different. There was no short-age of tropical rain forest down there, but it was not the in-country green—more the faded gray and brown of a Chinese watercolor.

Bob Cassaro had me in his back seat one afternoon and introduced me to Cambodia. SAC's B-52s had already begun the secret (to the American people, only) bombing of sanctuaries there, the results plain to see, but for now Misty was supposed to stay out. Not a rigid observer of formalities, Cass thought several spots worth watching, one of them what we called the Customs House, on the Kong River just inside Cambodia. Many shipments up the Siha-nouk Trail flowed through there. A large, central building bristled with gun pits dug around it, and we liked to wake up the gunners in the morning.

Cassaro was National Guard, from Albuquerque, what we called the Taco Guard. A really good guy, he wore a sawed-off, lever-action .30-30 strapped to his thigh, sort of like Chuck Connors of TV's *The Rifleman*. I worried the thing would break his leg if he ever got popped and had to step overboard. But he did, and it didn't.

Crawling in and out of the jet, the back-seater looked like a rich tourist, sporting the usual combat package plus binoculars and a pile of maps. Often, he'd bring a hefty, hand-held camera, stripped out of the combat documentation pod some F-100s carried at an inboard, underwing station. We'd modified this so-called arm-pit camera with a pistol grip so it snapped pictures as long as we held the trigger down. It was literally a handful under any kind of *g* load but produced remarkably sharp images. We set the theater standard for shots of river fords, gun emplacements, transportation choke points. We photographed every piece of jungle that looked like it would make a good truck stop and got pictures of such reso-lution that intel analysts could sometimes spot a lattice framework holding up camouflage, which the next day we dutifully blew away.

One afternoon I decided to enter the area a little farther north than usual. I let down into the south end of the A Shau Valley, intending to follow the road from there to Tchepone. Even in bright daylight, the A Shau was darkly forbidding, a spooky place.

Reconnoitering along the valley floor, I could still pull in the Armed Forces Radio station at Da Nang. In early 1969, Jimmy Webb's tune "Galveston" topped the charts. In the second verse, Glen Campbell sings,

> Galveston, oh Galveston
> I still hear your sea waves crashing
> While I watch the cannons flashing
> I clean my gun
> And dream of Galveston.

And at the exact moment he sang about cannons flashing, I saw gun muzzles winking at me from the wooded hillside.

⟶▲⟵

By the spring of 1969, the fast-FAC concept had proved its value in combat. But the Air Force had decided to begin phasing out the F-100; indeed, F-4s would soon displace us from Phu Cat. At some point, the Phantom would have to take up the fast-FAC role. So one day I recovered a Misty sortie into Da Nang to help get the F-4s of the 388th Fighter Wing in the business. The 388th Wing had already formed the cadre of an outfit called Stormy and flown a few missions into Laos. My old friend Steve Richie, who in a second Southeast Asia tour would become the Air Force's only Vietnam-era pilot ace, was one of the organizers. In time, Stormy assumed responsibility for the area north from Tchepone to Mu Gia, while Misty concentrated on the real estate south from Tchepone to the tri-border region.

At Da Nang, I jumped into an O-2, a twin-engine bug smasher, and rode along with a Covey slow-speed FAC.[42] These guys still

---

42 At a 2004 reunion of forward air controllers, held in San Antonio, Texas, I was honored for making "FAC history" by flying over the Ho Chi Minh Trail twice on the same day, once as a Misty and once as a Covey FAC.

worked in Laos, above us at medium altitude, and I wanted to find out what they were doing.

In war it's hard to know what the other guy is up to, which comes as no surprise. He's mostly out of sight and never happy to give up information. You have to take it away from him, producing what we call "intelligence." But it is also quite difficult to figure out what your own side is doing, which is a bit of a surprise. You'd think information would be shared willingly, but this is not so.

In Laos we were doing things that even Misty, on the trail from dawn to dusk every day, was only dimly aware of. Some of it concerned strings of electronic sensors the "pinball wizards" had installed under a highly classified program called Igloo White. Supposedly, this sensor net, nicknamed the McNamara Line, kept track of movement remotely, allowing for rapid response. As far as I could see, it was an expensive flop. We also kept friendly road-watch teams in there on the ground, much of the action under CIA or Army Special Forces control. This activity was hush-hush for obvious reasons. Each day intel briefers told us we shouldn't bomb at certain coordinates, nothing more. We knew about road-watch teams only because, quite often, one of them got in trouble and we'd hear all kinds of radio chatter about something called a "prairie-fire emergency." Covey FACs (and even more so, Raven FACs flying out of Thailand) worked with the guys on the ground, so part of the reason I rode along with Covey was to try to find out what was going on.

It's always wrong to think you know what the good guys are up to. You'll see some of the picture, but a lot of information will have to be extracted in much the same way we collect intelligence.

With the bombing stopped in the North, the Navy and our squadrons stationed in Thailand looked to Laos for action. As with in-country bombing, a FAC controlled all attacks, so pretty soon Misty and Stormy couldn't handle all the business. Other fast FACs stood up: Wolf operating out of Ubon, Laredo/Falcon from Udorn, Tiger from Korat. Following the Misty model, pilots volunteered for what was at that point in the war the most hazardous flying job in Southeast Asia. Over the three years from July 1967 to July 1970, 42 fast-FAC aircraft went down. The loss rate of 4.37 per 1,000 sorties far surpassed any other flying duty during this period. In the first six months of 1969, a span that included my time in Misty, we lost 14 fast-FAC aircraft.

"High threat" is a relative term, as we were showing here in Laos.

On 11 April I got in a fight with a two-position 23 mm gun site manned by NVA professionals, dangerous because they held guns tight and let us bomb all around them, taking a hand only if we went after the specific target they were assigned to protect. They opened up on us after a flight of fighters under my control attacked what I thought was an interesting-looking pull-off next to the trail, maybe the exit into a truck park. The guns were only a few meters from the pull-off, but dug in, well camouflaged, hidden from us until they opened fire. Now they were active, meaning we'd found us a real target.

I didn't much like marking guns, and that went double for 23 mil. In my opinion, it was the best gun they had, featuring a rapid rate of fire and a high-explosive shell. Larger stuff, 37 or 57, fired a clip of four or five rounds, then the gunner had to drop in another clip. The single-shot 85 mm was even worse from the gunner's point of view because he had to reload after every shot. But 23 mm was fed into the barrel from a 50-round belt, and the gun could be configured with two, or even four barrels. So the gunner could fire a nice fat burst, pause to see how he was doing, correct, then fire again—and again, without stopping to reload. It did belch fire and smoke every fourth or fifth round, as unignited gases cooked off, the gun's only real shortcoming. This must have taken some getting used to for the gunners, especially at night, when it gave away their position, big time. Even in daylight, they were fairly easy to spot once they started shooting.

I switched the fighters to attacking the guns and ended up having to mark them several times—uncomfortable work. For a job like this, I'd roll in, aim for no more than one-potato, two-potato, fire the Willie Pete, and immediately break hard left or right, lighting the burner and making a rolling reversal back to altitude. But even this must not become a routine. In order to stay unpredictable, you occasionally have to make your unpredictability unpredictable.

It was a pretty good fight, but we eventually silenced the guns. There was nothing unusual about the episode, sort of standard Misty fare, but I was subsequently cited for the action, the only combat decoration of any significance I received. The award nomination was submitted without my knowledge, and it was a pleasant surprise—probably cooked up by Bill Creech—when I learned that Gen. George Brown, current Seventh Air Force commander and a future Air Force chief of staff, as well as chairman of the Joint Chiefs of Staff, would hang the gong on me during one of his occasional passes through Phu Cat.

—··♠··—

In Laos, several new munitions were getting their first combat trial. One of them, the laser-guided bomb, would have a huge impact on aerial warfare.

During the early stages of the war, we sent hundreds of sorties against the North Vietnamese main highway bridge at Thanh Hoa. The bridge was never put out of service, becoming something of a symbol for both sides. Then in the spring of 1972, after the long bombing pause, we attacked the bridge again, sending eight F-4s in with laser-guided bombs. The first four aircraft got several hits and dropped a span. The second four got more hits and knocked the span into the water. No aircraft were lost, or even scratched, and the bridge was not used again until the war ended.

A military revolution occurs when a set of technologies and associated operational concepts transforms the nature and character of war. Having the technology in hand is not enough. In fact, the cultural transformation that must take place to make good use of the technology is probably more important.[43] According to some studies, roughly a generation passes before a truly new technology is accepted, becomes part of routine military operations.

We had in hand precision-guided air-to-ground munitions, a revolutionary technology, but much work remained before we could fully comprehend and integrate this radical innovation. In the end, instead of sending packages of aircraft to attack single targets, in a style we might call consecutive attack, we would send single aircraft to attack packages of targets, opening up a new world of parallel attack.

But just now Misty was helping give birth to the precocious infant. Early samples from a munitions program called Paveway had arrived in Thailand, and some Fighter Weapons School guys had come out from Nellis to test tactics, get some data, and do a little damage at the same time. They flew two-ship, one jet carrying a laser designator and the other hauling 2,000-pounders modified with seeker heads that sensed reflected laser energy and guided the bombs to home on the spot. If there was anything we'd been itching to hit, we put in these Paveway munitions. Often, we picked a stretch of road the truckers would have trouble bypassing, like a narrow passage along the side of some particularly rugged karst.

---

43 Among many familiar illustrations of the point:

1) In 1753, James Lind, a British naval surgeon, published *A Treatise on Scurvy*, saying it was caused from a "want of fresh vegetables and greens." He recommended that vessels of the Royal Navy carry an extract of lemons to prevent the malady. Twenty years later, Captain James Cook followed the advice during one of his voyages and reported the complete success of the antiscorbutic measure to the Admiralty, a result so important the Royal Society awarded Cook a medal. The Admiralty instituted the practice of issuing lime juice rations to sailors a mere two decades later, in 1795.

2) The program for the Army-Navy football game played on 29 November 1941 carried a picture of the battleship *Arizona*, plowing through heavy seas, with the note, "It is significant that despite the claims of air enthusiasts, no battleship has yet been sunk by bombs."

Just at sunset, we'd mark the spot, and Paveway would punch a humongous hole, dead center, blowing away the entire roadway. Then we'd run mine droppers across the crater and seed it with antipersonnel mines. Always, without exception, when we came by for a look the next morning, they'd either filled in the hole or bypassed it.

They owned the night.

—··▲··—

The trail was an anthill at night. We tried to do something about it. C-130s, call sign Spectre, went in at night with side-firing guns and infrared sighting systems, policing the road at lower altitudes than they could safely fly in daylight. They had fair success picking off vehicles, but the infrared avionics were not yet really good, and Laotian humidity didn't help.

One of the Thai-based F-4 squadrons switched entirely to night operations, picking up the call sign Night Owl. Its pilots learned which light sources in the cockpit they could dim and which they had to tape over and how to use early versions of night-vision goggles. They became real experts in the highly specialized tactics of low-altitude munitions delivery at night.

It was true nothing moved on the trail during daylight, while Misty was there, so some headquarters weenie deduced we should be up there at night. That's when we got to experiment with flare dropping.

We took the marking rockets off one wing and replaced them with a pod that held four parachute-retarded flares. Now we had flares on one side and Willie Pete on the other. The idea was to fly across heavily used parts of the trail, punch off a flare, circle back for a look at what was happening underneath it, and mark any movers for attack by fighters under flare light. At a minimum, we'd harass and slow down traffic, and maybe even bag a truck or two.

For these night sorties, the back-seater took along a Starlite scope, liberated from the Army. The Starlite amplified ambient light, and with it we hoped to pick out trucks in the murk. But the thing seemed to weigh about five pounds under one *g* and was too long to point out the side of the canopy, limiting us to a forward scan of about 20 degrees on each side of the nose. Then, when you did see something, it was little more than a smeary image because of the millisecond or so of latency in the light-amplification process. This was probably no big deal for snipers or troops using it from a stationary position, but for us, the thing was virtually useless.

I flew a couple of night sorties and didn't like it much. It was black as the inside of a domestic cat, the viz was crappy, and the bad guys didn't use headlights, so the first trick was to find the trail. We knew the road by heart but had no way to locate ourselves at night except by taking bearing and distance cuts on a navaid some distance away—OK for high-altitude navigation but not near good enough to bet your life on in this terrain. It was one thing working at night down in the delta, where it was dead flat. Here in Laos, there were mountains all over the place, and you had to descend well below the tops to drop flares, or they would ignite too high and burn out before lighting up the trail.

I did get good results, once, when lucky enough to pop a flare at just the right moment. The place jumped at night. But it was no fun, and I tried not to act too happy when the authorities decided to stop the exercise.

✈

Lacy Veach and Ron Standefer got smoked and jumped out on April Fools' Day. Luckily, we recovered them quickly. At the end, Misty's loss rate in Laos was no better than the very bad results we chalked up in the panhandle, but this was our only aircraft loss during my four months.

✈

In April, Dick Hepworth completed a tour and went back to his regular squadron. I moved up to commander, a nice honor since I was still pretty junior. Though technically not a squadron, Misty approached squadron size in terms of the number of pilots and was maybe even more important when it came to scope of responsibility.

Also in April 1969, the number of US troops in-country reached its peak, 543,400. So far, 33,641 had been killed, exceeding the number of combat deaths in Korea.

Now in the chain of command, I thought about casualties a good bit. I was signed up to stop traffic down the trail, even if it meant losing people, but I looked for ways to do it and still keep all my troops.

Up at Chu Lai, the Marines had A-4s and their own fast-FAC outfit, call sign Playboy. Though a jet, the A-4 didn't have an afterburner, the shortcoming not critical because they FACed in-country for their own guys, mostly in I Corps. They were curious about us, so we arranged an exchange. A really good officer named Larry Adkinson came down to Phu Cat to take a look at our operation, and I put him in my backseat. We flew the late-afternoon mission, ending up at Delta 43, one of our landmarks.

South of Tchepone, Delta 43 had some well-traveled underwater bridges at the bottom of a steep valley, with triple-A everywhere. It was early evening, dusk, the trail just starting to wake up, and I managed to take a few rounds of ground fire. One bullet sang by the canopy so close we heard the little sonic boom created by its wake. Larry, not accustomed to the safety margins we enjoyed because of higher speed, felt like the lieutenant who kept getting hosed in *The Bridges at Toko-Ri*. He yelled, "Jink! Jink!" I was already jinking, but he wanted a show of sincerity, so I jinked hard out of there, using a touch of burner.

Looking over what I could see of the jet, we'd obviously taken a hit, the telltale jaggies of a small hole pocking through the top of the left wing. OK, so with official battle damage, we could either take it east and get feet wet, or aim it at Thailand, where the people were friendly and we could go off base for dinner. I headed west.

Larry and I landed at Udorn and went to the club for an industrial-strength cerveza. We were sitting in a booth when someone lofted in a large firecracker. Turned out one of the pilots at Udorn had finished a tour and was celebrating, making a little noise. But Larry Adkinson was a Marine, and from Chu Lai, where they took

lots of incoming. When he unfolded off the floor, he was looking to
get even. Eventually, he quieted down, and we went off base for a
little dinner.

By comparison with the Thai version, Mexican hot peppers
should be labeled "suitable for sissies."

Fighter pilots are perfectionists, inhabiting what William
Langewiesche called "cockpits of perpetual, small disappointment."
So we were unhappy we couldn't hermetically seal the trail. *Any*
traffic got through, we took it as a personal slight. Still, we probably did a better job than we gave ourselves credit for.[44] According to the official intelligence estimate (for what that was worth),
in a typical month about 7,500 tons of materiel got on the trail at
the top, and 2,500 tons got off at the bottom. Some of the leak-
age represented cost of business on the trail itself, but the interdiction effort clearly took a toll. The problem was, we also estimated
Hanoi's side of the in-country war required 15 tons of supplies *a
day*. If this was correct, we were doing our best—and it was pretty
good by any objective measure—and the other guy still got about a
month's worth of stuff, every week.

You had to keep telling yourself the target was the truck, not
the trail. But the trail had a personality, was alive. Often on the
move in his early and middle years, Nguyen Sinh Cung constantly

---

44 In its postwar official history, *Victory in Vietnam*, the North is frank
about the disruption we caused:

> *Because of our difficulties in obtaining supplies . . .
> after the summer campaign of 1969 a major portion of
> our main force army was forced to withdraw to our base
> camps and regroup . . . By the end of 1969 the enemy
> had retaken almost all our liberated zones . . . Units
> were forced to begin alternately eating rice for one meal
> and manioc the next. Some of our cadre and soldiers
> became pessimistic . . . Some deserted their units to flee
> to rear areas, some even defected to the enemy.*

reinvented himself, accumulating at least 50 aliases, the final, apparently satisfactory formula being Ho Chi Minh—Ho, "Shedder of Light." By early 1969 the road to which we gave his last and most celebrated name had outdone him, the revisions coming every day. We attacked choke points, and bypasses appeared. We rolled avalanches into the roadbed, and it slithered to the other side of the hill. We made mud and soon found corduroy. We cratered fords that somehow filled up and widened. More a maze than a road, the trail disappeared, returned to view, dissolved, emerged, contracted, expanded, split, reunited, vanished, materialized. We blasted a big chunk of Laos, the 600-year-old monarchy, the Land of a Million Elephants, to bony, lunar dust. Yet somehow the Ho Chi Minh Trail, itself the enemy, was always there.

Killing it was like trying to put socks on an octopus.

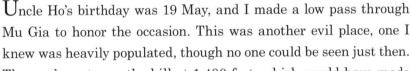

Uncle Ho's birthday was 19 May, and I made a low pass through Mu Gia to honor the occasion. This was another evil place, one I knew was heavily populated, though no one could be seen just then. The road went over the hill at 1,400 feet, which would have made for a considerable climb from the coastal plain in the early days of the trail, when porters carried the goods or strapped them to bicycles. Rugged peaks on either side of the pass topped out above 6,000 feet, reminding us the Annamites are an extension of the Himalayas. Everything about the place said, "Stick your nose in here if you want, Yankee Birdman, but be careful."

Misty kept the pass under close observation in daylight hours, but I did it by watching the Laotian exits. It was hard to recce the pass itself without making a shallow penetration into North Vietnam, at this point in the war something we were not supposed to do. Occasionally following instructions is another way fighter pilots maintain their unpredictability, but I found this order easy to obey.

My trailer mate, Gib Ahl, had increased his in-country mission total enough to qualify and joined the outfit as Misty 100. He was in my backseat one evening as we made a last run up the road a few kilometers north of Tchepone. I could barely make out the trail in civil twilight. Suddenly, we flashed by a single truck making good time to the south, one of those go-getters out for some mileage a little too early.

Ordinarily, we didn't make 360s on the trail. Survival depended on not coming back too quickly after going by, waking them up. If we saw something, we whistled past the graveyard, waited a while, then came back low and fast. Now, impending darkness wouldn't permit extended delay, but I pressed on anyway, as though I'd missed him in the gloom, continuing a lazy weave until out of earshot.

Then, in haste, I circled back. Estimating how far he would have driven, I was over the road just south of that point, set up for strafe, not jinking now, because I had to keep the guns trained on the trail. With unbelievable luck, I spotted him at the last moment and bunted the nose down hard to get the gun sight on his hood ornament for a split second. The cannon fired so rapidly you couldn't squeeze off a single round if you wanted to, like not being able to open and shut a refrigerator door without the light coming on. But the guns managed only the politest burp—a handful of rounds, surely the pure minimum. One round was enough. The truck, carrying ammo, cooked off in all directions, quite spectacular in the gathering darkness. Behind me, Gib celebrated his first result on the trail. Along the side of the road, a couple of 23 mm gunners joined in, sending elegant arcs of tracer toward us. I made another circle, jinking hard now, and a low, fast pass over the truck. Its door hung open, the driver splayed half in, half out of the cab.

Truckers were much admired by Misty. Their side called them "pilots of the ground," the metaphor causing no offense. We invented a teasing song about them—how lonely it was on the trail; how bad the food was when they got any; how they jacked it up to change tires, slippin' and slidin' in the mud; how they picked bugs out of their teeth when Misty poked holes in the windshield. But they did deadly serious work in the most dreadful conditions imaginable. They left their homes in the North and lived on the trail for months, even years, enduring monsoon weather, malaria, animal bites, constant hunger. Mail was collected once a month; an exchange of letters could take a whole season. They got to navigate through this desolate, beat-up countryside, in the dark, without headlights—a job that would be no fun on open turnpike at high noon, nobody shooting at you. And then we dropped *two million tons* of bombs on Laos—something like our total tonnage during all of World War II in *both* the European and Pacific theaters—most of it aimed at the trail. We seeded clouds to induce flooding, sprayed Agent Orange, mined the road, installed sensors of the electronic-monitoring McNamara Line. No doubt about it, we extracted a heavy price. In time, the North would fill 72 military cemeteries with the remains of those who built, manned and moved over the road. But move they did, putting through the cargo—the 122 mm rockets that pounded the Marines around Da Nang, the mines that killed our soldiers near the Parrot's Beak, the heavy equipment that in the end would surround and capture the Saigon of memory. Pumping hard, the truckers provided oxygen sustaining the North's ability to make war in the South. Their reward for each delivery: go get me some more.

The general view is that war long ago lost its personal dimension, the gory flesh-and-bone smell of face-to-face combat. Starting with spears, the technology for killing strangers has progressed through archery to long-range artillery and the ICBM, the workers now far back up the assembly line from the finished product. Even when armies do go toe-to-toe on a large scale, as in the Civil War or World War I, it has somehow gotten less personal, the sides mashed into fleshy, mindless, single-cell stuff, the fighting bacterial, formless. Mostly, nowadays, it's more antiseptic—rapid armored thrusts supported by air, the killing invisible, done at a remove.

But for some military elites—and here I'd include fighter pilots—combat retains a certain intimacy. The idea of fighting as just business, nothing personal, will survive the first whiz of bullets that pass close but die with the stilled breath of a good-guy truck driver.

—————

On 27 May, Maj. Clyde Seiler of the Colorado Air National Guard, who had returned to his unit at Phan Rang after Bill Creech removed him as Misty commander, was killed in action. His wings failed as he pulled up from a dive-bomb attack.

Chapter 17

Gutsy Gunner

O you leaden messengers,
That ride upon the violent speed of fire,
Fly with false aim.
      —Shakespeare, *All's Well That Ends Well*

In Laos, pilots being shot at had an understandable tendency to exaggerate the caliber and amount of ground fire. The guns were usually well hidden and often set up some distance from the airman's intended target. When fired on, the pilot had to guess at gun location and the type and number of rounds fired, important information if for no other reason than the matter would be probed by the intelligence mafia during mission debrief. At night, muzzle flash and the tracer stream provided visual clues. You could sometimes make out tracer even in daylight. The thing to remember: it's usually loaded every fifth round. You won't see the other four, and non-tracer ballistics are just different enough to be worrisome. As for muzzle flash, it could be pretty hard to see in bright daylight unless you were looking right down the barrel. Gun barrels smoke, and recoil kicks up dust around the site; sometimes you'd see these signs, sometimes not. Often the best indication somebody was shooting at you was a little row of puff clouds that appeared, often behind and above your flight path, when explosive rounds self-destructed as they slowed near the apex of their trajectory. These clouds get darker as gun caliber increases. In films about World War II, those black clouds appearing all around the B-17s are large-caliber triple-A rounds. If they detonated close to the airplane, it was probably because of proximity fusing; farther away, the round was self-destructing to keep metal from falling back in large chunks on the gunner's head. With small-caliber guns, you will not have this clue because the rounds are solid, not explosive, and do not self-destruct.

So, pilots could have trouble figuring out just what was being shot at them. Plus, they might get a tad excited. A rule of thumb: if they reported 57 mm, it was more likely 37, maybe even 23. If they reported heavy, it was probably moderate, or even light. Misty saw a lot of triple-A and wanted to report it accurately, but how should we train a new Misty who, when he first comes to us, is likely one of these guys who's been overguessing the caliber and intensity of ground fire?

By and large, we couldn't count on North Vietnamese gunners to give helpful triple-A demos. In some places—Tchepone was one—you could always get shot at, but over most of the trail, the NVA showed rather good fire discipline. They must have had orders to react only when the specific real estate they were assigned to defend came under attack. We could pound away at other nearby spots and induce no response. But point your nose at their target and you kicked over a hornet's nest. Perhaps their restraint had something to do with the difficulty of getting ammunition down the trail. Whatever the reason, it was always hard to guess if NVA gunners would shoot. When they did, it could be quite a show, but the element of unpredictability made for haphazard training at best; they were certainly not dependable enough for inclusion in the new-Misty orientation package.

We did have one trustworthy gunner located a few kilometers north of Delta 87, a prominent checkpoint on the trail. He had a 14.5 mm (about .50 caliber) heavy machine gun—what we called

Southeast Asia, 1968–69

The boys took care of Ellie while I was in Vietnam.

Getting ready to launch with "slick" bombs and fuse extenders ("daisy cutters"), Phu Cat, January 1969. We sometimes used daisy cutters so the bomb would go off a little before ground impact, producing better blast effects.

The Misty squadron logs 10,000 flying hours on the Ho Chi Minh Trail. Standing, second and third from left, Tony McPeak and Ron Fogleman, two future Air Force chiefs. Next to Fogleman, Dick Hepworth, eighth commander of Misty. Standing, far left, Bill Creech, later the enormously influential commander of Tactical Air Command. Standing far right, Leroy Manor, commander of the 37th Fighter Wing.

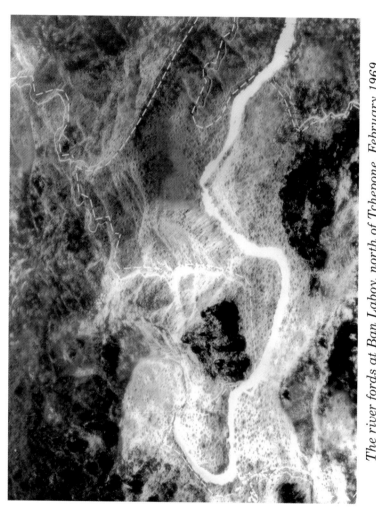

The river fords at Ban Laboy, north of Tchepone, February 1969, showing (dashed line) the Ho Chi Minh Trail and its bypasses. We reduced much of Laos to bony, lunar dust.

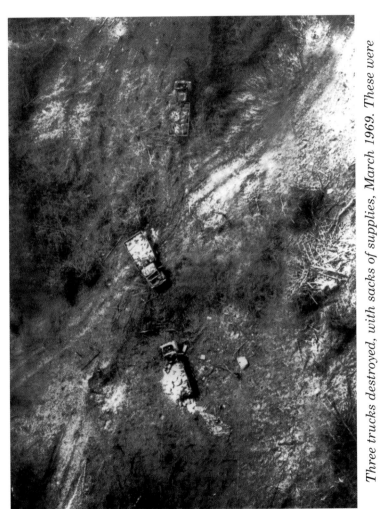

Three trucks destroyed, with sacks of supplies, March 1969. These were Russian-built ZIL 157s, good trucks, but pounded hard by us and the trail.

In April 1969, I became the ninth
commander of the Misty squadron.

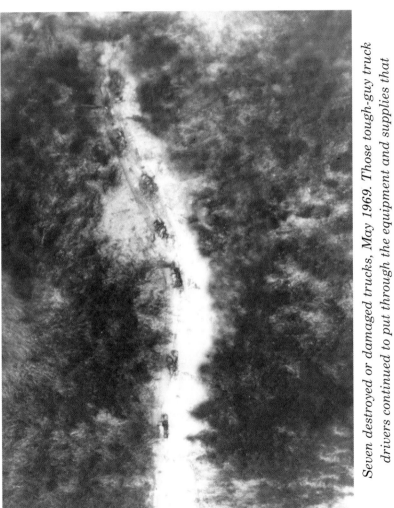

Seven destroyed or damaged trucks, May 1969. Those tough-guy truck drivers continued to put through the equipment and supplies that would, in the end, surround and capture the Saigon of memory.

Mistys join up at the Air Force Association's Iron Gate Ball, New York City, 1993. From left, Dave Skilling, Matt Husson, me, Bud Day (wearing the Medal of Honor), Ray Lee, Bob Cassaro, Lacy Veach, Gib Ahl. Behind Cassaro and Veach, Chris Kellum.

a Zip gun, from ZPU, the Russian nomenclature for the weapon. Zip came in various flavors, with up to four barrels, each capable of hosing off 600 rounds a minute. This guy had the four-barrel version—a quad Zip.

North of Delta 87, the trail ran through rugged, forested country. The gunner had set up housekeeping on the edge of a cliff. His position was well camouflaged, the foliage changed regularly to keep it natural looking. He had every reason to believe he was invisible, not knowing a stratum of rock ran across the face of the cliff, forming what looked from the air like a hand, complete with a Monty Python-style thumb and extended index finger. The gun was located at the end of the finger.

There was no way this gunner was regular NVA; he had to be Pathet Lao. Entirely lacking in fire discipline, he always shot as we went by. Better yet, he never hit anybody because he understood nothing about lead for target motion. He blazed away, aiming directly at us, the bullet stream passing harmlessly behind. This combination of personal qualities made him ideal training material. Whenever the outfit got a new pilot, we made it a point to fly by this guy's hangout. In the backseat for one of his first Misty rides, our recruit would never spot the gun, but we'd say, "Look at the end of the finger, about where the fingernail should be." To the gunner, we looked like we were just doing road recce, but we'd roll the aircraft so as to be canopy-up to his gun as we went by. We could count on the muzzles to twinkle at us in their distinctive box pattern. "That," we'd say to the new guy, "is quad Zip." He wasn't protecting anything special, and we didn't want him to know we had him located, so we left him alone otherwise. We came to appreciate his trustworthiness. He never let us down.

One morning the weather was unworkable just about everywhere in Laos. Incoming Air Force and Navy flights stacked up, and Hillsboro was looking for something to bomb. There was a little sucker hole right over our Zip gunner's head, so I told them to send us the iron, feeling sad we were about to lose our training aid.

Marking guns was never going to be my favorite activity. In the contest with gunners, here was our Achilles heel: aiming at him, as we must to put a marking rocket on his position, solved his tracking problem. From his point of view, we stayed at a constant azimuth and elevation and sooner or later would fly into range. In this special case, he didn't have to correct for target motion; we just got bigger in his sights.[45]

Going after a gun, I tried to talk the attack pilot's eyes to the target so I wouldn't have to mark it. But this particular morning they were dumping ordnance on us so fast there was no time for subtlety. It was one pass, haul ass for everybody. Anyway, we ended up marking him several times. He obliged by shooting at us, every pass we made.

We went to the tanker and came back twice, in the end putting in maybe a dozen flights. Some of the bombing was not so good, but some was quite respectable, especially a four-ship of F-105s with 2,000-pounders that must have made his ears ring. No doubt, it was a memorable day for him. He'd spent months minding his own business at some quiet corner of the trail, then all hell broke loose. But one way or another, he shot back at everybody who rolled in on him.

When we ran out of flights to control, I made one last pass to assess the damage, low and fast with lots of crossing angle. All the camouflage had been blown away from his position, but there he was, still standing, and still hosing away, aiming, as I knew he would, right at our canopy.

So we didn't get him. And the next day he was gone.

I often thought we should strike a special Misty medal for the guy. On one side it would say, "World's Gutsiest Gunner," on the other, "World's Dumbest Gunner." Either way, we never saw him again.

---

45 Which is why you should never—repeat, never—strafe guns. Getting into a gunfight with guns takes what should be an overwhelming combat advantage and turns it into a 50-50 proposition.

Logbook: Misty

1969	Sorties	Combat Hours
Feb	23	87.4
Mar	27	95.4*
Apr	24	83.8
May	24	97.7
Total	98	364.3

Qualifications:

Forward Air Controller (Air)

* Does not include the O-2 slow-FAC (Covey) sortie flown out of Da Nang that added 4.3 hours, giving me 99.7 combat hours in March, the closest I ever got to 100 flying hours in a month.

Chapter 18

Trees in Contact

It was the most important part. Time was Vietnam. But it became so immeasurable in a man's emotions, some days so long and some so short, that it was irrelevant, except for what it did to the face of a calendar.

—James Webb, *Fields of Fire*

In the spring of 1969, our operation at Phu Cat was winding down. F-4s would soon come to the base, displacing the F-100s. Misty would have to relocate to Tuy Hoa and become part of the 31st Wing. In mid-May, I flew down there for a look at the digs being offered and to get acquainted with my new masters.

Bruce W. Carr, famous fighter pilot and the 31st Wing's deputy for operations, would be the boss. I figured I'd impress the heck out of him, being semi-famous myself. Plus, he was getting Misty, the crown jewel of F-100 operations. I walked into his office prepared to be modest about our accomplishments, bringing along some prize-winning pictures from our armpit-camera collection. I got wire-brushed. To say the least, Bruce W. Carr was unimpressed. As far as he was concerned, Misty had to date been a large pain in the butt, an annoyance that kept some of his best pilots at Phu Cat with no measurable effect on the flow of goods and services down the trail. "Pretty pictures? Who needs 'em? Out of my office. See you next week."

—..▲..—

Nobody ever called Bruce W. Carr anything but Bruce W. Carr. Not to his face, of course, but away and out of earshot—Bruce W. Carr. Not Bruce, not Bruce Carr, certainly not Colonel Carr. Just Bruce W. Carr, spoken as though it were one word. After his first aerial victory in World War II, Bruce W. Carr's commander chewed him out for being too aggressive. He responded so vigorously he was arrested for insubordination and nearly court-martialed. Transferred to a squadron with better leadership, he ended up among our leading P-51 aces with 15 kills and was himself brought down by ground fire three times.

He created one of the Air Force's great legends when forced to bail out behind German lines. Eluding capture for four days, hungry and tired, he was about to give himself up. Instead, he sneaked onto a Luftwaffe airfield, somehow managed to get a Focke-Wulf 190 started up and flew it back home. The Allies would have loved to get their hands on a mint-condition specimen of this formidable airplane, nicknamed *Wurger* ("Butcherbird") by the Germans. But as he circled the field trying to figure out how to get the wheels down, "friendly" defenses looked like they were about to open up, so Bruce W. Carr bellied it in.

Tall and skinny, with a monument for a nose, he had a disregard for danger that verged on contempt. He cared about courage and flying skill and absolutely nothing else.

—..▲..—

As soon as Misty completed the move to Tuy Hoa, Bruce W. Carr scheduled himself for a sortie in my backseat. It was the standard road patrol, three-plus hours of jinking, high-speed recce, down in the weeds. Not much action, although I ended up marking some well-known gun positions—probably empty—for flights Hillsboro dumped on us. I put in one mark after a hard pull into the vertical, floating the nose over at nothing miles per hour and squeezing off a Willie Pete going straight down. I sometimes used this trick when marking active triple-A because most guns are either hard or impossible to elevate all the way to 90 degrees, so the gunners can't shoot straight up. But this gun site wasn't active, as far as I could see, and anyway I wouldn't normally do this without warning the guy in back. To keep going straight down you have to bunt it a little, which lifts you in the seat and presents a plan-form, pie-in-the-face view of the ground—an uncomfortable feeling when you're not flying the airplane. Plus, I managed to pry him loose from some pocket change with the tanker hookup challenge. But he hadn't exactly sweet-talked me when I showed up at Tuy Hoa the first time.

When we got back, I managed to trick the airplane into a kissy touchdown and acted nonchalant, an unspoken claim the landing barely met standards. As we pulled into the de-arm area, Bruce W. Carr unstrapped so he could reach up to hit me hard on the shoulder. I'd flown my last Misty mission. A fire truck came out to hose me down and my guys appeared with some champagne.

Early in its history, Misty had lost a few pilots on their last missions. So, by tradition, we never told a guy when it was his last one. Sometime toward the end of his Misty tour, we'd just water him down and send him back to his line squadron. This was what Bruce W. Carr had done to me.

So I never got my 100 Misty missions. He stopped me at 98.

Having taken Misty away from me a little early, Bruce W. Carr booted me upstairs. I became chief of the wing's Standardization and Evaluation Division, reporting directly to Bruce W. Carr. I ran a small office—just me and a couple of other instructor pilots administering periodic flying checks to the wing's aircrews, and an NCO who assisted with written exams and kept track of paperwork. All wings had such shops, check rides being part of normal peacetime harassment. Here in Vietnam, flight checks were usually tacked on a combat sortie. If the pilot was an element or flight lead, he briefed and led, with me in the formation. If he qualified only as a wingman, I briefed and led a standard combat sortie.

Bruce W. Carr scheduled himself for an annual proficiency check. He was a flight lead, of course, but told me to brief and lead. Actually, what he wanted was to get on my wing and do formation aerobatics. So, at the end of a routine bombing sortie, I put him in close and we did a couple of rolls. He could handle it, so I took him through a loop or two. All of which stretched regulations.

That night he had a party in his hooch and invited me. All was forgiven. Riding in my backseat for a Misty mission and doing some illicit aerobatics made us friends for life.[46]

In May the *New York Times* broke the news about the "secret" bombing of Cambodia. Obsessed with information leaks, Nixon ordered wiretaps on the telephones of 13 government officials and four journalists.

Also in May 1969, 46 men of the 101st Airborne died during a fierce, 10-day battle for Hamburger Hill, in the A Shau Valley. After the hill was captured, our troops were ordered to abandon it, and the NVA moved back in. This turned out to be the last large-scale "search and destroy" mission by US troops.

Tuy Hoa was a big change from Phu Cat. Right on the water, it was a beach resort, lacking only the resort part. I occupied the seaside half of the trailer nearest the beach, no obstacle between

---

46 In 1994, my final year as Air Force chief of staff, I returned to Europe for the 50th anniversary celebration of D-day. A gala dinner was held at the Guildhall in Portsmouth, the spot from which many of the invasion ships embarked. Seated at a raised platform: Queen Elizabeth, President Clinton, and many other heads of state. I was at one of the Guildhall's long tables with my colleague, Air Chief Marshall Mike Graydon, head of the RAF. On the bench directly opposite, looking uncomfortable in a civilian black-tie outfit, was my old buddy, Bruce W. Carr.

me and open water, a few meters from the door. I stocked up on
.38 ammo and hoped Charlie wasn't a strong swimmer.

Nearly all of the missions I flew out of Tuy Hoa were against
in-country targets, and here I assign to the word "target" its most
relaxed meaning. Mainly, we attacked infrastructure, hoping, I
suppose, to make it more difficult for VC or NVA troops to live off
the land. Often it came down to blowing up hooches in government-
declared free-fire zones. The Saigon regime had supposedly
rounded up and relocated all the friendlies out of these zones so
we were cleared to attack anything that moved or could possibly
support the insurgency. But we also bombed tree lines at the edge
of built-up areas, spots where an active imagination could picture
troops gathering; or jungle trails, fancying this would impede
enemy movement; or thickly wooded areas close to trails, pinning
our hopes on their potential to hide equipment and supplies. At
the end of each sortie, the FAC graded our work. Here might be
a summary involving grass huts, haystacks, and a small sluice
gate: "Seven military structures destroyed, two supply caches
uncovered, one water support system damaged." Every day an
impressive scorecard flowed from each of the fighter wings into the
headquarters at Saigon, creating the statistical certainty of victory.

The pilots knew better. Our nickname for these missions was
"trees in contact," a corruption of "troops in contact," one of the few
mission categories that was not pointless.

Troops in contact. Supposedly, people on the ground shooting at
each other. The Army often gave the term a more liberal interpre-
tation, but when it was authentic, this was the best kind of mission
because there was actual trouble and our side needed help.

In late June, I led a four-ship to the aid of the Special Forces
camp at Ben Het. Like many others, this small station was located
in the Central Highlands, where Special Forces A teams worked
with Montagnards, gathering intelligence and setting ambushes.

These were tough guys, often under attack because their camps were plopped down astride infiltration routes. Ben Het was the archetype, only six miles from the tri-border juncture, in the middle of rush-hour traffic.

The appearance of these camps was always the same and would be recognized at once by engineers who designed the fortress systems that replaced medieval castles. An opening in the forest was found or created to clear interlocking fields of fire and a double or triple row of concertina wire was strung around a central redoubt of low, sandbagged huts with tin roofs. Dug in and resupplied by air, the Snake Eaters could hold out indefinitely, or until the NVA brought in heavy weapons.

When we arrived on scene at Ben Het, the bad guys were already inside the wire. I saw what looked like bunk-bed mattresses laid over the concertina at several places, each mattress forming a sort of bridge. The camp looked tiny, maybe 200 meters wide at the outer wire. I told the FAC I'd bomb this close to friendlies only as a last resort. He said, "OK, how about strafing between the rows of wire?"—which we did, carefully, but with enthusiasm.

Fighter aircraft from all over the country converged on Ben Het and eventually lifted the siege. We all welcomed this kind of sortie. But far more often it was trees in contact instead.

One thing the Air Force can do is generate combat power. By mid-1969, we'd built an elaborate base structure, turned on the pipeline, and settled into a routine, producing awesome sortie rates, at least during daylight hours. In an endless loop, aircraft launched, delivered munitions and returned to be armed and launched again. We could and did suspend operations in the North from time to time as part of various diplomatic initiatives, but the in-country treadmill had no pause feature.

Unhappily, the targets were not so well organized. Even high-intensity combat is often by nature episodic, with battles coming after prolonged calms of preparation. Even so, in contemporary, industrial-age conflict, our style of nonstop sortie generation is a good match to the requirement because we can discover and attack the other side's preparations. Here, in-country in 1969, our highly developed technique for producing a large, steady stream of daylight combat sorties went one-on-one with a yesteryear target array that presented itself rarely, suddenly, in low profile, and usually at night. As a consequence, we very seldom had a target worth attacking. But we produced and consumed the sorties anyway, as though to make the machine work we had to exercise it.

It is the targets that give a war its character. The decisive operational question: "What's the target?" The essential intelligence: "Where's the target?"

As for the first question, the overall theater commander has ultimate responsibility for target selection, but if we are to win at reasonable cost the process must be "joint." That is, the senior airman and his staff should qualify and nominate air targets for the commander's review and approval. This did not happen in South Vietnam. Bright, well-intentioned Army officers, who thought they knew something about air fighting (or thought they didn't need to), picked all the targets. The Air Force, with plenty of hands-on, hard-won experience, was excluded from participation. We'd earned a place at the targeting table but were never given one, a sad failure to make effective joint use of armed forces.

Regarding intelligence, the failure was as serious and more obvious. We invested an enormous amount of time, money, and talent on the intelligence problem and, in the end, never could reliably locate the targets we knew were there.

Success on the battlefield requires that the marriage of intelligence to operations be fruitful. If intelligence is barren, there won't be offspring, no matter how potent the operator.

After each sortie, we de-armed, taxied back to the revetments and shut down. The crew chief was the first guy up the ladder, wanting a debrief. They worked their tails off getting the birds ready, out in the weather, 18 hours a day, no beefs. They saw us go away and saw us come back, and very seldom got to see results.

I usually tried to make something up, sort of like what Westy did for LBJ.

Basically, every fighter sortie flown in Vietnam, even the safest, most prosaic mud mover, counted as combat. But as the 31st Wing's chief check pilot, I flew sorties for which I never gave myself combat credit. For instance, a colonel arrived at Tuy Hoa with virtually no qualifications in the F-100. For some reason, he'd been assigned a senior position in the wing without having gone through the normal stateside F-100 conversion course. He was a nice man and a fine officer, but we'd have to start him with takeoffs and landings and work our way through the basics of formation, instruments, night, and so on, leading to bomb dropping. By then, maybe he could handle wingman duties. He couldn't realistically expect ever to become a qualified element or flight lead in the one year maximum he'd be with the wing. Because of his rank and position, I assigned myself to supervise his checkout, flying six or seven sorties with him, including some at the end that featured bombing trees in contact. I signed him off, hoping he'd devote as much time as possible to office duties. The system recorded all my flights with the colonel as combat sorties. I counted only the last ones, in which we expended ordinance.

In another case, a captain from the Air National Guard was having great difficulty in one of the squadrons. By this point in the war, we'd called up entire Air Guard squadrons, which were performing well in-theater. In addition, stateside Guard units were canvassed for volunteers to fill in-country slots with either active or recalled Guard squadrons. This fellow was one of these individual replacements. Back home, he was current and qualified in the F-100, but when he reported to Tuy Hoa, he scared the pants off everybody on account of his lack of proficiency at instruments. Instructor pilots in his squadron would not sign off a theater checkout. His commander nominated him for one last check ride before shipping him home. Being rejected for work in Vietnam did not happen often, especially for an experienced fighter pilot who had disrupted his civilian life to volunteer for combat. In this unusual circumstance, rather than hand off responsibility to one of my other check pilots, I did the final pass/fail ride myself.

The captain had only to demonstrate he could fly blind, by reference to instruments alone. He got in the backseat of an F-100F and went under the bag shortly after takeoff. It would be an easy test: make the standard instrument departure, navigate to a couple of nearby radio aids, proceed to Tuy Hoa's initial approach fix and fly the published letdown to the base. If he couldn't do these simple tasks, he might kill himself in bad weather, not a good outcome for sure, but the concern was he might also kill a wingman.

Although the briefed flight profile was dead simple, as soon as I gave him the aircraft to fly, it was your basic animal act. For the life of me, I couldn't figure out what he was trying to do. Twice, I took control of the jet, asked him to come out from under the hood and got him lined up to start over, hoping he could pick up the profile and finish the mission. At length, we arrived at what he thought was the initial approach fix for Tuy Hoa. I said nothing, though we were nowhere near the fix. He began the letdown. I let him continue until we reached altitude minimums for the published approach. At this point, we should have been lined up with the end of the runway, about ready to land. In fact, we had leveled, below approach minimums, over open water. Though land was in sight, the base was not.

I said, "OK, pop the hood and have a look," after which I took the airplane, cleaned it up, and flew back to the base. The captain was going home early.

That evening, he was at the bar and offered to buy me a drink. He explained he would catch the courier to Saigon next morning. From there, a "freedom flight" would take him back to "the world."

He had no hard feelings, actually thanked me, realizing he'd be a threat to himself and others if we kept him around.

He told me something of his background: a successful business-man whose personal life had fallen apart, a messy divorce in progress. I got the impression he'd volunteered for Vietnam to get away from all that. As a reason for being here, it didn't pass the Farmer Jones logic test, but then the rationale for any of us being here was not so hot.

The captain and I had flown another "combat" sortie I wouldn't credit. In all, my official record shows 285 combat missions. By my count, I flew 269—maybe half of them against trees in contact.

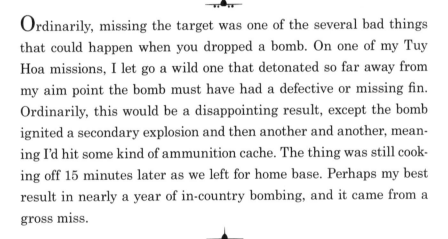

Ordinarily, missing the target was one of the several bad things that could happen when you dropped a bomb. On one of my Tuy Hoa missions, I let go a wild one that detonated so far away from my aim point the bomb must have had a defective or missing fin. Ordinarily, this would be a disappointing result, except the bomb ignited a secondary explosion and then another and another, meaning I'd hit some kind of ammunition cache. The thing was still cooking off 15 minutes later as we left for home base. Perhaps my best result in nearly a year of in-country bombing, and it came from a gross miss.

Back home in New York state, Woodstock kicked off in August, a three-day, free festival of peace, love, and rock 'n' roll. Half a million people showed up to watch an unbelievable cast: Janis Joplin, The Grateful Dead, Jimi Hendrix, The Band, Joe Cocker, The Who, Jefferson Airplane, to name a few. For some Americans, it was unpatriotic, plain and simple, an insult carrying all the earmarks of the hippie counterculture. Thing is, in-country, this was the music we listened to, the volume turned up.

I took a four-ship into southeastern Laos one late-summer after-noon, the weather good for once. A Misty FAC put us in on an underwater bridge that served as a river ford. Immediately, we woke up some guns—looked like 23 mil—meaning we were after something they wanted to protect. We could see the gun positions easily once they opened up, and I switched to dropping on them. No sweat in a jet, but my wingman tracked the guns too long and took a round close along the fuselage. The bullet left a nice groove in his vertical stabilizer and knocked the rudder completely off the airplane. I got on his wing, and we went home. He did a nice job with a straight-in approach and landing.

In a dozen or so years flying fighters, I hadn't lost a wingman—and didn't want to start now.

—✈—

Ho Chi Minh died 2 September 1969, age 79, of a heart attack. His will, read publically, urged the North to fight "until the last Yankee is gone."

—✈—

The 20 mm round is what's fired through the cannon of most Air Force fighters. It comes in several versions, the most common being: ball (solid metal, nonexplosive, used for target practice), armor piercing incendiary (API), and high explosive incendiary (HEI). In combat, we usually carried a four-to-one mix of API/HEI, explosive rounds that detonated on contact.

Returning from a target in I Corps, I followed the usual practice of checking in with the FAC who controlled a free-fire zone. My flight had expended its bombs on a "suspected storage area," but we still had a load of 20 mm. The FAC directed us toward the bend of a river. At a point where the river exited heavy jungle, there was a clearing and a small herd of water buffalo. They were easy to see; he didn't have to mark them.

Strafe. From the German *strafen*, "to punish."

We began, and immediately the animals panicked, scattering in all directions. Still, firing nearly 5,000 rounds a minute from each of our aircraft, they were impossible to miss. What happens to a water buffalo hit by 20 mil is not pleasant. At the end, the FAC gave us our score: "Ten enemy transport systems destroyed."

I believe there is no dishonor in killing enemy in combat. But this was some enemy, some combat.

Stateside, Dennis Hopper wrote, directed and starred in *Easy Rider*, a movie about two young men who go looking for America and can't find it.

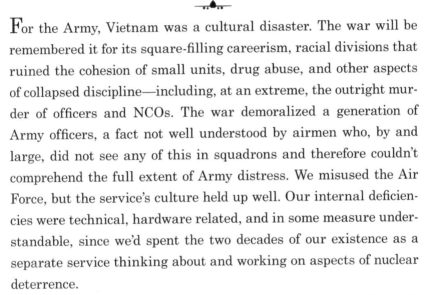

For the Army, Vietnam was a cultural disaster. The war will be remembered it for its square-filling careerism, racial divisions that ruined the cohesion of small units, drug abuse, and other aspects of collapsed discipline—including, at an extreme, the outright murder of officers and NCOs. The war demoralized a generation of Army officers, a fact not well understood by airmen who, by and large, did not see any of this in squadrons and therefore couldn't comprehend the full extent of Army distress. We misused the Air Force, but the service's culture held up well. Our internal deficiencies were technical, hardware related, and in some measure understandable, since we'd spent the two decades of our existence as a separate service thinking about and working on aspects of nuclear deterrence.

To be sure, the Air Force could not put deterrence on the back burner, since we were still locked in confrontation with the Soviets, but a couple of technical shortcomings could be put right without damaging the Cold War effort—and maybe even helping it. Based on what I saw, we needed first to equip our aircraft with infrared or other sensors useful in finding and identifying targets at night, then develop tactics for night attack and train using the tactics. "Winning the day" used to mean winning, full stop, but in Vietnam it meant winning the day.

Second, we had to achieve precision accuracy with high explosives. Freefall, or "dumb" bombs are inherently inaccurate, and we

knew that, so we compensated by dropping more bombs. It didn't
work. A good example was the Arc Light attacks staged by B-52s
out of Guam and Thailand. Our bombers flew in at high altitude
and dumped as many as 108 500-pound bombs each on jungle targets picked by MACV. (There was a Strategic Air Command liaison
cell in the Saigon headquarters, but MACV's effective monopoly
on decision-making showed.) Arc Lights were said to be chillingly
impressive if you were on the ground nearby, so they may have
had psychological impact. Moreover, we dropped so many bombs
that some damage must have been done, if only by chance. But at
the end of the day, this was monkey killing on a grand scale, in
large part because target intelligence was so poor, but also because
even though targets might have been down there somewhere, these
munitions had little chance of scoring hits.

For fighters, the primary method of aiming unguided bombs
was to give them a vector toward the target by diving at it. For
one thing, this pretty much limited us to daylight, good-weather
attack, meaning our effectiveness against mobile targets depended
a great deal on enemy cooperation. A shallower dive angle got us
closer to the target before release, making for better accuracy, but
also sharply increased exposure to ground fire—and anyway was
no money-back guarantee of accuracy because of the many variables involved in unguided weapon delivery.

With fighters as with bombers, we tried to offset inaccuracy with
increased firepower—by sending more aircraft, flying more sorties,
dropping more bombs—employing mass. Mass is, after all, a principle of war. But precision is itself a kind of mass—the best kind, in
that power is applied right to the target.

We needed to move quickly to guided air-to-ground weaponry,
and ultimately to autonomous, or self-guided munitions that could
be used day or night, good weather or bad. This sort of explosive
would be more expensive than freefall bombs, and also much more
cost effective, not only because it hit what we aimed at, but also

because eventually we would be able to release at standoff ranges and altitudes, sharply reducing the threat from air defenses.

—..▲..—

On 2 November, Lt. Col. Larry Whitford, Misty's 11th commander, was shot down in Laos on his 21st mission. With him was Capt. Patrick Henry Carroll, flying his 70th Misty sortie. The government would carry them as missing for some years before making a presumptive finding of killed in action.

—..▲..—

It is an article of faith with airmen that air warfare is of a piece. In application, an air campaign can have various phases or aspects, such as establishing control of the air, deep bombardment, or close support for surface forces, but the instruments of airpower—the pilots, aircraft, and munitions—have the inherent flexibility for rapid concentration and retasking. Therefore, the highest and best use of airpower is achieved only when it comes under central direction. Had we acted in accordance with this view, we would have considered all air operations in Southeast Asia part of a system and organized an integrated air campaign, led by a senior airman.[47]

In fact, we fought several separate air wars. MACV, under Westmoreland and later Abrams, ran the in-country air war, using a 1920s model in which the Air Force served as an Army auxiliary—a sort of winged artillery. In practical terms, our presence meant the Army couldn't be defeated militarily, a live possibility if we hadn't been there. As for the more purposeful uses of airpower, MACV was clueless.

The second air war, the on-and-off bombing of the North, was run by the White House, reaching through the Joint Chiefs of Staff and Adm. Ulysses S. Grant Sharp, head of Pacific Command.

---

47 The most likely candidate would have been the commander of Seventh Air Force. For much of the period, this would have been Gen. William W. "Spike" Momyer, an experienced and able tactician.

Because of inability or unwillingness to conduct coordinated air operations, the North Vietnamese landscape was subdivided by Admiral Sharp into "route packages," each package assigned to either the Air Force or Navy.

Chopping up the real estate in this way was a classic mistake. Air operations enjoy considerable freedom from the constraints of geography, including those synthetic lines people draw on maps, a fact accounting for much of the leverage airpower brings to the fight. Sadly we gave away this edge, increasing our exposure and driving up losses. But in the end it probably made little difference, the mistake overshadowed by even more important shortcomings in technology and, especially, strategic direction.

For instance, our bombing was interrupted 16 times by pauses designed to give the North an opportunity to rethink its convictions. As it happened, conviction was their strong suit. The breaks in the action did little to enhance our negotiating position, but each time we went back the air defenses were rested, repaired and improved. In the end, nearly 1,100 aircraft were shot down in the North (North Vietnam staked claims to 3,300) and more than 800 aviators killed or captured.

The third and fourth of the air wars were fought in Laos. It's difficult even to describe the dog's breakfast of command arrangements, which anyway evolved in the ebb and flow of time. Seventh Air Force, answering to MACV, called the shots in Steel Tiger, the campaign to stop traffic down the Ho Chi Minh Trail. Farther north in Laos, Seventh Air Force was also involved in the attempt to tilt the odds in favor of a weak Royal Laotian government in the civil war it would eventually lose. This effort, called Barrel Roll,[48] was in principle under the control of Pacific Command but during the most critical period real authority was in the hands of our embassy in Vientiane. Ambassador William H. Sullivan (known as "Field Marshal") was

---

48 The terms "Steel Tiger" and "Barrel Roll" applied to both the geographic area and the operations conducted in these areas.

especially forceful in exercising this responsibility. Meanwhile, Strategic Air Command retained tasking authority for B-52s flying into Laos from Guam and U Tapao, Thailand. In addition, Air America flew combat sorties under the separate auspices of the CIA. The resulting air operations in Laos could scarcely be described as "joint," let alone "integrated." Thus, if our strategic direction was defective, command arrangements were, if anything, worse.

The Air Force spent as much time in Southeast Asia as any other service (and more money), deploying a third of our airplanes and losing 2,257 of them. We dropped nearly three times as much bomb tonnage as we had in World War II. In the end, 2,700 airmen did not come back. Lacking a single air commander to unify the work in the service of a commonsense concept of operations, the entire undertaking was a fiasco.

Why were we losing? That was the easy one. Our strategic, operational and technical defects were everywhere visible: inaccurate weaponry, zero capability at night, Army mismanagement, valueless intelligence, the lack of a sane, integrated air campaign—all these factors present and obvious at first hand. But in the middle of the in-country war and at the height of our military presence, there was a harder question, one that has echoed over the years: Why are we here?

You could make a case for intervention, and successive American administrations tried. We might prevent a Communist takeover of the South, just as Truman had kept North Korea from swallowing its southern neighbor. It was clear that if we could do this, success would have wider, potentially very important consequences.[49]

---

49 For one thing, an extra million Vietnamese might be alive today. And because the "Vietnam syndrome" all but paralyzed American use of military power for a decade, Leonid Brezhnev stepped up subversion in Central America and Africa and in 1979 invaded Afghanistan, confident that Washington would not act.

But we were on the wrong side of history, fighting a national independence movement intent on dissolving the residue of French and Japanese imperialism. It would be a stretch, but we could imagine a South Vietnamese government that was competent and honest. Even so, the mere fact of our support would undermine its legitimacy with its own people. There was really no way we could rescue the Saigon regime.

Moreover, it was obvious from the beginning that the outcome was far more important to the other side than it was to us, conditions strategically lopsided in their favor. Throughout the conflict, our design was to fight a limited war with a limited aim—the preservation of the South—against an enemy who fought an all-out war with the single-minded goal of reuniting the country, no matter how long it took or how much it cost. In the end, the North did lose more than one million dead and 300,000 missing—staggering numbers, something like 5 percent of the population it controlled. But the North Vietnamese believed, correctly as it turned out, that they could endure punishment longer and more stoically than we could dish it out.

In *Apocalypse Now*, Lieutenant Colonel Kilgore is the Patton-esque battalion commander whose nutty, marvelous "I love the smell of napalm in the morning" speech ends with the line: "Someday this war is gonna end." Kilgore makes the assertion wistfully, without conviction, but he's dead right. A country like ours will tolerate foolishness for a while, but not forever.

—··▲··—

Richard Nixon won the 1968 election in part because of his "secret plan" to end the war. Unwrapped in July 1969, the plan, later labeled the Nixon Doctrine, called for Asian nations to be more self-reliant in defense matters. In keeping with this idea, the administration announced a program of "Vietnamization," under which we would hand more responsibility for the war to the South Vietnamese. Because of our help so far, the South had already produced formidable armed forces, was well on the way to being able to defend itself. In addition, we'd leave behind vast quantities of military hardware, further increasing their fighting power. All this meant we could start bringing American troops home.

Vietnamization was a lie. As with any good lie, it contained an element of truth. The truth: we were getting out. As part of the drawdown, people nearing their end of tour were ordered home. I therefore left Tuy Hoa in November 1969, having been in-country only 11 months.

By early 1971, SAMs had appeared in the passes at Mu Gia and Ban Karai. They pushed into Tchepone in the spring of 1972, joining at least 800 triple-A guns in southern Laos. MiGs occasionally pulled contrails overhead. By the spring of 1974, the North Vietnamese could travel on pavement from Mu Gia all the way into South Vietnam. With five main arteries, 29 branches, and many cutoffs and bypasses, it all added up to 12,000 miles of road, much of it two-lane highway.

Da Nang fell on 29 March 1975; Qui Nhon two days later. Phu Cat was captured with 60 flyable aircraft sitting on the ramp. Nha Trang gave up on 3 April, the battle there lasting only a couple of hours. The magnificent deep-water facility at Cam Ranh Bay changed hands the same day after 30 minutes of fighting. Saigon surrendered on 30 April and within 24 hours was officially (unlike the trail) given Ho Chi Minh's name.

It was not a swarm of VC guerrillas that fell on Saigon, but columns of Russian-made T-54 tanks, leading a modern field army complete with artillery and SAMs, all brought down the trail by those tough-guy truckers.

The war was always the South's to win, and it couldn't. It was always ours to lose, and we did.

Logbook: Vietnam

1968–69	Sorties	Hours
Combat	269	626.7
Other	16	19.2
Total	285	645.9

Logbook: Career to Date

Dec 57–Nov 69	Flying Hours
F-100	2464.3
F-104	674.1
F-4	3.0
T-33	28.7
Total Jet	3170.1
A-1	0.5
C-117	2.4
O-2	4.3
L-20/U-6	28.6
Total Rated	3205.9
Student	239.5
Total Time	3445.4

Appendix: Flying Lessons

——✈——

Air: Pictures of Earth, taken from space, show how thin our atmosphere is, standing in relation to the planet something like the apple's skin to the rest of the apple. Air clings to Earth, half of it within three nautical miles of the surface.

The downward pressure exerted by the weight of air can be measured. The classic way of doing this is to put an evacuated tube into an open dish of mercury. In standard, sea-level conditions, air pressure forces mercury up the tube to a height of 29.92 inches. The pressure will drop about an inch for every thousand feet of altitude gained. Thus, an observer stationed at 5,000 feet gets a standard day reading of 24.92 inches of mercury. Denver will nearly always have a lower reading than New Orleans, the reason weather stations adjust the observation to a sea-level equivalent when reporting altimeter settings.

When we inhale at sea level, we breathe air that is about 20 percent oxygen. We get the same 20 percent at 10,000 feet, but the number of oxygen molecules per breath is fewer because the reduced weight of air pressing down from above allows atmospheric gases to spread out, to become less densely packed. At 18,000 feet, each individual breath delivers to the lungs about half the number of oxygen molecules we're used to getting at sea level.

The consequences of oxygen reduction can be compensated for by living or training at high altitude, or by hyperventilation—breathing deeply and rapidly, which has its own adverse effects—but for most of us some impairment of physical capacity, especially eyesight, begins to occur around 8,000 feet pressure altitude. The rule adopted by the FAA is, if you fly above a cockpit altitude of 12,500 feet for more than 30 minutes, you need supplemental oxygen, and if you fly above 14,000 feet, you need oxygen immediately and continuously. This 12.5/14 rule, written when oxygen systems were costly and scarce, is a compromise based more on politics than physiology. At 12,500 feet, you can fly through mountain passes, making nearly all continental US airspace open to those who do not have oxygen aboard. Standard military systems begin delivering supplemental oxygen at 8,000 feet, and Air Force regulations prohibit flight above 14,000 feet without it.

Air continues thinning as we climb. Just where the transition from air to space occurs is somewhat arbitrary. The Air Force awards astronaut wings to pilots whose trajectory carries them above 50 miles, but this number is a legal fiction, the atmosphere, for all practical purposes, left far behind at this trifling distance from the surface.

—✦—

Airspeed: Speed is what sustains flight, and knowing about it is the pilot's most essential information requirement, which is why the first true aircraft instrument was an airspeed indicator. But airspeed reveals itself in a dance of veils: "indicated" and "calibrated" and "equivalent" and "true"—the mnemonic is "ICE-T"— all different and all of consequence in various contexts.

Measuring airspeed starts with the knowledge that quiet air has a standard day ambient, or static pressure of 29.92 inches of mercury at sea level. We all have observed that moving air (wind) generates dynamic pressure—engineers call this "q"—that varies with speed. The sum of these two—static plus dynamic—is total, or ram pressure.

It's pretty easy to find a spot somewhere on the aircraft—often on the front end, where airflow is least disturbed—to place a sensor called a pitot tube that faces into the wind and reads ram pressure. It's not so easy to find a place where a static reading can be taken because airflow over and around aircraft surfaces distorts the measurement. But a static port has to be put somewhere— sometimes on the side of the pitot tube itself, sometimes elsewhere on the aircraft—to try to measure ambient pressure in the free air stream. The pitot-static system can then subtract static from ram and display the result, dynamic pressure, as indicated airspeed. Thus, an airspeed indicator is a pressure gauge, measuring speed only indirectly, the reading an analogue relating dynamic air pressure to velocity.

As a first approximation, the airplane takes off, lands, stalls, spins, or whatever else you want it to do, based on indicated airspeed. The most significant operating limits—for instance, the speed at which landing gear and flaps may be safely lowered—are expressed in indicated airspeed because that's what the pilot sees on the face of the instrument and can act on.

Calibrated airspeed is the result of correcting for errors mostly due to location of the static pressure sensor. The distribution of static pressures around an aircraft can vary a good deal in differing conditions of flight. By design, the static port should be located at a spot where these differences are small in the range of flight conditions critical to aircraft performance.

Equivalent airspeed is the result of correcting for compressibility. In designing a simple airspeed indicator, the assumption is made that air is not compressible, but of course it is. Most manufacturers rig airspeed indicators so that compressibility error is zero for any airspeed at sea level and negligible below 10,000 feet and about 250 knots. But the error increases with altitude and airspeed. When you make allowance for compressibility you arrive at equivalent airspeed.

Thus several factors can create a measurable difference between what the instrument is telling you and your actual speed through the air mass. But for most flight conditions, the adjustments needed to get from indicated to calibrated to equivalent are small and have little practical consequence. This is not so for the last correction commonly applied, the one taking us to true airspeed. True airspeed is velocity through the air mass. To measure it, equivalent airspeed must be corrected for air density, which as we have seen decreases a lot with altitude. This means that as an aircraft climbs into thinner air, maintaining constant dynamic pressure—indicated airspeed—results in faster and faster travel. At jet cruising altitudes, an indicated airspeed around 300 knots typically translates to a true airspeed around 500 knots. This is the big advantage achieved by jet aircraft.

As noted, pilots use "ICE-T" to remember the order in which corrections are applied to get from indicated to calibrated to equivalent to true airspeed. Of course, this is not the end of the story, since true airspeed must itself be adjusted for wind to get ground speed. But "ICE-T-G" is not so elegant a memory jogger.

The Anglo-American format measures airspeed in knots, "knot" being the nickname for nautical miles per hour. This is handy for navigators because a nautical mile is one minute of longitude at the equator, or of latitude anywhere on the globe. A nautical mile equals close to 6,080 feet, about 1.15 statute miles, so 500 knots is 575 mph.

For high-speed flight, the various miles-per-hour measures are usurped by the decimals of Mach number.

—◆—

Dynamic pressure (q): Quiet air has a standard day, ambient (static) pressure of 29.92 inches of mercury at sea level. Moving air—wind—generates dynamic pressures that vary with speed. The relationship is explained by a famous formula: dynamic pressure = $\frac{1}{2}pV^2$, where p is air density and V is velocity.

Dynamic pressure is the common denominator of aerodynamic forces, appearing so often in the equations that it is usually abbreviated to the single letter q. As can be seen, q varies directly with air density and the square of velocity. This has lots of practical consequences. For instance, in a descent, as the thickness of the air increases, velocity must be reduced to maintain the same dynamic pressures on the aircraft.

For the fighter pilot, one of the toughest flying environments is low altitude, high-speed flight, a regime that pilots call "high *q*." Aircraft structures likely get their hardest test when high *q* is combined with high *g*, as in the pull-up from a dive bomb attack, or to do vertical rolls through the Diamond Bomb Burst.

g: A load of about 9.8 meters per second squared, the approximate acceleration due to gravity at sea level on the Earth's surface (written here in lowercase and italics to distinguish it from "G," Newton's gravitational constant, and "g," the international abbreviation for gram).

The work a wing can do, as measured by the number of *g*'s it can pull, increases with the square of airspeed. Say that an aircraft is slowed in level, 1 *g* flight, and wing stall occurs at 150 knots (approximately true for the F-100). If this wing's speed is doubled to 300 knots, and AOA is increased to obtain maximum lift, a load factor of 4 *g*'s is available prior to stall. If speed is tripled to 450 knots, 9 *g*'s can be pulled, which, in the case of the F-100, would exceed the aircraft's structural limits.

At the 425-knot entry speed Thunderbird solo pilots used, *g* available was about 7.33, which was the aircraft's positive-*g* limit, meaning the aircraft had the structural strength to pull this load repeatedly over its useful life, without coming unglued. Thus, for the F-100, 425 knots was a special, very important speed, *Va*, or maneuver speed—what fighter pilots call corner velocity—the lowest speed at which you can load the aircraft to its limiting *g* without stalling. This is as slow as you want to be entering a fight. More is better, but you have to keep in mind that above corner velocity it's possible to over-*g* the airplane.

Civilian pilots often look at *Va* in reverse. If you stay below *Va*, the airplane will stall before it exceeds its limit-*g* load, so you can yank as hard as you want and maybe the wings won't fall off.

Caterpillar Club: An association of pilots who have abandoned aircraft in flight and whose lives have therefore been saved by the parachute. (Paratroops do not qualify, as they jump out on purpose.) So called because some caterpillars produce silk like that used to make early parachutes. Silk has not been used for this purpose for many years. Whereas pilots used to "hit the silk," nowadays they "make a nylon letdown."

The Caterpillar Club gained widespread publicity during the Battle of Britain, when many RAF pilots became members, but its existence predates the Second World War. Lindbergh was an early member, making in all four emergency jumps. Jimmy Doolittle had three. Membership is becoming less common now, as aircraft reliability is much improved. My Caterpillar Club membership dates from 21 October 1967.

CEP: Circular Error Probable. In managing air combat operations, planners must calculate the number of explosives needed to achieve desired damage levels. Start by drawing a circle around the target, the radius of which is an informed guess that half the bombs will fall inside the circle. This planning CEP is essential in figuring how many and what kind of aircraft to task against a target.

The early aviation enthusiasts asserted that airpower would shortly constitute both a quicker and a more humane way of waging war. The assessment of end results was correct, but the timing was off. The forecast dividends required hitting what was aimed at and, until quite recently, we could not reliably do this. For all bombs dropped on Germany in World War II, our CEP was on the order of 1,000 meters, meaning half the munitions landed a kilometer or more away from the target. (This was called precision daylight bombing.) With this sort of accuracy, you need to send thousand-bomber raids—which we did—and you'll need to send them back again—which we also did. We lost bomber crews at a murderous rate, killed tens of thousands of civilians who were well away from industrial or military targets, and German production of many strategic goods increased right up to the end of the war.

By the time of Vietnam, our CEP had improved by an order of magnitude, but even 100 meters is not good enough against point targets—which is most targets. In early Rolling Thunder operations, we sent 873 sorties against the Thanh Hoa Bridge, lost 11 aircraft and achieved nothing useful.

This is a strange result, in a way, because already by the 1950s we had solved the accuracy problem for a whole class of very tough targets: opposing aircraft. An independent Air Force quickly recognized that unguided munitions (i.e., bullets) weren't good enough for the air-to-air fight. Starting with the Navy's Sidewinder, we introduced the more expensive, but much more cost-effective, guided munitions that revolutionized air-to-air combat.

Why did it take us so long to apply the same thinking to ground targets? The answer cannot be that we worked on the simplest problem. A bridge or building just sits there, inviting attack, a whole lot easier target than a fast-moving, piloted aircraft in a dynamic, swirling dogfight. It could be because what we care about is air-to-air fighting, which is what the Army believes. If so, I find the error forgivable. The air fight is the one we have to win. Airpower cannot always assure horizontal victory, but if we don't win in the vertical, nothing else works.

In any case, by the end of Vietnam, we were using guided air-to-ground munitions, giving us another order of magnitude improvement in bombing results. That is, our CEP with these munitions was on the order of 10 meters, good enough against nearly all targets of interest. In 1972, we sent two four-ship flights against the same Thanh Hoa Bridge, knocked it out of action and got everybody home safe. And when Desert Storm came along, we were able (finally) to deliver on the promise of airpower, to make the fight both shorter and less deadly. Billy Mitchell would have been proud.

It makes a difference when you hit what you aim at.

Index